# Criminal Procedures

## *2002 Supplement*

2002 Supplement

# Criminal Procedures

## *Cases, Statutes, and Executive Materials*

### Marc L. Miller
*Professor of Law*
*Emory University*

### Ronald F. Wright
*Professor of Law*
*Wake Forest University*

ASPEN LAW & BUSINESS
A Division of Aspen Publishers, Inc.
New York      Gaithersburg

Copyright © 2002 by Marc L. Miller and Ronald F. Wright

Permissions
Aspen Law & Business
1185 Avenue of the Americas
New York, NY 10036

Printed in the United States of America

1 2 3 4 5 6 7 8 9 0

**Library of Congress Cataloging-in-Publication Data**

Miller, Marc L. (Marc Louis)
    Criminal procedures : cases, statutes, and
executive materials / Marc L. Miller,
Ronald F. Wright.
        p. cm.
    Includes bibliographical references.
    ISBN 1-56706-645-3 (casebound)
    ISBN 0-7355-3343-1 (supplement)
    1. Criminal procedure—United States—
Cases. I. Miller, Marc L., 1959–   ;
Wright, Ronald F., 1959–  .  II. Title.
KF9618.M52   1998
345.73´05—dc21                        98-14160
                                            CIP

# About Aspen Law & Business
# Legal Education Division

With a dedication to preserving and strengthening the long-standing tradition of publishing excellence in legal education, Aspen Law & Business continues to provide the highest quality teaching and learning resources for today's law school community. Careful development, meticulous editing, and an unmatched responsiveness to the evolving needs of today's discerning educators combine in the creation of our outstanding casebooks, coursebooks, textbooks, and study aids.

**ASPEN LAW & BUSINESS**
**A Division of Aspen Publishers, Inc.**
**A Wolters Kluwer Company**
*www.aspenpublishers.com*

# Contents

Contents

Contents

Contents

# Preface

A casebook supplement serves several functions. One is to keep teachers and students "current" with the material. The goal of staying current assumes there is constant change. Criminal procedure changes constantly in some ways but is relatively stable in others (at least as measured in months or a few years). In terms of basic doctrine, most aspects of criminal procedure have changed only modestly over the past few years. This is particularly true for a book, such as this one, that emphasizes nationwide trends within state criminal justice systems. Such nationwide changes take much longer to develop than any shifts in a single jurisdiction.

Doctrinal change can happen quickly in cutting-edge areas such as community policing. In other parts of the criminal process, the basic doctrine remains stable, but new applications of the doctrine have taken center stage. One illustration is the dramatic debate in the past few years over the use of criminal "profiles" and related charges that some police enforce a crime called "driving while black" (or "DWB"). Another is the debate in Los Angeles about proper remedies for police misconduct in light of a massive corruption scandal centering on the Rampart District.

Traditionally, casebook supplements contain materials that will appear in the next printed edition of the casebook. This supplement is somewhat different. Some of the materials in this supplement will appear in the next edition; other materials will not. Many decisions from the U.S. Supreme Court (along with some from the state supreme courts) seem on a first reading to make a dramatic shift in law and practice. However, after some time for analysis and reflection, most decisions merely restate or apply established concepts. A casebook supplement is a good opportunity to test the staying power of new cases, statutes, and policies.

The materials in this supplement are divided by chapter and section. We indicate where the materials fit with those in the casebook itself. In the first ten chapters of the supplement, page numbers refer both to the hardbound comprehensive casebook and to the first of our two paperback volumes ("Criminal Procedures: The Police"). In the latter half of the supplement, each chapter receives two numbers: one for the hardbound volume, and a second chapter number for those using the paperback volume ("Criminal Procedures: Prosecution and Adjudication") focused on the material for the Criminal Procedure II—or "bail to jail"—law school course. Page numbers in the latter half of the supplement also are matched to both the hardbound and paperback editions.

For most chapters, the additions are modest—a few notes and one or two short cases or documents. For some chapters, the materials are more substantial and may occupy a full day of class discussion. For example, the New Jersey Attorney General's report on racial profiling and DWB, which appears in the supplement materials for Chapter 2, is an extraordinary document and deserves, in our view, careful reading and discussion. That document explores low-level stops and searches, intentional and unintentional racial discrimination, and the capacities of different branches of government to deal with discrimination.

Chapter 2 reprints several U.S. Supreme Court opinions on the questions of reasonable suspicion and stops, such as Florida v. J.L., Illinois v. Wardlow, and City of Indianapolis v. Edmond. Chapter 4 covers United States v. Drayton, the Supreme Court's most recent consent case. Chapter 5 offers the Court's recent decision involving an arrest for a seatbelt violation, Atwater v. City of Lago Vista, while Chapter 7 reprints the Court's latest effort to adapt the law of searches to modern technology in Kyllo v. United States. Chapter 8 covers Dickerson v. United States, the Supreme Court's recent reaffirmation of the *Miranda* doctrine. Chapter 15 reprints and analyzes some of the key provisions from the Civil Asset Forfeiture Reform Act of 2000, P.L. No. 106-185. Chapter 20 covers the Supreme Court's recent effort to control legislative power to define "elements" of a crime, in Apprendi v. New Jersey, along with follow-up cases such as Harris v. United States.

Thus, we aim for this supplement to add both currency and conversation to the casebook. We hope that teachers and students will help us on both of these fronts by offering suggestions about materials we have included and those we might include in later supplements and in later editions.

## Web Resources

This supplement is consistent with our larger goal of creating materials to extend the scope and depth of the core casebook. We have created Internet web pages for this casebook to enrich the resources available for students using this casebook. Our goal is not to create an electronic coursebook. Instead, the electronic resources broaden, deepen, and enliven the core text.

The *Criminal Procedures* web pages include materials allowing students to test and expand their knowledge, such as practice problems, exams, short excerpts of articles on criminal procedure, a virtual library with a few police manuals and prosecutorial policies that would otherwise be difficult to obtain, and links to criminal justice resources on the web. The address for these pages is http://www.crimpro.com (or simply "crimpro"). We welcome suggestions for materials to post on the web pages or to publish in this printed supplement.

We hope you find that the casebook, this supplement, and the web pages—together—offer a complete, coherent, and challenging set of tools for learning about criminal procedure.

Marc Miller
Ron Wright

July 2002

# Table of Cases

# Table of Cases

# Chapter 1

## The Border of Criminal Procedure: Daily Interactions Between Citizens and Police

### B. Police Enforcement of Civility

**Page 20.** **Add this material after the notes.**

5. *Officer Manners: Police civility guidelines.* New York City's mayor and police chief have promulgated civility guidelines for police officers. The guidelines appear on a card given to all NYPD officers. Both sides of this card are duplicated below.

---

**NYPD DEPARTMENT VALUES**
In partnership with the community we pledge to:
- Protect the lives and property of our fellow citizens and impartially enforce the law.
- Fight crime both by preventing it and by aggressively pursuing violators of the law.
- Maintain a higher standard of integrity than is generally expected of others because so much is expected of us.
- Value human life, respect the dignity of each individual and render our services with courtesy and civility.
- *Remember to treat people in the same way you would expect to be treated.*

---

**WHEN ADDRESSING THE PUBLIC**

- Address and introduce yourself to members of the public during the course of your duties as appropriate. Use terms such as Mr., Ms., Sir or Ma'am, Hello and Thank You. Refer to teenagers as young lady or young man.
- Respect each individual, his or her cultural identity, customs and beliefs.
- Evaluate carefully every situation that leads to contact with the public and conduct yourself in a professional manner.
- Explain to the public in a courteous, professional demeanor the reason for your interaction with them and apologize for any inconvenience.
- Think tactics in every encounter.

---

Reporters had a field day. One article observed that "no one ever has portrayed New York's police officers as urban Andy Griffiths, aw-shucksing and Mornin' Ma'am-ing their way through the mean streets." See Sir, You're Busted: Giuliani Pushes Lesson in Good Manners for Police, The Commercial Appeal, Apr. 7, 1999, at A4. Another article quoted Mayor Giuliani's explanation of how the politeness policy could apply to arrests: "To say to even the worst criminal you're arresting, 'You're under arrest, sir,' it will channel some of the natural human emotions of anger." Henri Cauvin and John Marzulli, Nice NYPD on

Way—Giuliani Orders Police to Show Good Manners, N.Y. Daily
News, Apr. 7, 1999 at 4. The article continued:

> James Savage, president of the Patrolmen's Benevolent Association, called the plan
> "patronizing" to cops. "To inspire and to order are two different things," he said.
> Reaction from the rank and file was mixed. "I already treat people with respect,"
> said a cop at the 7th Precinct on the lower East Side. "They're going to want us to
> be robots soon," said another cop.

Should polite cops be granted greater discretion and power than impolite
cops?

## C. Traditional and Community Policing

**Page 21.   Add this material at the bottom of the page after the text.**

There are historic antecedents for the culture of community crime
control. In the following passage, Professor Jonathan Simon describes
the thousand-year-old tradition of "frankpledge" in England, where each
frankpledge group (originally 100 households) was held responsible for
making collective financial restitution for any property loss unless they
came up with the perpetrators within a specified time.

> In large portions of England from the tenth through the fifteenth centuries the lower
> orders of free adult males were members of a system of more or less compulsory
> collective security known as frankpledge. The system imposed on them a legal
> obligation to report offenses committed by other members of the group and to be
> financially obligated for any failure to produce the offender at presentment. . . .
> The central ritual of frankpledge was the so-called view of the frankpledge. In
> idealized form this was a royal review of the assembled freemen of a lordship or
> village. In its peak years during the twelfth and thirteenth centuries it provided an
> occasion when virtually the entire male population of the lower classes assembled
> before representatives of the crown and local elites. With the freemen or their
> representative chiefs assembled, both royal and local officials undertook to collect
> taxes and fines, register newcomers, and record the circumstances of the people.
> The frankpledge system integrated crime control into the everyday lives of the
> common people and local government. Rather than an arm of state power,
> frankpledge is best seen as a mechanism for mobilizing local power in a manner
> which was in part constitutive of state power.

Simon, Poor Discipline: Parole and the Social Control of the Underclass 18-20 (1993). The frankpledge system created strong incentive for private social control of criminal behavior. Is it compatible with a mobile society? How does the relationship between citizen and police officer in a community policing model resemble the frankpledge?

## D.  Curfew Laws

**Page 36.   Add this material after the notes.**

Closely related to curfew laws are gang or loitering ordinances that create a basis for police action where none would otherwise exist. These laws exist not only at the border of criminal procedure, but at the borders of government powers and individual rights more generally. These cases raise the most basic questions of our government: Why have a government? What powers *must* government have? What powers *may* government have? What powers must government *not* have? To what extent do the answers to these questions change as the context changes, such as in a crime wave?

In 1992, the city of Chicago passed an ordinance, §8-4-015 of the Municipal Code, giving police authority to disrupt loitering by gang members.

(a) Whenever a police officer observes a person whom he reasonably believes to be a criminal street gang member loitering in any public place with one or more other persons, he shall order all such persons to disperse and remove themselves from the area. Any person who does not promptly obey such an order is in violation of this section.

(b) It shall be an affirmative defense to an alleged violation of this section that no person who was observed loitering was in fact a member of a criminal street gang.

(c) As used in this section:

(1) "Loiter" means to remain in any one place with no apparent purpose.

(2) "Criminal street gang" means any ongoing organization, association in fact or group of three or more persons, whether formal or informal, having as one of its substantial activities the commission of one or more [enumerated] criminal acts . . . , and whose members individually or collectively engage in or have engaged in a pattern of criminal gang activity. . . .

(e) Any person who violates this Section is subject to a fine of not less than $100 and not more than $500 for each offense, or imprisonment for not more than six months, or both. In addition to or instead of the above penalties, any person who

4

violates this section may be required to perform up to 120 hours of community service. . . .

In 1997 the Illinois Supreme Court held that the ordinance violated the U.S. Constitution. City of Chicago v. Jesus Morales, 687 N.E.2d 53 (Ill. 1997). The city petitioned the U.S. Supreme Court for certiorari. News reports recounted the concerns of Attorney General Reno that the ordinance was unconstitutional, and stated that she refused to support Chicago without the explicit direction of President Clinton. President Clinton reportedly gave that order. The Supreme Court's decision follows.

## City of Chicago v. Jesus Morales
### 527 U.S. 41 (1999)

STEVENS, J.

In 1992, the Chicago City Council enacted the Gang Congregation Ordinance, which prohibits "criminal street gang members" from "loitering" with one another or with other persons in any public place. The question presented is whether the Supreme Court of Illinois correctly held that the ordinance violates the Due Process Clause of the Fourteenth Amendment to the Federal Constitution.

Before the ordinance was adopted, the city council's Committee on Police and Fire conducted hearings to explore the problems created by the city's street gangs, and more particularly, the consequences of public loitering by gang members. Witnesses included residents of the neighborhoods where gang members are most active, as well as some of the aldermen who represent those areas. . . . The council found that a continuing increase in criminal street gang activity was largely responsible for the city's rising murder rate, as well as an escalation of violent and drug-related crimes. It noted that in many neighborhoods throughout the city, "the burgeoning presence of street gang members in public places has intimidated many law abiding citizens." Furthermore, the council stated that gang members "establish control over identifiable areas . . . by loitering in those areas and intimidating others from entering those areas; and [m]embers of criminal street gangs avoid arrest by committing no offense punishable under existing laws when they know the police are present. . . ."

Two months after the ordinance was adopted, the Chicago Police Department promulgated General Order 92-4 to provide guidelines to govern its enforcement. That order purported to establish limitations on the enforcement discretion of police officers "to ensure that the anti-gang loitering ordinance is not enforced in an arbitrary or discriminatory way." The limitations confine the authority to arrest gang members who violate the ordinance to sworn "members of the Gang Crime Section" and certain other designated officers, and establish detailed criteria for defining street gangs and membership in such gangs. In addition, the order directs district commanders to "designate areas in which the presence of gang members has a demonstrable effect on the activities of law abiding persons in the surrounding community," and provides that the ordinance "will be enforced only within the designated areas." The city, however, does not release the locations of these "designated areas" to the public. During the three years of its enforcement, the police issued over 89,000 dispersal orders and arrested over 42,000 people for violating the ordinance.[7] . . .

The basic factual predicate for the city's ordinance is not in dispute. As the city argues in its brief, "the very presence of a large collection of obviously brazen, insistent, and lawless gang members and hangers-on on the public ways intimidates residents, who become afraid even to leave their homes and go about their business. That, in turn, imperils community residents' sense of safety and security, detracts from property values, and can ultimately destabilize entire neighborhoods." The findings in the ordinance explain that it was motivated by these concerns. We have no doubt that a law that directly prohibited such intimidating conduct would be constitutional,[17] but this ordinance broadly covers a significant amount of additional activity. Uncertainty

---

7. City of Chicago, R. Daley & T. Hillard, Gang and Narcotic Related Violent Crime: 1993-1997, p. 7 (June 1998). The city believes that the ordinance resulted in a significant decline in gang-related homicides. It notes that in 1995, the last year the ordinance was enforced, the gang-related homicide rate fell by 26%. In 1996, after the ordinance had been held invalid, the gang-related homicide rate rose 11%. However, gang-related homicides fell by 19% in 1997, over a year after the suspension of the ordinance. . . .

17. In fact the city already has several laws that serve this purpose. See, e.g., Ill. Comp. Stat. ch. 720 §§5/12-6 (1998) (Intimidation); 570/405.2 (Streetgang criminal drug conspiracy); 147/1 et seq. (Illinois Streetgang Terrorism Omnibus Prevention Act); 5/25-1 (Mob action). . . .

6

about the scope of that additional coverage provides the basis for respondents' claim that the ordinance is too vague.

[T]he freedom to loiter for innocent purposes is part of the "liberty" protected by the Due Process Clause of the Fourteenth Amendment. We have expressly identified this "right to remove from one place to another according to inclination" as "an attribute of personal liberty" protected by the Constitution. Williams v. Fears, 179 U.S. 270 (1900); see also Papachristou v. Jacksonville, 405 U.S. 156 (1972).[20] Indeed, it is apparent that an individual's decision to remain in a public place of his choice is as much a part of his liberty as the freedom of movement inside frontiers that is "a part of our heritage," Kent v. Dulles, 357 U.S. 116 (1958), or the right to move "to whatsoever place one's own inclination may direct" identified in Blackstone's Commentaries. 1 W. Blackstone, Commentaries on the Laws of England 130 (1765). . . .

Vagueness may invalidate a criminal law for either of two independent reasons. First, it may fail to provide the kind of notice that will enable ordinary people to understand what conduct it prohibits; second, it may authorize and even encourage arbitrary and discriminatory enforcement.

[T]he term "loiter" may have a common and accepted meaning, but the definition of that term in this ordinance — "to remain in any one place with no apparent purpose" — does not. It is difficult to imagine how any citizen of the city of Chicago standing in a public place with a group of people would know if he or she had an "apparent purpose." If she were talking to another person, would she have an apparent purpose?

---

20. Petitioner cites historical precedent against recognizing what it describes as the "fundamental right to loiter." While antiloitering ordinances have long existed in this country, their pedigree does not ensure their constitutionality. In 16th-century England, for example, the "Slavery acts" provided for a 2-year enslavement period for anyone who "liveth idly and loiteringly, by the space of three days." Note, Homelessness in a Modern Urban Setting, 10 Fordham Urb. L.J. 749, 754, n. 17 (1982). In *Papachristou* we noted that many American vagrancy laws were patterned on these "Elizabethan poor laws." . . . In addition, vagrancy laws were used after the Civil War to keep former slaves in a state of quasi slavery. In 1865, for example, Alabama broadened its vagrancy statute to include "any runaway, stubborn servant or child" and "a laborer or servant who loiters away his time, or refuses to comply with any contract for a term of service without just cause." T. Wilson, Black Codes of the South 76 (1965). . . . Neither this history nor the scholarly compendia in Justice Thomas' dissent persuades us that the right to engage in loitering that is entirely harmless in both purpose and effect is not a part of the liberty protected by the Due Process Clause.

If she were frequently checking her watch and looking expectantly down the street, would she have an apparent purpose? . . .

The city's principal response to this concern about adequate notice is that loiterers are not subject to sanction until after they have failed to comply with an officer's order to disperse. "[W]hatever problem is created by a law that criminalizes conduct people normally believe to be innocent is solved when persons receive actual notice from a police order of what they are expected to do." We find this response unpersuasive for at least two reasons.

*unpers. b/c*

First, the purpose of the fair notice requirement is to enable the ordinary citizen to conform his or her conduct to the law. No one may be required at peril of life, liberty or property to speculate as to the meaning of penal statutes. Although it is true that a loiterer is not subject to criminal sanctions unless he or she disobeys a dispersal order, the loitering is the conduct that the ordinance is designed to prohibit.[28] If the loitering is in fact harmless and innocent, the dispersal order itself is an unjustified impairment of liberty. . . . Because an officer may issue an order only after prohibited conduct has already occurred, it cannot provide the kind of advance notice that will protect the putative loiterer from being ordered to disperse. Such an order cannot retroactively give adequate warning of the boundary between the permissible and the impermissible applications of the law.

Second, the terms of the dispersal order compound the inadequacy of the notice afforded by the ordinance. It provides that the officer "shall order all such persons to disperse and remove themselves from the area." This vague phrasing raises a host of questions. After such an order issues, how long must the loiterers remain apart? How far must they move? If each loiterer walks around the block and they meet again at the same location, are they subject to arrest or merely to being ordered to disperse again? . . .

Lack of clarity in the description of the loiterer's duty to obey a dispersal order might not render the ordinance unconstitutionally vague

---

28.   In this way, the ordinance differs from the statute upheld in Colten v. Kentucky, 407 U.S. 104 (1972). There, we found that the illegality of the underlying conduct was clear. "Any person who stands in a group of persons along a highway where the police are investigating a traffic violation and seeks to engage the attention of an officer issuing a summons should understand that he could be convicted under . . . Kentucky's statute if he fails to obey an order to move on."

if the definition of the forbidden conduct were clear, but it does buttress our conclusion that the entire ordinance fails to give the ordinary citizen adequate notice of what is forbidden and what is permitted. The Constitution does not permit a legislature to set a net large enough to catch all possible offenders, and leave it to the courts to step inside and say who could be rightfully detained, and who should be set at large. This ordinance is therefore vague not in the sense that it requires a person to conform his conduct to an imprecise but comprehensible normative standard, but rather in the sense that no standard of conduct is specified at all. *no standard of conduct specified*

The broad sweep of the ordinance also violates the requirement that a legislature establish minimal guidelines to govern law enforcement. There are no such guidelines in the ordinance. In any public place in the city of Chicago, persons who stand or sit in the company of a gang member may be ordered to disperse unless their purpose is apparent. The mandatory language in the enactment directs the police to issue an order without first making any inquiry about their possible purposes. It matters not whether the reason that a gang member and his father, for example, might loiter near Wrigley Field is to rob an unsuspecting fan or just to get a glimpse of Sammy Sosa leaving the ballpark; in either event, if their purpose is not apparent to a nearby police officer, she may — indeed, she "shall" — order them to disperse. . . .

It is true, as the city argues, that the requirement that the officer reasonably believe that a group of loiterers contains a gang member does place a limit on the authority to order dispersal. That limitation would no doubt be sufficient if the ordinance only applied to loitering that had an apparently harmful purpose or effect, or possibly if it only applied to loitering by persons reasonably believed to be criminal gang members. But this ordinance, for reasons that are not explained in the findings of the city council, requires no harmful purpose and applies to nongang members as well as suspected gang members. . . .

Finally, in its opinion striking down the ordinance, the Illinois Supreme Court refused to accept the general order issued by the police department as a sufficient limitation on the "vast amount of discretion" granted to the police in its enforcement. We agree. That the police have adopted internal rules limiting their enforcement to certain designated areas in the city would not provide a defense to a loiterer who might be arrested elsewhere. Nor could a person who knowingly loitered with a

9

well-known gang member anywhere in the city safely assume that they would not be ordered to disperse no matter how innocent and harmless their loitering might be. . . .

We recognize the serious and difficult problems testified to by the citizens of Chicago that led to the enactment of this ordinance. We are mindful that the preservation of liberty depends in part on the maintenance of social order. However, in this instance the city has enacted an ordinance that affords too much discretion to the police and too little notice to citizens who wish to use the public streets. . . .

O'CONNOR, J., concurring in part and concurring in the judgment.

I agree with the Court that Chicago's Gang Congregation Ordinance is unconstitutionally vague. . . . I share Justice Thomas' concern about the consequences of gang violence, and I agree that some degree of police discretion is necessary to allow the police to perform their peacekeeping responsibilities satisfactorily. A criminal law, however, must not permit policemen, prosecutors, and juries to conduct "a standardless sweep . . . to pursue their personal predilections."

[The ordinance] fails to provide police with any standard by which they can judge whether an individual has an "apparent purpose." Indeed, because any person standing on the street has a general "purpose" — even if it is simply to stand — the ordinance permits police officers to choose which purposes are permissible. Under this construction the police do not have to decide that an individual is "threaten[ing] the public peace" to issue a dispersal order. [T]he ordinance applies to hundreds of thousands of persons who are not gang members, standing on any sidewalk or in any park, coffee shop, bar, or other location open to the public. . . .

Nevertheless, there remain open to Chicago reasonable alternatives to combat the very real threat posed by gang intimidation and violence. For example, the Court properly and expressly distinguishes the ordinance from laws that require loiterers to have a "harmful purpose," from laws that target only gang members, and from laws that incorporate limits on the area and manner in which the laws may be enforced. In addition, the ordinance here is unlike a law that "directly prohibit[s]" the "presence of a large collection of obviously brazen, insistent, and lawless gang members and hangers-on on the public ways," that intimidates residents. Indeed, as the plurality notes, the city of Chicago has several laws that do exactly this. . . . Chicago's general disorderly conduct provision allows the police to arrest those who knowingly "provoke, make or aid in making a breach of peace." . . .

BREYER, J., concurring in part and concurring in the judgment.

The ordinance before us creates more than a "minor limitation upon the free state of nature." The law authorizes a police officer to order any person to remove himself from any "location open to the public, whether publicly or privately owned," Chicago Municipal Code §8-4-015(c)(5), i.e., any sidewalk, front stoop, public park, public square, lakeside promenade, hotel, restaurant, bowling alley, bar, barbershop, sports arena, shopping mall, etc., but with two, and only two, limitations: First, that person must be accompanied by (or must himself be) someone police reasonably believe is a gang member. Second, that person must have remained in that public place "with no apparent purpose."

The first limitation cannot save the ordinance. Though it limits the number of persons subject to the law, it leaves many individuals, gang members and nongang members alike, subject to its strictures. Nor does it limit in any way the range of conduct that police may prohibit. The second limitation is . . . not a limitation at all. Since one always has some apparent purpose, the so-called limitation invites, in fact requires, the policeman to interpret the words "no apparent purpose" as meaning "no apparent purpose except for. . . ." And it is in the ordinance's delegation to the policeman of open-ended discretion to fill in that blank that the problem lies. To grant to a policeman virtually standardless discretion to close off major portions of the city to an innocent person is, in my view, to create a major, not a "minor," limitation upon the free state of nature. . . .

The ordinance is unconstitutional, not because a policeman applied this discretion wisely or poorly in a particular case, but rather because the policeman enjoys too much discretion in every case. [T]he city of Chicago may no more apply this law to the defendants, no matter how they behaved, than could it apply an (imaginary) statute that said, "It is a crime to do wrong," even to the worst of murderers. . . .

SCALIA, J., dissenting.

The citizens of Chicago were once free to drive about the city at whatever speed they wished. At some point Chicagoans (or perhaps

Illinoisans) decided this would not do, and imposed prophylactic speed limits designed to assure safe operation by the average (or perhaps even subaverage) driver with the average (or perhaps even subaverage) vehicle. This infringed upon the "freedom" of all citizens, but was not unconstitutional.

Similarly, the citizens of Chicago were once free to stand around and gawk at the scene of an accident. At some point Chicagoans discovered that this obstructed traffic and caused more accidents. They did not make the practice unlawful, but they did authorize police officers to order the crowd to disperse, and imposed penalties for refusal to obey such an order. Again, this prophylactic measure infringed upon the "freedom" of all citizens, but was not unconstitutional.

Until the ordinance that is before us today was adopted, the citizens of Chicago were free to stand about in public places with no apparent purpose — to engage, that is, in conduct that appeared to be loitering. In recent years, however, the city has been afflicted with criminal street gangs. As reflected in the record before us, these gangs congregated in public places to deal in drugs, and to terrorize the neighborhoods by demonstrating control over their "turf." Many residents of the inner city felt that they were prisoners in their own homes. Once again, Chicagoans decided that to eliminate the problem it was worth restricting some of the freedom that they once enjoyed. The means they took was similar to the second, and more mild, example given above rather than the first: Loitering was not made unlawful, but when a group of people occupied a public place without an apparent purpose and in the company of a known gang member, police officers were authorized to order them to disperse, and the failure to obey such an order was made unlawful. The minor limitation upon the free state of nature that this prophylactic arrangement imposed upon all Chicagoans seemed to them (and it seems to me) a small price to pay for liberation of their streets. The majority today invalidates this perfectly reasonable measure . . . by elevating loitering to a constitutionally guaranteed right, and by discerning vagueness where . . . none exists. . . .

I turn first to the support for the proposition that there is a constitutionally protected right to loiter — or, as the plurality more favorably describes it, for a person to "remain in a public place of his choice." . . . The plurality tosses around the term "constitutional right" in

*no evid. for no rt. to loiter*

this renegade sense, because there is not the slightest evidence for the existence of a genuine constitutional right to loiter. . . .

There are innumerable reasons why it may be important for a constable to tell a pedestrian to "move on" — and even if it were possible to list in an ordinance all of the reasons that are known, many are simply unpredictable. Hence the (entirely reasonable) Rule of the City of New York which reads: "No person shall fail, neglect or refuse to comply with the lawful direction or command of any Police Officer, Urban Park Ranger, Parks Enforcement Patrol Officer or other [Parks and Recreation] Department employee, indicated by gesture or otherwise." 56 RCNY §1-03(c)(1) (1996). . . .

Finally, I address . . . the proposition that the Ordinance is vague. It is not. . . . The criteria for issuance of a dispersal order under the Chicago Ordinance could hardly be clearer. . . .    *not vague*

The Court [argues] that the "apparent purpose" test is too elastic because it presumably allows police officers to treat de minimis "violations" as not warranting enforcement. But such discretion . . . is no different with regard to the enforcement of this clear ordinance than it is with regard to the enforcement of all laws in our criminal-justice system. Police officers (and prosecutors) have broad discretion over what laws to enforce and when. . . .    *P.O.'s always have broad discr.*

The plurality points out that Chicago already has several laws that reach the intimidating and unlawful gang-related conduct the Ordinance was directed at. The problem, of course, well recognized by Chicago's City Council, is that the gang members cease their intimidating and unlawful behavior under the watchful eye of police officers, but return to it as soon as the police drive away. The only solution, the council concluded, was to clear the streets of congregations of gangs, their drug customers, and their associates. . . .

The fact is that the present ordinance is entirely clear in its application, cannot be violated except with full knowledge and intent, and vests no more discretion in the police than innumerable other measures authorizing police orders to preserve the public peace and safety. [T]he majority's real quarrel with the Chicago Ordinance is simply that it permits (or indeed requires) too much harmless conduct by innocent citizens to be proscribed. . . .

But in our democratic system, how much harmless conduct to proscribe is not a judgment to be made by the courts. So long as

13

constitutionally guaranteed rights are not affected, and so long as the proscription has a rational basis, all sorts of perfectly harmless activity by millions of perfectly innocent people can be forbidden — riding a motorcycle without a safety helmet, for example, starting a campfire in a national forest, or selling a safe and effective drug not yet approved by the FDA. All of these acts are entirely innocent and harmless in themselves, but because of the risk of harm that they entail, the freedom to engage in them has been abridged. The citizens of Chicago have decided that depriving themselves of the freedom to "hang out" with a gang member is necessary to eliminate pervasive gang crime and intimidation—and that the elimination of the one is worth the deprivation of the other. This Court has no business second-guessing either the degree of necessity or the fairness of the trade. . . .

THOMAS, J., dissenting.

The duly elected members of the Chicago City Council enacted the ordinance at issue as part of a larger effort to prevent gangs from establishing dominion over the public streets. By invalidating Chicago's ordinance, I fear that the Court has unnecessarily sentenced law-abiding citizens to lives of terror and misery. . . .

Gangs fill the daily lives of many of our poorest and most vulnerable citizens with a terror that the Court does not give sufficient consideration, often relegating them to the status of prisoners in their own homes. The city of Chicago has suffered the devastation wrought by this national tragedy. Last year, in an effort to curb plummeting attendance, the Chicago Public Schools hired dozens of adults to escort children to school. The youngsters had become too terrified of gang violence to leave their homes alone. The children's fears were not unfounded. In 1996, the Chicago Police Department estimated that there were 132 criminal street gangs in the city. Between 1987 and 1994, these gangs were involved in 63,141 criminal incidents, including 21,689 nonlethal violent crimes and 894 homicides. Many of these criminal incidents and homicides result from gang "turf battles," which take place on the public streets and place innocent residents in grave danger. . . .

As part of its ongoing effort to curb the deleterious effects of criminal street gangs, the citizens of Chicago sensibly decided to return to basics. The ordinance does nothing more than confirm the well-established principle that the police have the duty and the power to maintain the public peace, and, when necessary, to disperse groups of individuals who threaten it. . . .

The plurality's sweeping conclusion that this ordinance infringes upon a liberty interest protected by the Fourteenth Amendment's Due Process Clause withers when exposed to the relevant history: Laws prohibiting loitering and vagrancy have been a fixture of Anglo-American law at least since the time of the Norman Conquest. The American colonists enacted laws modeled upon the English vagrancy laws, and at the time of the founding, state and local governments customarily criminalized loitering and other forms of vagrancy. Vagrancy laws were common in the decades preceding the ratification of the Fourteenth Amendment, and remained on the books long after.

[I]t is important to note that the ordinance does not criminalize loitering per se. Rather, it penalizes loiterers' failure to obey a police officer's order to move along. A majority of the Court believes that this scheme vests too much discretion in police officers. Nothing could be *[P.O.'s not too much disc-]* further from the truth. Far from according officers too much discretion, the ordinance merely enables police officers to fulfill one of their traditional functions. Police officers are not, and have never been, simply enforcers of the criminal law. They wear other hats—importantly, they have long been vested with the responsibility for preserving the public peace. See, e.g., O. Allen, Duties and Liabilities of Sheriffs 59 (1845) ("As the principal conservator of the peace in his county, and as the calm but irresistible minister of the law, the duty of the Sheriff is no less important than his authority is great"). Nor is the idea that the police are also peace officers simply a quaint anachronism. In most American jurisdictions, police officers continue to be obligated, by law, to maintain the public peace. . . .

In order to perform their peace-keeping responsibilities satisfactorily, the police inevitably must exercise discretion. Indeed, by empowering them to act as peace officers, the law assumes that the police will exercise that discretion responsibly and with sound judgment. That is not to say that the law should not provide objective guidelines for the police, but simply that it cannot rigidly constrain their every action. By directing a police officer not to issue a dispersal order unless he "observes a person whom he reasonably believes to be a criminal street gang member loitering in any public place," Chicago's ordinance strikes an appropriate balance between those two extremes. Just as we trust officers to rely on their experience and expertise in order to make spur-of-the-moment determinations about amorphous legal standards such as "probable cause" and "reasonable suspicion," so we must trust them to determine whether a group of loiterers contains individuals (in this case members of criminal street gangs) whom the city has determined threaten the public peace. . . .

The plurality also concludes that the definition of the term loiter . . . fails to provide adequate notice. . . . The plurality underestimates the intellectual capacity of the citizens of Chicago. Persons of ordinary intelligence are perfectly capable of evaluating how outsiders perceive their conduct . . . . Members of a group standing on the corner staring blankly into space, for example, are likely well aware that passersby would conclude that they have "no apparent purpose." . . .

Today, the Court focuses extensively on the "rights" of gang members and their companions. It can safely do so—the people who will have to live with the consequences of today's opinion do not live in our neighborhoods. Rather, the people who will suffer from our lofty pronouncements are people . . . who have seen their neighborhoods literally destroyed by gangs and violence and drugs. They are good, decent people who must struggle to overcome their desperate situation, against all odds, in order to raise their families, earn a living, and remain good citizens. As one resident described, "There is only about maybe one or two percent of the people in the city causing these problems maybe, but it's keeping 98 percent of us in our houses and off the streets and afraid to shop." By focusing exclusively on the imagined "rights" of the two percent, the Court today has denied our most vulnerable citizens the very thing that Justice Stevens elevates above all else—the "freedom of movement." And that is a shame. I respectfully dissent.

## NOTES

1.  *Order maintenance.* Is order maintenance by the police a crime control function or a community caretaker function? Is gang control the same as order maintenance? Should police have the general authority to ask citizens to "move on"? Will such statutes survive attacks under the federal constitution after *Morales*? If you were a member of the Chicago

City Council, could you draft a constitutional gang ordinance that would serve similar purposes to the ordinance struck down in *Morales*? State and federal cases on gang and order maintenance provisions are uncommon. Why? Are challenges to such laws likely to become more frequent after *Morales* and in light of community policing and crime control efforts?

2. *Community crime control.* Scholars have begun to argue that community policing is only the tip of a much larger iceberg, in the form of community crime control. Hearkening back to work by sociologists in the 1930s and 1940s, these scholars argue that crime policies, including police authority, must be understood in the context of "place" or "social meaning." So long as the notion of community is kept local and democratic, should community representatives (the police) have greater powers, such as the power to direct people to "move on"?

Pursuing this theme of localized and contextual understandings of crime and police power, Professor Tracey Meares has argued that "loitering laws enhance liberty of minority individuals in inner city communities." See Meares, Place and Crime, 73 Chi.-Kent L. Rev. 669 (1998) ("[T]he law abider-focused social organization improvement model of law enforcement may not look at all like any type of law enforcement that we've ever seen. Such a model likely involves explicit and strong relationships between the police and organizations that have not typically worked with the police in the past in poor, minority neighborhoods, such as the church."). See also Dan Kahan, Social Meaning and the Economic Analysis of Crime, 27 J. Legal Stud. 609 (1998).

In February 2000, the city of Chicago amended its anti-loitering ordinance to address the Court's concerns as expressed in *Morales*. The new ordinance prohibits loitering "under circumstances that would warrant a reasonable person to believe the purpose *or effect* of that behavior is to enable a criminal street gang to establish control over identifiable areas" (emphasis added). The ordinance itself now requires the police superintendent to designate "hot zones" of gang or narcotics activity, where the police may enforce the ordinance. The superintendent must consult community groups (along with various law enforcement officials) when designating the hot zones. Will the amended ordinance survive a constitutional challenge? Does it reinforce community crime control efforts?

⌐→ *new ordinance enacted after case brought*

17

# Chapter 2

# Brief Searches and Stops

## A. Brief Investigative Stops of Suspects

### 2. Grounds for Stops: Articulable, Individualized Reasonable Suspicion

**Page 60.** Add this material before the notes.

**Illinois v. William aka "Sam" Wardlow**
528 U.S. 119 (2000)

REHNQUIST, C.J.

Respondent Wardlow fled upon seeing police officers patrolling an area known for heavy narcotics trafficking. Two of the officers caught up with him, stopped him and conducted a protective pat-down search for weapons. Discovering a .38-caliber handgun, the officers arrested Wardlow. We hold that the officers' stop did not violate the Fourth Amendment to the United States Constitution.

On September 9, 1995, Officers Nolan and Harvey were working as uniformed officers in the special operations section of the Chicago Police Department. The officers were driving the last car of a four car caravan converging on an area known for heavy narcotics trafficking in order to investigate drug transactions. The officers were traveling together because they expected to find a crowd of people in the area, including lookouts and customers.

As the caravan passed 4035 West Van Buren, Officer Nolan observed respondent Wardlow standing next to the building holding an opaque bag. Respondent looked in the direction of the officers and fled. Nolan and Harvey turned their car southbound, watched him as he ran through the gangway and an alley, and eventually cornered him on the street. Nolan then exited his car and stopped respondent. He immediately conducted a protective pat-down search for weapons because in his experience it was common for there to be weapons in the near vicinity of narcotics transactions. During the frisk, Officer Nolan squeezed the bag respondent was carrying and felt a heavy, hard object similar to the shape of a gun. The officer then opened the bag and discovered a .38-caliber handgun with five live rounds of ammunition. The officers arrested Wardlow. The Illinois trial court denied respondent's motion to suppress, finding the gun was recovered during a lawful stop and frisk. Following a stipulated bench trial, Wardlow was convicted of unlawful use of a weapon by a felon. The [state Supreme Court reversed], concluding that the gun should have been suppressed because Officer Nolan did not have reasonable suspicion. . . . [1]

This case, involving a brief encounter between a citizen and a police officer on a public street, is governed by the analysis we first applied in Terry v. Ohio, 392 U.S. 1 (1968). In *Terry*, we held that an officer may, consistent with the Fourth Amendment, conduct a brief, investigatory stop when the officer has a reasonable, articulable suspicion that criminal activity is afoot. While "reasonable suspicion" is a less demanding standard than probable cause and requires a showing considerably less than preponderance of the evidence, the Fourth Amendment requires at least a minimal level of objective justification for making the stop. United States v. Sokolow, 490 U.S. 1 (1989). The officer must be able to articulate more than an "inchoate and unparticularized suspicion or hunch" of criminal activity.

Nolan and Harvey were among eight officers in a four car caravan that was converging on an area known for heavy narcotics trafficking,

---

1. The state courts have differed on whether unprovoked flight is sufficient grounds to constitute reasonable suspicion. See, e.g., State v. Anderson, 454 N.W.2d 763 (Wis.1990) (flight alone is sufficient); Platt v. State, 589 N.E.2d 222   (Ind.1992) (same); Harris v. State, 423 S.E.2d 723 (Ga. 1992) (flight in high crime area sufficient); State v. Hicks, 488 N.W.2d 359 (Neb. 1992) (flight is not enough); State v. Tucker, 642 A.2d 401 (N.J. 1994) (same). . . .

and the officers anticipated encountering a large number of people in the area, including drug customers and individuals serving as lookouts. It was in this context that Officer Nolan decided to investigate Wardlow after observing him flee. An individual's presence in an area of expected criminal activity, standing alone, is not enough to support a reasonable, particularized suspicion that the person is committing a crime. Brown v. Texas, 443 U.S. 47 (1979). But officers are not required to ignore the relevant characteristics of a location in determining whether the circumstances are sufficiently suspicious to warrant further investigation. Accordingly, we have previously noted the fact that the stop occurred in a "high crime area" among the relevant contextual considerations in a *Terry* analysis.

In this case, moreover, it was not merely respondent's presence in an area of heavy narcotics trafficking that aroused the officers' suspicion but his unprovoked flight upon noticing the police. Our cases have also recognized that nervous, evasive behavior is a pertinent factor in determining reasonable suspicion. Headlong flight—wherever it occurs—is the consummate act of evasion: it is not necessarily indicative of wrongdoing, but it is certainly suggestive of such. In reviewing the propriety of an officer's conduct, courts do not have available empirical studies dealing with inferences drawn from suspicious behavior, and we cannot reasonably demand scientific certainty from judges or law enforcement officers where none exists. Thus, the determination of reasonable suspicion must be based on commonsense judgments and inferences about human behavior. We conclude Officer Nolan was justified in suspecting that Wardlow was involved in criminal activity, and, therefore, in investigating further.

Such a holding is entirely consistent with our decision in Florida v. Royer, 460 U.S. 491 (1983), where we held that when an officer, without reasonable suspicion or probable cause, approaches an individual, the individual has a right to ignore the police and go about his business. And any refusal to cooperate, without more, does not furnish the minimal level of objective justification needed for a detention or seizure. But unprovoked flight is simply not a mere refusal to cooperate. Flight, by its very nature, is not "going about one's business"; in fact, it is just the opposite. Allowing officers confronted with such flight to stop the fugitive and investigate further is quite consistent with the individual's right to go about his business or to stay put and remain silent in the face of police questioning.

Respondent and *amici* also argue that there are innocent reasons for flight from police and that, therefore, flight is not necessarily indicative of ongoing criminal activity. This fact is undoubtedly true, but does not establish a violation of the Fourth Amendment. Even in *Terry*, the conduct justifying the stop was ambiguous and susceptible of an innocent explanation. The officer observed two individuals pacing back and forth in front of a store, peering into the window and periodically conferring. All of this conduct was by itself lawful, but it also suggested that the individuals were casing the store for a planned robbery. *Terry* recognized that the officers could detain the individuals to resolve the ambiguity.

In allowing such detentions, *Terry* accepts the risk that officers may stop innocent people. Indeed, the Fourth Amendment accepts that risk in connection with more drastic police action; persons arrested and detained on probable cause to believe they have committed a crime may turn out to be innocent. The *Terry* stop is a far more minimal intrusion, simply allowing the officer to briefly investigate further. If the officer does not learn facts rising to the level of probable cause, the individual must be allowed to go on his way. But in this case the officers found respondent in possession of a handgun, and arrested him for violation of an Illinois firearms statute. . . .

STEVENS, J., dissenting in part.

The State of Illinois asks this Court to announce a "bright-line rule" authorizing the temporary detention of anyone who flees at the mere sight of a police officer. Respondent counters by asking us to adopt the opposite per se rule—that the fact that a person flees upon seeing the police can never, by itself, be sufficient to justify a temporary investigative stop of the kind authorized by *Terry*. The Court today wisely endorses neither per se rule. . . .

Although I agree with the Court's rejection of the per se rules proffered by the parties, unlike the Court, I am persuaded that in this case the brief testimony of the officer who seized respondent does not justify the conclusion that he had reasonable suspicion to make the stop.

. . . The question in this case concerns "the degree of suspicion that attaches to" a person's flight—or, more precisely, what "commonsense conclusions" can be drawn respecting the motives behind that flight. A

pedestrian may break into a run for a variety of reasons—to catch up
with a friend a block or two away, to seek shelter from an impending
storm, to arrive at a bus stop before the bus leaves, to get home in time
for dinner, to resume jogging after a pause for rest, to avoid contact with
a bore or a bully, or simply to answer the call of nature—any of which
might coincide with the arrival of an officer in the vicinity. A pedestrian
might also run because he or she has just sighted one or more police
officers. [T]here are unquestionably circumstances in which a person's
flight is suspicious, and undeniably instances in which a person runs for
entirely innocent reasons.[3]

Given the diversity and frequency of possible motivations for flight,
it would be profoundly unwise to endorse either per se rule. The
inference we can reasonably draw about the motivation for a person's
flight, rather, will depend on a number of different circumstances.
Factors such as the time of day, the number of people in the area, the
character of the neighborhood, whether the officer was in uniform, the
way the runner was dressed, the direction and speed of the flight, and
whether the person's behavior was otherwise unusual might be relevant
in specific cases. . . .

Illinois contends that unprovoked flight is "an extreme reaction,"
because innocent people simply do not "flee at the mere sight of the
police." . . . Even assuming we know that a person runs because he sees
the police, the inference to be drawn may still vary from case to case.
[A] reasonable person may conclude that an officer's sudden appearance
indicates nearby criminal activity. And where there is criminal activity
there is also a substantial element of danger—either from the criminal or
from a confrontation between the criminal and the police. These
considerations can lead to an innocent and understandable desire to quit
the vicinity with all speed.

Among some citizens, particularly minorities and those residing in
high crime areas, there is also the possibility that the fleeing person is

---

3. Compare, e.g., Proverbs 28:1 ("The wicked flee when no man pursueth: but the
righteous are as bold as a lion") with Proverbs 22:3 ("A shrewd man sees trouble coming
and lies low; the simple walk into it and pay the penalty"). I have rejected reliance on the
former proverb in the past, because its "ivory-towered analysis of the real world" fails to
account for the experiences of many citizens of this country, particularly those who are
minorities. See California v. Hodari D., 499 U.S. 621, 630, n.4 (1991) (Stevens, J.,
dissenting). That this pithy expression fails to capture the total reality of our world,
however, does not mean it is inaccurate in all instances.

entirely innocent, but, with or without justification, believes that contact with the police can itself be dangerous, apart from any criminal activity associated with the officer's sudden presence.[7] . . .

Guided by that totality-of-the-circumstances test, the Court concludes that Officer Nolan had reasonable suspicion to stop respondent. In this respect, my view differs from the Court's. The entire justification for the stop is articulated in the brief testimony of Officer Nolan, [who stated,] "He looked in our direction and began fleeing."

No other factors sufficiently support a finding of reasonable suspicion. Though respondent was carrying a white, opaque bag under his arm, there is nothing at all suspicious about that. Certainly the time of day—shortly after noon—does not support Illinois' argument. Nor were the officers "responding to any call or report of suspicious activity in the area." Officer Nolan did testify that he expected to find "an enormous amount of people," including drug customers or lookouts . . . . This observation, in my view, lends insufficient weight to the reasonable suspicion analysis; indeed, in light of the absence of testimony that anyone else was nearby when respondent began to run, this observation points in the opposite direction.

The State, along with the majority of the Court, relies as well on the assumption that this flight occurred in a high crime area. Even if that assumption is accurate, it is insufficient because even in a high crime neighborhood unprovoked flight does not invariably lead to reasonable suspicion. On the contrary, because many factors providing innocent motivations for unprovoked flight are concentrated in high crime areas, the character of the neighborhood arguably makes an inference of guilt

---

7. See Johnson, Americans' Views on Crime and Law Enforcement: Survey Findings, National Institute of Justice Journal 13 (Sept.1997) (reporting study by the Joint Center for Political and Economic Studies in April 1996, which found that 43% of African-Americans consider "police brutality and harassment of African-Americans a serious problem" in their own community); President's Comm'n on Law Enforcement and Administration of Justice, Task Force Report: The Police 183-184 (1967) (documenting the belief, held by many minorities, that field interrogations are conducted "indiscriminately" and "in an abusive . . . manner," and labeling this phenomenon a "principal problem" causing "friction" between minorities and the police); see also Casimir, Minority Men: We Are Frisk Targets, N.Y. Daily News, Mar. 26, 1999, p. 34 (informal survey of 100 young black and Hispanic men living in New York City; 81 reported having been stopped and frisked by police at least once; none of the 81 stops resulted in arrests).

less appropriate, rather than more so. Like unprovoked flight itself, presence in a high crime neighborhood is a fact too generic and susceptible to innocent explanation to satisfy the reasonable suspicion inquiry. It is the State's burden to articulate facts sufficient to support reasonable suspicion. In my judgment, Illinois has failed to discharge that burden. . . .

# Florida v. J.L.
## 529 U.S. 266 (2000)

GINSBURG, J.

The question presented in this case is whether an anonymous tip that a person is carrying a gun is, without more, sufficient to justify a police officer's stop and frisk of that person. We hold that it is not.

On October 13, 1995, an anonymous caller reported to the Miami-Dade Police that a young black male standing at a particular bus stop and wearing a plaid shirt was carrying a gun. So far as the record reveals, there is no audio recording of the tip, and nothing is known about the informant. Sometime after the police received the tip—the record does not say how long—two officers were instructed to respond. They arrived at the bus stop about six minutes later and saw three black males "just hanging out [there]." One of the three, respondent J.L., was wearing a plaid shirt. Apart from the tip, the officers had no reason to suspect any of the three of illegal conduct. The officers did not see a firearm, and J.L. made no threatening or otherwise unusual movements. One of the officers approached J.L., told him to put his hands up on the bus stop, frisked him, and seized a gun from J.L.'s pocket. The second officer frisked the other two individuals, against whom no allegations had been made, and found nothing.

J.L., who was at the time of the frisk "10 days shy of his 16th birthday," was charged under state law with carrying a concealed firearm without a license and possessing a firearm while under the age of 18. He moved to suppress the gun as the fruit of an unlawful search, and the trial court granted his motion. [The Supreme Court of Florida held the search invalid under the Fourth Amendment.]

In the instant case, the officers' suspicion that J.L. was carrying a weapon arose not from any observations of their own but solely from a call made from an unknown location by an unknown caller. Unlike a tip from a known informant whose reputation can be assessed and who can be held responsible if her allegations turn out to be fabricated, "an anonymous tip alone seldom demonstrates the informant's basis of knowledge or veracity." Alabama v. White, 496 U.S. 325 (1990). As we have recognized, however, there are situations in which an anonymous tip, suitably corroborated, exhibits "sufficient indicia of reliability to provide reasonable suspicion to make the investigatory stop." The question we here confront is whether the tip pointing to J.L. had those indicia of reliability.

In *White*, the police received an anonymous tip asserting that a woman was carrying cocaine and predicting that she would leave an apartment building at a specified time, get into a car matching a particular description, and drive to a named motel. Standing alone, the tip would not have justified a . . . stop. Only after police observation showed that the informant had accurately predicted the woman's movements, we explained, did it become reasonable to think the tipster had inside knowledge about the suspect and therefore to credit his assertion about the cocaine. Although the Court held that the suspicion in *White* became reasonable after police surveillance, we regarded the case as borderline. Knowledge about a person's future movements indicates some familiarity with that person's affairs, but having such knowledge does not necessarily imply that the informant knows, in particular, whether that person is carrying hidden contraband. We accordingly classified *White* as a "close case."

The tip in the instant case lacked the moderate indicia of reliability present in *White* and essential to the Court's decision in that case. The anonymous call concerning J.L. provided no predictive information and therefore left the police without means to test the informant's knowledge or credibility. That the allegation about the gun turned out to be correct does not suggest that the officers, prior to the frisks, had a reasonable basis for suspecting J.L. of engaging in unlawful conduct: The reasonableness of official suspicion must be measured by what the officers knew before they conducted their search. All the police had to go on in this case was the bare report of an unknown, unaccountable informant who neither explained how he knew about the gun nor supplied any basis for believing he had inside information about J.L. If *White* was a close case on the reliability of anonymous tips, this one surely falls on the other side of the line.

Florida contends that the tip was reliable because its description of the suspect's visible attributes proved accurate: There really was a young black male wearing a plaid shirt at the bus stop. . . . An accurate description of a subject's readily observable location and appearance is of course reliable in this limited sense: It will help the police correctly identify the person whom the tipster means to accuse. Such a tip, however, does not show that the tipster has knowledge of concealed criminal activity. The reasonable suspicion here at issue requires that a tip be reliable in its assertion of illegality, not just in its tendency to identify a determinate person.

A second major argument advanced by Florida and the United States as *amicus* is, in essence, that the standard [reasonable suspicion] analysis should be modified to license a "firearm exception." Under such an exception, a tip alleging an illegal gun would justify a stop and frisk even if the accusation would fail standard presearch reliability testing. We decline to adopt this position.

Firearms are dangerous, and extraordinary dangers sometimes justify unusual precautions. Our decisions recognize the serious threat that armed criminals pose to public safety; Terry v. Ohio, 392 U.S. 1 (1968), which permits protective police searches on the basis of reasonable suspicion rather than demanding that officers meet the higher standard of probable cause, responds to this very concern. But an automatic firearm exception to our established reliability analysis would rove too far. Such an exception would enable any person seeking to harass another to set in motion an intrusive, embarrassing police search of the targeted person simply by placing an anonymous call falsely reporting the target's unlawful carriage of a gun. Nor could one securely confine such an exception to allegations involving firearms. Several Courts of Appeals have held it per se foreseeable for people carrying significant amounts of illegal drugs to be carrying guns as well. If police officers may properly conduct *Terry* frisks on the basis of bare-boned tips about guns, it would be reasonable to maintain . . . that the police should similarly have discretion to frisk based on bare-boned tips about narcotics. [T]he Fourth Amendment is not so easily satisfied.

The facts of this case do not require us to speculate about the circumstances under which the danger alleged in an anonymous tip might be so great as to justify a search even without a showing of reliability. We do not say, for example, that a report of a person carrying a bomb need bear the indicia of reliability we demand for a report of a person carrying a firearm before the police can constitutionally conduct a frisk. Nor do we hold that public safety officials in quarters where the reasonable expectation of Fourth Amendment privacy is diminished, such as airports and schools, cannot conduct protective searches on the basis of information insufficient to justify searches elsewhere.

[We] hold that an anonymous tip lacking indicia of reliability of the kind contemplated in . . . *White* does not justify a stop and frisk whenever and however it alleges the illegal possession of a firearm. The judgment of the Florida Supreme Court is affirmed.

KENNEDY, J., concurring.

It seems appropriate to observe that a tip might be anonymous in some sense yet have certain other features, either supporting reliability or narrowing the likely class of informants, so that the tip does provide the lawful basis for some police action. One such feature, as the Court recognizes, is that the tip predicts future conduct of the alleged criminal. There may be others. For example, if an unnamed caller with a voice which sounds the same each time tells police on two successive nights about criminal activity which in fact occurs each night, a similar call on the third night ought not be treated automatically like the tip in the case now before us. In the instance supposed, there would be a plausible argument that experience cures some of the uncertainty surrounding the anonymity, justifying a proportionate police response. In today's case, however, the State provides us with no data about the reliability of anonymous tips. Nor do we know whether the dispatcher or arresting officer had any objective reason to believe that this tip had some particular indicia of reliability.

If an informant places his anonymity at risk, a court can consider this factor in weighing the reliability of the tip. An instance where a tip might be considered anonymous but nevertheless sufficiently reliable to justify a proportionate police response may be when an unnamed person driving a car the police officer later describes stops for a moment and, face to face, informs the police that criminal activity is occurring. This too seems to be different from the tip in the present case.

Instant caller identification is widely available to police, and, if anonymous tips are proving unreliable and distracting to police, squad cars can be sent within seconds to the location of the telephone used by the informant. Voice recording of telephone tips might, in appropriate cases, be used by police to locate the caller. It is unlawful to make false reports to the police, and the ability of the police to trace the identity of anonymous telephone informants may be a factor which lends reliability to what, years earlier, might have been considered unreliable anonymous tips. These matters, of course, must await discussion in other cases, where the issues are presented by the record.

**Page 61.   Add this material after the notes.**

6. *Limits on reasonable suspicion: the "innocent activity" doctrine.* Typically the government must affirmatively show that reasonable suspicion existed for a stop. Does a suspect undermine this showing by arguing that behavior of this sort is often innocent? A few state courts say that reasonable suspicion does not exist where the suspect's behavior was "as consistent with innocent activity as with criminal activity." See Irwin v. Superior Court of Los Angeles County, 462 P.2d 12, 14 (Cal. 1969). Most states have now rejected that formulation as being unworkable. See Woods v. State, 956 S.W.2d 33 (Tex. Crim. App. 1997); Arvizu v. United States, 122 S. Ct. 744 (2002) (experienced police officers can draw inferences from cumulative effects of various facts that standing alone contribute little to reasonable suspicion calculus).

## 3.   Pretextual Stops

**Page 82.   Replace the *Tate* case with the following materials.**

# State v. Thomas Ladson
979 P.2d 833 (Wash. 1999)

SANDERS, J.

The issue is whether pretextual traffic stops violate article I, section 7, of the Washington Constitution. We find they do and [affirm] the trial court's suppression order.

The facts are basically undisputed. On October 5, 1995 City of Lacey police officer Jim Mack and Thurston County sheriff's detective Cliff Ziesmer were on proactive gang patrol. The officers explained they do not make routine traffic stops while on proactive gang patrol although they use traffic infractions as a means to pull over people in order to initiate contact and questioning. The trial court factually found: While on gang patrol, officer Mack selectively enforces traffic violations depending on whether he believes there is the potential for intelligence gathering in such stops.

On the day in question Richard Fogle attracted the attention of officers Mack and Ziesmer as he drove by. Fogle and his passenger Thomas Ladson are both African-American. Although the officers had never seen Ladson before, they recognized Fogle from an unsubstantiated street rumor that Fogle was involved with drugs. The trial court found, "Officer Mack's suspicions about Fogle's reputed drug dealing was his motivation in finding a legal reason to initiate the stop of Fogle's vehicle."

The officers tailed the Fogle vehicle looking for a legal justification to stop the car. They shadowed the vehicle while it refueled at a local filling station and then finally pulled Fogle over several blocks later on the grounds that Fogle's license plate tabs had expired five days earlier. The officers do not deny the stop was pretextual.

The police then discovered Fogle's driver's license was suspended and arrested him on the spot. After securing Fogle in handcuffs in the squad car, the police conducted a full search of the car "incident to Fogle's arrest." Then they turned their attention to the passenger, Thomas Ladson. They ordered Ladson to exit the vehicle, patted him down, and required him to stand against the car while they searched its interior. The police searched Ladson's jacket which was in the passenger's seat and found a small handgun. Ladson was placed under arrest and searched. On Ladson's person and in his jacket the police found several baggies of marijuana and some $600 in cash.

Ladson was charged with unlawful possession of a controlled substance with intent to deliver while armed with a deadly weapon, and possession of a stolen firearm. Ladson filed a pretrial motion to suppress the evidence on the grounds it was obtained during an unconstitutional pretextual traffic stop. The trial court agreed and granted the motion ruling, "Pretextual stops by law enforcement officers are violative of the Constitution."

The State appealed and shortly thereafter the United States Supreme Court decided Whren v. United States, 517 U.S. 806 (1996), holding pretextual traffic stops do not violate the Fourth Amendment to the United States Constitution. [Ladson argues in this court that] article I, section 7, of the state constitution provides broader protection than does the Fourth Amendment in the area of pretextual traffic stops and contend[s that] article I, section 7, renders pretextual traffic stops unconstitutional. . . .

It is already well established that article I, section 7, of the state constitution has broader application than does the Fourth Amendment of the United States Constitution. Washington Constitution article I, section 7, provides: "No person shall be disturbed in his private affairs, or his home invaded, without authority of law." Article I, section 7, is explicitly broader than that of the Fourth Amendment as it clearly recognizes an individual's right to privacy with no express limitations and places greater emphasis on privacy. Further, while the Fourth Amendment operates on a downward ratcheting mechanism of diminishing expectations of privacy, article I, section 7, holds the line by pegging the constitutional standard to those privacy interests which citizens of this state have held, and should be entitled to hold, safe from governmental trespass absent a warrant.

[T]he essence of this, and every, pretextual traffic stop is that the police are pulling over a citizen, not to enforce the traffic code, but to conduct a criminal investigation unrelated to the driving. Therefore the reasonable articulable suspicion that a traffic infraction has occurred which justifies an exception to the warrant requirement for an ordinary traffic stop does not justify a stop for criminal investigation. . . .

We have observed that ultimately our state constitutional provision is designed to guard against "unreasonable search and seizure, made without probable cause." However, the problem with a pretextual traffic stop is that it is a search or seizure which cannot be constitutionally justified for its true reason (i.e., speculative criminal investigation), but only for some other reason (i.e., to enforce traffic code) which is at once lawfully sufficient but not the real reason. Pretext is therefore a triumph of form over substance; a triumph of expediency at the expense of reason. But it is against the standard of reasonableness which our constitution measures exceptions to the general rule, which forbids search or seizure absent a warrant. Pretext is result without reason. . . .

The question, then, becomes whether the fact that someone has committed a traffic offense, such as failing to signal or eating while driving, justifies a warrantless seizure which would not otherwise be permitted absent that "authority of law" represented by a warrant. The State argues it does. The State asks this court to approve the use of pretext to justify a warrantless seizure. We decline the invitation. Article I, section 7, forbids use of pretext as a justification for a warrantless search or seizure because our constitution requires we look beyond the formal justification for the stop to the actual one. In the case of pretext, the actual reason for the stop is inherently unreasonable, otherwise the use of pretext would be unnecessary. . . .

The ultimate teaching of our case law is that the police may not abuse their authority to conduct a warrantless search or seizure under a narrow exception to the warrant requirement when the reason for the search or seizure does not fall within the scope of the reason for the exception.

But in this case the state asks us to abandon our commitment against pretext and significantly undermine the vitality of article I, section 7, in favor of the lower standard under the Fourth Amendment announced in Whren v. United States, 517 U.S. 806 (1996) . . . .[10]

We conclude the citizens of Washington have held, and are entitled to hold, a constitutionally protected interest against warrantless traffic stops or seizures on a mere pretext to dispense with the warrant when the true reason for the seizure is not exempt from the warrant requirement. We therefore hold pretextual traffic stops violate article I, section 7,

---

10.   We note if we were to depart from our holdings and allow pretextual traffic stops, Washington citizens would lose their privacy every time they enter their automobiles. The traffic code is sufficiently extensive in its regulation that "[w]hether it be for failing to signal while changing lanes, driving with a headlight out, or not giving 'full time and attention' to the operation of the vehicle, virtually the entire driving population is in violation of some regulation as soon as they get in their cars, or shortly thereafter." Peter Shakow, Let He Who Never Has Turned Without Signaling Cast the First Stone: An Analysis of Whren v. United States, 24 Am. J. Crim. L. 627, 633 (1997). Thus, nearly every citizen would be subject to a *Terry* stop simply because he or she is in his or her car. But we have repeatedly affirmed that Washingtonians retain their privacy while in the automobile and we will do so today. . . .

32

because they are seizures absent the "authority of law" which a warrant would bring. Const. art. I, §7.

When determining whether a given stop is pretextual, the court should consider the totality of the circumstances, including both the subjective intent of the officer as well as the objective reasonableness of the officer's behavior. We recognize the Court of Appeals has held that the test for pretext is objective only. See State v. Chapin, 879 P.2d 300 (Wash. App. 1994). But an objective test may not fully answer the critical inquiry: Was the officer conducting a pretextual traffic stop or not? We cannot agree with *Chapin* and disapprove it to the extent it limits the query to objective factors alone. . . .

Here, the initial stop, which is a seizure for constitutional purposes, was without authority of law because the reason for the stop (investigation) was not exempt from the warrant requirement. It is elementary that "[i]f the initial stop was unlawful, the subsequent search and fruits of that search are inadmissible. . . ."

MADSEN, J., dissenting.

Under article I, section 7 of the Washington Constitution, the motive of a law enforcement officer is irrelevant when assessing the constitutionality of a stop for a minor traffic infraction. Article I, section 7 prohibits searches and seizures "without authority of law." A constitutionally valid statute may provide "authority of law" within the meaning of article I, section 7, and such authority is provided by state statutes which enable law enforcement officers to stop vehicles and cite the drivers for traffic and equipment violations. Nothing in the statutes limits an officer's authority to make a traffic stop depending upon the motive of the officer, nor is a stop prohibited depending upon the duties to which the officer is assigned.

However, the scope of such a traffic stop is strictly limited by existing statutes and decisional law. Unless there is justification independent of the traffic infraction justifying the initial stop, an officer is prohibited from any detention or search beyond that necessary to issue a citation. The majority collapses the justification for a traffic stop into the question of scope. I dissent.

Article I, section 7, prohibits searches and seizures made "without authority of law." The authority of law required by Const. art. I, §7 . . . includes authority granted by a valid (i.e., constitutional) statute, the common law or a rule of this court. Under RCW 46.64.015 . . . an officer may issue a notice of a traffic infraction at the request of another law enforcement officer in whose presence the infraction was committed.

[The] statutes establish that an officer must have probable cause to believe that a traffic infraction has been committed in order to make a stop. Because the relevant statutes encompass a probable cause standard, they codify a constitutionally valid standard for warrantless traffic stops. Certainly there is no dispute in this case that absent pretextual motive, an officer is constitutionally entitled to stop a vehicle without a warrant where a minor traffic infraction has been committed in the officer's presence.

However, the scope of a stop for a minor traffic violation is limited. With certain express exceptions, the officer may detain the driver only for the period of time reasonably necessary to issue and serve a citation and notice. The officer is not, without other justification, entitled to further detain the occupants of the vehicle nor to conduct a warrantless search. . . . An officer's motive in stopping a vehicle to investigate a "hunch," or to engage in a fishing expedition makes no difference — the scope of a stop for a minor traffic infraction is still limited. The officer cannot lawfully exceed that scope. If the officer exceeds that scope, with nothing more than the traffic stop as justification, any evidence unlawfully obtained must be suppressed. . . .

I would hold that the officer's motive does not turn a stop based upon probable cause that a traffic violation has occurred into an unlawful stop. . . . Our expectations are that we will be stopped and cited for traffic infractions, and we cannot reasonably expect that we are protected from such a stop depending on the officer's other motives.

Of course, once the initial stop is made, there may be other justification to detain or search independent of the traffic or equipment violation which justified the initial stop. For example, an officer may stop for a traffic infraction, such as speeding. The officer also suspects that the driver may be involved in illegal drug activity. When the officer approaches the vehicle to issue and serve a citation and notice, and the officer immediately smells marijuana or sees readily identifiable illegal drugs, the officer then has probable cause to arrest the driver of the vehicle and to conduct a warrantless search. The officer is not justified in doing so based upon the traffic stop, nor based upon suspicion of illegal activity, but rather based upon probable cause ("plain smell" or "plain view") that a crime is being committed independent of the traffic offense. . . .

Finally, I note that should there be any allegations that an officer's motive in making a traffic stop is relevant because a particular class has been targeted, the Supreme Court has stated: "We of course agree . . . that the Constitution prohibits selective enforcement of the law based on considerations such as race. But the constitutional basis for objecting to intentionally discriminatory application of laws is the Equal Protection Clause, not the Fourth Amendment." *Whren*, 517 U.S. at 813. Similarly, article I, section 7, does not require inquiry into the motive of an officer making a traffic stop, even if discrimination is alleged. Discriminatory motive is relevant, however, under the equal protection and privileges and immunities clauses. . . .

**Page 85.    Add this material at the end of note 1.**

The trend toward the death of the pretext doctrine has continued. Several states where pretext claims remained part of the jurisprudence before *Whren* have issued clear statements rejecting the doctrine. See, e.g., State v. Vineyard, 958 S.W.2d 730 (Tenn. 1997). The intermediate appellate courts in Georgia appear to have rejected Tate v. State (reprinted in the casebook), though the Supreme Court of Georgia has yet to speak on the subject. See State v. Kirbabas, 502 S.E.2d 314 (Ga. Ct. App. 1998). A few states, like Washington, continue to apply the pretext concept for both brief stops and searches. See, e.g., State v. Varnado, 582 N.W.2d 886 (Minn. 1998); State v. Holmes, 569 N.W.2d 181 (Minn. 1997) (rejecting inventory search of automobile where officer's sole motivation was to discover a gun). Remnants of the pretext concept exist in other cases in which the defendant claims that the officers did not have reasonable suspicion at all.

**Page 87.    Add this material before section B.**

7. *Pretext, subjective expectations and privacy rights.*  With the U.S. Supreme Court's decision in Whren v. United States (1996), the pretext doctrine seemed like it was on the ropes, remaining active only in a handful of states. Then, in April 2000, the U.S. Supreme Court decided Bond v. United States, 529 U.S. 334 (2000).  In *Bond*, the Court held

that an officer's "physical manipulation of a bus passenger's carry-on luggage" was a search. The majority asserted that *Bond* was merely a case distinguishing between "searches" and investigations of items left in plain sight (or casual contact). It was not, the Court said, a case about the officer's subjective intent. From the court's perspective, the contact with the bag was more than "plain sight" since "physically invasive inspection is simply more intrusive than purely visual inspection."

But the dissenters, Justices Breyer and Scalia, suggested that the case was indeed about the officer's subjective intent. They noted that squeezing of softsided luggage is a typical occurrence. Justice Breyer suggested that what distinguishes the Border Patrol agent's squeeze from a more ordinary squeeze is that

> the agent's purpose here—searching for drugs—differs dramatically from the intention of a driver or fellow passenger who squeezes a bag in the process of making more room for another parcel. But in determining whether an expectation of privacy is reasonable, it is the effect, not the purpose, that matters. [A] Fourth Amendment rule that turns on purpose could prevent police alone from intruding where other strangers freely tread. And the added privacy protection achieved by such an approach would not justify the harm worked to law enforcement—at least that is what this Court's previous cases suggest.

In footnote 2, the majority opinion cited *Whren* and pointed out that the parties "agree that the subjective intent of the law enforcement officer is irrelevant in determining whether that officer's actions violate the Fourth Amendment. This principle applies to the agent's acts in this case as well; the issue is not his state of mind, but the objective effect of his actions." Is pretext—now in the nascent form of subjective officer expectations—alive after all? If not, will state and federal courts be developing "squeeze" and "fondle" jurisprudence, for years to come?

## 4.   DWB ("Driving While Black")

The racial implications of issues such as pretextual stops and the use of criminal profiles to establish reasonable suspicion have not disappeared, even though the courts generally have not regulated these police techniques. Defendants have only rarely convinced courts to outlaw the use of pretextual stops or criminal profiles, but a related claim has achieved more success outside the courts. The related claim is that police stop motorists based at least partly on their race. Such claims are often described in public debates as the creation of a crime called "driving while black" or "DWB." The police response to such charges is similar to their response to claims of pretext: First, police say, they stop only drivers who are breaking some law, and second, they stop drivers who satisfy established profiles for serious criminals.

Claims of DWB have been especially strong for parts of Interstate 95, especially the stretch of highway between Washington and New York known as the New Jersey Turnpike, and the stretch of highway from Northern Florida through Georgia. Claims of DWB are difficult for a criminal defendant to litigate, though litigation is currently pending in both federal and state courts. But both state and federal governments have begun to investigate patterns of traffic and drug stops on highways. A few jurisdictions have passed statutes requiring collection on data. Consider the following report by the New Jersey Attorney General, developed both to guide New Jersey police and "as a guide for other state and local jurisdictions throughout the country."

## INTERIM REPORT OF THE STATE POLICE
## REVIEW TEAM REGARDING ALLEGATIONS
## OF RACIAL PROFILING
### Peter Verniero, Attorney General (April 20, 1999)

. . . This Interim Report specifically focuses on the activities of state troopers assigned to patrol the New Jersey Turnpike. [T]he Turnpike is widely believed to be a major drug corridor, thereby providing the State Police with both the impetus and the opportunity to engage in drug interdiction tactics that appear to be inextricably linked to the "racial profiling" controversy. [B]ased upon the information that we reviewed, minority motorists have been treated differently than nonminority motorists during the course of traffic stops on the New Jersey Turnpike. For the reasons set out fully in this Report, we conclude that the problem of disparate treatment is real — not imagined. This problem . . . is more complex and subtle than has generally been reported.

[We] define "racial profiling" broadly to encompass any action taken by a state trooper during a traffic stop that is based upon racial or ethnic stereotypes and that has the effect of treating minority motorists differently than nonminority motorists. We have thus elected not to limit our review to a trooper's initial decision to order a vehicle to pull over. Rather, we also consider a host of other actions that may be taken by State Police members throughout the course of a traffic stop, such as ordering the driver or passengers to step out, subjecting the occupants to questions that are not directly related to the motor vehicle violation that gave rise to the stop, summoning a drug-detection canine to the scene, or requesting permission to conduct a consent search of the vehicle and its contents. . . .

Our review has revealed two interrelated problems that may be influenced by the goal of interdicting illicit drugs: (1) willful misconduct by a small number of State Police members, and (2) more common instances of possible de facto discrimination by officers who may be influenced by stereotypes and may thus tend to treat minority motorists differently during the course of routine traffic stops, subjecting them more routinely to investigative tactics and techniques that are designed to ferret out illicit drugs and weapons. . . .

The obvious and necessary remedy to deal with those officers who intentionally violate the civil rights of minority motorists is to ensure swift discipline and criminal prosecutions, taking full advantage of New Jersey's official misconduct laws. . . . As to the problem occasioned by the disparate treatment of minorities based on subtle or even subconscious stereotypes, the solution lies not only in clearly and precisely explaining once and for all what conduct is prohibited, but also, as importantly, in clearly explaining in *positive* terms how stops are to be conducted. . . .

Our review has shown that over the years, conflicting messages have been sent regarding the official policy to prohibit any form of race-based profiling. This situation should be rectified by developing a clear and consistent message. We propose that as a matter of policy for the New Jersey State Police, race, ethnicity, and national origin should not be used at all by troopers in selecting vehicles to be stopped or in exercising discretion during the course of a stop (other than in determining whether a person matches the general description of one or more known suspects). In making this recommendation, we propose going beyond the minimum requirements of federal precedent because, simply, it is the right thing to do and because the Executive Branch, no less than its judicial counterpart, has an independent duty to ensure that our laws are enforced in a constitutional, efficient, and even-handed fashion. . . .

*Stops.* We have received and compiled information regarding stops by troopers assigned to the Moorestown and Cranbury stations from the monthly stop data. . . . Four of every ten stops (40.6 percent) made during the period for which data are available involved black, Hispanic, Asian or other nonwhite people. . . .

*Searches.* It is obvious from the data provided that very few stops result in the search of a motor vehicle. For example, in those instances for which we have data permitting comparisons between stops and searches, only 627 (0.7 percent) of 87,489 stops involved a search. [T]he available data indicate that the overwhelming majority of searches (77.2 percent) involved black or Hispanic persons. Specifically, of the 1,193 searches for which data are available, 21.4 percent involved a white person, more than half (53.1 percent) involved a black person, and almost one of every four (24.1 percent) involved a Hispanic person.

. . . Not surprisingly, most consent searches do not result in a "positive" finding. . . . Specifically, 19.2 percent of the searches we considered resulted in an arrest or seizure of contraband. Accounting for race and ethnicity, 10.5 percent of the searches that involved white motorists resulted in an arrest or seizure of contraband, 13.5 percent of the searches that involved black motorists resulted in an arrest or seizure, and 38.1 percent of the searches of Hispanic motorists resulted in an arrest or seizure.

*Arrests.* [During the years 1996 through 1998], there were a total of 2,871 arrests [for crimes other than drunk driving]. Of these, 932 (32.5 percent) involved white persons, 1,772 (61.7 percent) involved black persons, and 167 (5.8 percent) involved persons of other races.

## Interpretations of the Data and Areas of Special Concern

. . . Information and analysis compiled by the Public Defender's Office . . . suggests that troopers who enjoyed a wider ambit of discretion, by virtue of the nature of their duty assignment, stopped and ticketed minority motorists more often. Specifically, the Public Defender's statistical expert compared the tickets issued on 35 randomly selected days by three different State Police units: (1) the Radar Unit, which uses radar-equipped vans and chase cars and exercises comparatively little discretion; (2) the Tactical Patrol Unit, which focuses on motor vehicle enforcement in particular areas and exercises somewhat greater discretion; and, (3) the Patrol Unit, which is responsible for general law enforcement and exercises the most discretion. [T]he Radar Unit was found to have issued 18% of its tickets to African-Americans, the Tactical Patrol Unit issued 23.8% of its tickets to African-Americans, and the Patrol Unit issued 34.2% of its tickets to African-Americans. . . . We are concerned by what may be a pattern that when state troopers are permitted more discretion by virtue of their duty assignment, they tended during the time periods examined to ticket African-Americans more often. . . .

One need not be a racist to violate the Equal Protection Clause. . . . Many if not most of the problems and concerns we address in this Report will require that the State Police take a new look at the issue of racial profiling precisely because honest, nonbigoted officers throughout the ranks of the State Police could scarcely believe that they were engaged in or tolerated any form of discrimination.

The potential for the disparate treatment of minorities during routine traffic stops may be the product of an accumulation of circumstances that can contribute to the use of race or ethnicity-based criteria by creating the unintended message that the best way to catch drug traffickers is to focus on minorities. To some extent, the State Police as an organization may have been caught up in the martial rhetoric of the "war on drugs," responding to the call to arms urged by the public, the Legislature, and the Attorney General's Statewide Narcotics Action Plans of 1987 and 1993.

[T]he officially stated policy has always been to condemn reliance upon constitutionally impermissible factors. The message in these official policies, however, was not always clear and may have been undermined by other messages in both official and unofficial policies.    . . . The State Police official policy prohibiting racial profiling was announced in a 1990 Standard Operating Procedure. Ironically, the problem of the reliance upon stereotypes may have unwittingly been exacerbated by the issuance of this [1990 Procedure. It] included a discussion of the "sufficiency of objective facts to establish reasonable suspicion or probable cause," explaining that . . . personal characteristics such as race, age, sex, length of hair, style of dress, type of vehicle, and number of occupants of a vehicle "may not be utilized as facts relevant to establish reasonable suspicion or probable cause *unless the [State Police] member can identify and describe the manner in which a characteristic is directly and specifically related to particular criminal activity.*" (Emphasis added.) [This] portion of the Standard Operating Procedure, read literally, suggests that a person's race *may* be relied upon by a State Police member if he or she is able to identify and describe the manner in which race is directly and specifically related to a particular criminal activity. This exception has the very real capacity to swallow the rule, and opens the door (or at least fails to shut the door) to the use of stereotypes, especially those that have been "validated" by tautological and self-serving intelligence reports and profiles. . . .

With respect to training programs, no one can seriously question the right, indeed the obligation, of the State Police to alert troopers to the existence and activities of criminal organizations that they might encounter. . . . The problem, however, is that in providing this kind of training, inadequate attention may have been paid to the possibility that subtle messages in these lectures and videos would reinforce preexisting stereotypes by, for example, focusing mostly on criminal groups that happen to be comprised of minority citizens or foreign nationals. These kinds of messages may have been further reinforced by statistics compiled by State Police and disseminated to troopers in seminars and bulletins. The very fact that information concerning the racial characteristics of drug traffickers was provided to troopers assigned to patrol duties could have suggested that such characteristics are a legitimate, relevant factor to be taken into account or "kept in mind" in exercising police discretion during a traffic stop.

The State Police reward system, meanwhile, gave practical impetus to the use of these inappropriate stereotypes about drug dealers. [E]vidence has surfaced that minority troopers may also have been caught up in a system that rewards officers based on the quantity of drugs that they have discovered during routine traffic stops. (An internal audit of State Police motor vehicle stops recorded on the Moorestown Station radio logs between May 1, 1996 and July 31, 1996 shows that 34.3% of the 3,524 stops that were conducted by nonminority troopers involved minority motorists. An essentially identical proportion (33.3%) of the 1,751 total stops that were conducted by minority troopers involved minority motorists.) . . . The typical trooper is an intelligent, rational, ambitious, and career-oriented professional who responds to the prospect of rewards and promotions as much as to the threat of discipline and punishment. The system of organizational rewards, by definition and design, exerts a powerful influence on officer performance and enforcement priorities. . . .

## The Critical Distinction Between Legitimate Crime Trend Analysis and Impermissible Racial Profiling

Today we propose to make clear, as a matter of policy if not settled law, that race, ethnicity, and national origin are inappropriate factors that State Police members should not rely upon at all in selecting vehicles to be stopped or in exercising discretion during the course of a stop (other than in determining whether a person matches the general description of one or more known suspects).

[We] start with a discussion of the legitimate use of law enforcement's "collective knowledge and experience." Sophisticated crime analysis is sorely needed if police agencies are to remain responsive to emerging new threats and enforcement opportunities. The law is thus well-settled that in appropriate factual circumstances, police may piece together a series of acts, which by themselves seem innocent, but to a trained officer would reasonably indicate that criminal activity is afoot. State v. Patterson, 270 N.J. Super. 550, 557 (Law Div. 1993). As the court in *Patterson* correctly noted, "it is appropriate and legitimate police work to develop a so-called 'profile' based upon observations made in investigating the distribution or transportation of illicit drugs." Using these and other means, the police can develop a pattern of criminal wrongdoing that justifies their suspicions when they observe features that are in accord with the principal aspects of that pattern. . . . This regularized police experience reflects the collection of historical and intelligence information, careful crime trend analysis, and an examination of the methods of operations, the so-called "modus operandi," of drug traffickers and others engaged in various types of criminal activity. . . .

While police agencies are permitted, indeed are expected, to conduct crime trend analysis and to train officers as to those facts and circumstances that, while innocent on their face, provide a reasonable basis for suspecting criminal activity, the law also provides that certain factors may not be considered by law enforcement. In State v. Kuhn, 213 N.J. Super. 275 (App. Div. 1986), the court held that police are not permitted to draw any inferences of criminal activity from a suspect's race. The court in State v. Patterson expounded on this point, noting that, "[c]ertainly the police cannot conclude that all young, male African-Americans are suspected of involvement in the illicit drug trade." . . .

One need not be a constitutional scholar to understand that race, ethnicity, or national origin cannot be the sole basis for initiating a motor vehicle stop. On this point, everyone seems to agree. The law is far less clear, and opinions within and outside the criminal justice system become far more diverse, with respect to the question whether there are any circumstances when police may legitimately consider these kinds of personal traits and characteristics in drawing rational inferences about criminal activity. No one disputes, of course, that police can take a person's race into account in deciding whether the person is the individual who is described in a "wanted" bulletin; in this instance, race or ethnicity is used only as an "identifier." The issue, rather, and one that has not yet been definitely or at least uniformly resolved by the courts, is whether race, ethnicity, or national origin may be considered as one among an array of factors to infer that a particular individual is more likely than others to be engaged in criminal activity.

We believe that when finally confronted with this issue, the New Jersey Supreme Court would likely . . . hold, based upon independent state constitutional grounds if necessary, that race may play no part in an officer's determination of whether a particular person is reasonably likely to be engaged in criminal activity. In any event, . . . we need not wait for the courts to reach this conclusion before we propose a clear rule to be followed by state troopers assigned to patrol duties. . . .

## The Importance of Perceptions

Our findings and our proposed remedial steps are based in part on statistics . . . that document actual practices and procedures. We think it important to add, however, that law enforcement policy cannot be divorced from public opinion and public perceptions. The New Jersey State Police, no less than any other law enforcement agency, [must] remain responsive to public needs and expectations if it is to achieve its ultimate mission to protect and to serve. [P]erceptions concerning the magnitude and impact of the problem vary widely . . . .

To help to explain the nature of these issues we now confront and to put the problem and the proposed remedial steps in perspective, we find it useful to cite to a *Star Ledger/Eagleton* poll that was conducted in early May 1998. The poll showed that while the overall job performance rating of the State Police is quite positive in New Jersey, there is a major racial divide among Garden State residents. Black and white New Jerseyans have markedly different views of troopers' fairness in the enforcement of the laws, even-handed treatment of all drivers, judgment in deciding whom to pull over, and courteousness in dealing with stopped motorists. The poll revealed that the vast majority of African-Americans in New Jersey feel that State Police members treat minorities worse than others, and that troopers target cars to pull over based on the race and age of the people in the cars. In stark contrast, the majority of white New Jerseyans feel that troopers treat all motorists the same and seem highly satisfied with all aspects of their job performance. . . .

### The Circular Illogic of Race-Based Profiles

. . . We turn now to the specific assumption that is at the heart of the racial profiling controversy: the notion that a disproportionate percentage of drug traffickers and couriers are black or Hispanic, so that race, ethnicity, or national origin can serve as a reliable, accurate predictor of criminal activity. The proponents of this view point to empirical evidence, usually in the form of arrest and conviction statistics, that would appear at first blush to demonstrate quite conclusively that minorities are disproportionately represented among the universe of drug dealers.

The evidence for this conclusion is, in reality, tautological and reflects as much as anything the initial stereotypes of those who rely upon these statistics. To a large extent, these statistics have been used to grease the wheels of a vicious cycle—a self-fulfilling prophecy where law enforcement agencies rely on arrest data that they themselves generated as a result of the discretionary allocation of resources and targeted drug enforcement efforts. . . .

The most obvious problem in relying on arrest statistics, of course, is that these numbers refer only to persons who were found to be involved in criminal activity. . . . Arrest statistics, by definition, do not show the number of persons who were detained or investigated who, as it turned out, were not found to be trafficking drugs or carrying weapons. Consistent with our human nature, we in law enforcement proudly display seized drug shipments or "hits" as a kind of trophy, but pay scant attention to our far more frequent "misses," that is, those instances where stops and searches failed to discover contraband. . . .

## Remedial Steps

[T]he State Police has already undertaken a series of initiatives to address these issues, beginning in 1990 with a comprehensive Standard Operating Procedure governing the conduct of motor vehicle stops. That SOP included a number of important and innovative safeguards, including a requirement that state troopers have a reasonable, articulable suspicion to believe that evidence of a crime would be found before asking for permission to conduct a consent search, and a requirement that all consents to search be reduced to writing.

The State Police have also issued policies and procedures that require troopers to advise the dispatcher as to the racial characteristics of motorists who are stopped, that require troopers to record this information on patrol logs, and that prohibit the practice of "spotlighting" vehicles to ascertain the racial characteristics of the occupants of vehicles that have not yet been ordered to pull over. . . . Most recently, pursuant to the Governor's and Attorney General's initiative, State Police vehicles were equipped with video cameras that can be used to provide conclusive evidence of the conduct of motor vehicle stops. . . .

[A] trooper who is bent on finding drugs will . . . engage in comparatively protracted patrol stops, since his or her objective would not be simply to issue a summons or warning, but rather to undertake a full-blown criminal investigation. For this reason, we propose the establishment of a system that would allow supervisors and the State Police hierarchy to monitor the duration of road stops. If, for example, the median length of patrol stops by a given officer is shown to be correlated to the race, ethnicity, or national origin of motorists, that circumstance would trigger the "early warning system" and require appropriate follow-up investigation and explanation. . . .

The Department of Law and Public Safety should prepare and make public on a quarterly basis aggregate statistics compiled pursuant to the databases created in accordance with the recommendations of this Interim Report, detailing by State Police station the proportion of minority and nonminority citizens who were subject to various actions taken by State Police members during the course of traffic stops.

The Superintendent should within 120 days of this Report issue a comprehensive Standard Operating Procedure creating and establishing a protocol for the use of an "early warning system" to detect and deter the disparate treatment of minority citizens by State Police members assigned to patrol duties. . . . The protocol for use of the "early warning system" should provide for the routine supervisory review of videotapes, patrol officer logs, Traffic Stop Report forms, Search Incident forms, and any other patrol work product. The protocol should also provide for regularly conducted audits of enforcement patterns including traffic stops, the issuance of motor vehicle summons, and search and arrest activity. . . .

The Superintendent should within 90 days of this Report issue a single, comprehensive Standard Operating Procedure [regarding traffic stops]. In preparing the Standard Operating Procedure, the following should be considered:

1.  Before exiting his or her police vehicle, a State Police member will inform the dispatcher of the exact reason for the stop (e.g., speeding, 70 mph), a description of the vehicle and, when possible, a description of its occupants (i.e., the number of occupants and the apparent race and gender).

2.  A system should be established to monitor the exact duration of all stops.

3.  When the patrol vehicle is equipped with a video camera, the State Police person will ensure that the camera is activated before exiting the patrol vehicle and will not turn the camera off until the detained vehicle has been released and departs the scene.

4.  In the case of routine stops, the State Police member will at the outset of the stop introduce him or herself by name and inform the driver as to the reason for the stop. The member should not wait for the driver to inquire as to the reason for the stop, which may not be readily apparent to the driver. . . .

6.  At the conclusion of the vehicle stop, the State Police person will inform the dispatcher as to the stop outcome (e.g., warning, summons, etc.). . . .

7.  All State Police members conducting a motor vehicle traffic stop must utilize a Traffic Stop Report form, which shall record all officer action information necessary for immediate supervisory review or to supplement information recorded by the Computer Aided Dispatch System. . . .

8.  All Traffic Stop Report forms are to be reviewed by supervisory personnel at the conclusion of all duty shifts. The information contained in the reports should be entered into the "early warning system" database. . . .

Although the racial profiling issue has gained state and national attention recently, the underlying conditions that foster disparate treatment of minorities have existed for decades in New Jersey and throughout the nation, and will not be changed overnight. Even so, we firmly believe that this Interim Report represents a major step, indeed a watershed event, signaling significant change. We thus hope that this Report, once fully implemented through the issuance of new and comprehensive Standard Operating Procedures, a monitoring system, training, and other reforms, will ensure that New Jersey is a national leader in addressing the issue of racial profiling.

### *NOTES*

1.  *DWB claims.*   Claims that police officers stop drivers because of their race and not their behavior are not new, but have become much more prominent over the past several years after a series of prominent law review articles, litigation in New Jersey (the *Soto* case) and Maryland (the *Wilkins* case), and new and proposed state and federal legislation. See Tracey Maclin, Race and the Fourth Amendment, 51 Vand. L. Rev. 333 (1998); David Harris, "Driving While Black" and All Other Traffic Offenses: The Supreme Court and Pretextual Traffic Stops, 87 J. Crim. L. & Criminology 544 (1997); Randall Kennedy, Race, Crime and Law (1997). See also American Civil Liberties Union, Driving While Black: Racial Profiling on Our Nation's Highways (June 1999). The focus on I-95 is not accidental. Both state and federal

authorities have established programs targeting traffickers that run their wares between Florida and New York.

2.   *DWB legislation.* With DWB making little or no headway as a constitutional claim, state legislatures have taken the lead in efforts to monitor, limit, and sanction racially biased traffic stops.  Is the DWB problem one of evidence and proof, law and procedure, or institutional or individual culture and bias?

The statutes pursue different strategies. An Oklahoma statute, 22 Okla. Stat. §34.3, directly forbids the use of race as the "sole" basis for stopping or detaining a person, and makes racial profiling a misdemeanor. The statute also calls for law enforcement agencies to adopt and publicize "a detailed written policy that clearly defines the elements constituting racial profiling." A California statute, Penal Code §13519.4, requires training of officers in topics related to cultural diversity. A Missouri statute, Mo.Stat. §590.650, provides for mandatory collection of data about the race of motorists whom the police stop and search. Which of these strategies is most likely to reveal the amount and cause of racial profiling?  To reduce the amount of racial profiling?

3.   *DWB and police expertise.*   Does the report of the New Jersey Attorney General create a convincing case that racial profiling has occurred on the New Jersey Turnpike? If not, what additional information would be necessary to make the argument airtight? Is the New Jersey report right that clearer policies, better data, and better training are the answer for DWB? If not, what other responses might a legislature, the executive branch, or the courts have? Consider the views of novelist and former police officer Joseph Waumbaugh:

[I]t is obvious that one's race must not be the sole reason for being detained by police. But in an age of exquisite racial sensitivity, I wonder if we may be going too far. . . .

Police have always been acutely aware of crime statistics that are categorized by the sex, age and race of perpetrators. . . . As police attempt to cull potential lawbreakers from honest citizens, sex, age, race, clothing and lots of subtleties go into the process. In truth, criminals seldom oblige by committing that "furtive gesture" we hear so much about in courtrooms from police officers struggling to justify their having had "probable cause" to stop, frisk and interrogate. "Cops' instinct" doesn't cut much slack in courts of law. And those who think that only blacks are singled out by race should see what happens to young white men at the hands of police in inner-city neighborhoods. Cops expect that nonblacks who don't "belong" will be in possession of drugs or weapons, and act accordingly. When it comes to the current outcry over racial profiling, the question should be: Is the component of race now to be wholly excluded from the probable-cause equation for good street cops doing their best trying to decide whether or not someone "fits" in a given situation? If the answer is yes, then in the future the aforementioned white lawbreakers will be very happy when they cruise black neighborhoods unmolested, looking to score some crack. And wasn't it the Rev. Jesse Jackson who confessed a few years ago to feelings of fear when he encounters young men on the streets at night, and relief if he sees that the young men are not black? Apparently, when Mr. Jackson goes for a stroll, he finds racial profiling to be a prudent exercise.

Trust Cops' Intuition, Wall Street Journal, May 19, 1998, at A22.

4. *Litigating DWB.* If racial bias in stops, searches and arrests is so high, why have so few defendants challenged police action on these grounds, at least as far as indicated by published case reports? Note the concern of the New Jersey Attorney General's Office that its report might encourage such litigation.

We cannot prevent defendants from raising these issues in future motions to suppress evidence, but we wish to make clear that as to any such future challenges, we will be prepared to fully and fairly litigate the question whether any particular defendant was, in fact, a victim of unconstitutional conduct by the State Police warranting the suppression of reliable evidence of guilt. . . .

# B. Brief Administrative Stops

**Page 93.   Add this material before the notes.**

## City of Indianapolis v. James Edmond
**531 U.S. 32 (2000)**

O'CONNOR, J.

. . . In August 1998, the city of Indianapolis began to operate vehicle checkpoints on Indianapolis roads in an effort to interdict unlawful drugs. The city conducted six such roadblocks between August and November that year, stopping 1,161 vehicles and arresting 104 motorists. Fifty-five arrests were for drug-related crimes, while 49 were for offenses unrelated to drugs. The overall "hit rate" of the program was thus approximately nine percent.

The parties stipulated to the facts concerning the operation of the checkpoints by the Indianapolis Police Department (IPD) for purposes of the preliminary injunction proceedings instituted below. At each checkpoint location, the police stop a predetermined number of vehicles. Approximately 30 officers are stationed at the checkpoint. Pursuant to written directives issued by the chief of police, at least one officer approaches the vehicle, advises the driver that he or she is being stopped briefly at a drug checkpoint, and asks the driver to produce a license and registration. The officer also looks for signs of impairment and conducts an open-view examination of the vehicle from the outside. A narcotics-detection dog walks around the outside of each stopped vehicle.

The directives instruct the officers that they may conduct a search only by consent or based on the appropriate quantum of particularized suspicion. The officers must conduct each stop in the same manner until particularized suspicion develops, and the officers have no discretion to stop any vehicle out of sequence. The city agreed in the stipulation to operate the checkpoints in such a way as to ensure that the total duration of each stop, absent reasonable suspicion or probable cause, would be five minutes or less.

The affidavit of Indianapolis Police Sergeant Marshall DePew . . . provides further insight concerning the operation of the checkpoints. According to Sergeant DePew, checkpoint locations are selected weeks in advance based on such considerations as area crime statistics and traffic flow. The checkpoints are generally operated during daylight hours and are identified with lighted signs reading, "NARCOTICS CHECKPOINT ___ MILE AHEAD, NARCOTICS K-9 IN USE, BE PREPARED TO STOP." Once a group of cars has been stopped, other traffic proceeds without interruption until all the stopped cars have been processed or diverted for further processing. Sergeant DePew also stated that the average stop for a vehicle not subject to further processing lasts two to three minutes or less.

Respondents James Edmond and Joell Palmer were each stopped at a narcotics checkpoint in late September 1998. Respondents then filed a lawsuit on behalf of themselves and the class of all motorists who had been stopped or were subject to being stopped in the future at the Indianapolis drug checkpoints. Respondents claimed that the roadblocks violated the Fourth Amendment of the United States Constitution and the search and seizure provision of the Indiana Constitution.

Respondents requested declaratory and injunctive relief for the class, as well as damages and attorney's fees for themselves. . . .

The Fourth Amendment requires that searches and seizures be reasonable. A search or seizure is ordinarily unreasonable in the absence of individualized suspicion of wrongdoing. While such suspicion is not an irreducible component of reasonableness, we have recognized only limited circumstances in which the usual rule does not apply. For example, we have upheld certain regimes of suspicionless searches where the program was designed to serve "special needs, beyond the normal need for law enforcement." See, e.g., Vernonia School Dist. 47J v. Acton, 515 U.S. 646 (1995) (random drug testing of student-athletes); Treasury Employees v. Von Raab, 489 U.S. 656 (1989) (drug tests for United States Customs Service employees seeking transfer or promotion to certain positions); Skinner v. Railway Labor Executives' Assn., 489 U.S. 602 (1989) (drug and alcohol tests for railway employees involved in train accidents or found to be in violation of particular safety regulations). We have also allowed searches for certain administrative purposes without particularized suspicion of misconduct, provided that those searches are appropriately limited. See, e.g., New York v. Burger, 482 U.S. 691 (1987) (warrantless administrative inspection of premises of "closely regulated" business).

We have also upheld brief, suspicionless seizures of motorists at a fixed Border Patrol checkpoint designed to intercept illegal aliens, United States v. Martinez-Fuerte, 428 U.S. 543 (1976), and at a sobriety checkpoint aimed at removing drunk drivers from the road, Michigan Dept. of State Police v. Sitz, 496 U.S. 444 (1990). In addition, in Delaware v. Prouse, 440 U.S. 648 (1979), we suggested that a similar type of roadblock with the purpose of verifying drivers' licenses and vehicle registrations would be permissible. In none of these cases, however, did we indicate approval of a checkpoint program whose primary purpose was to detect evidence of ordinary criminal wrongdoing.

In *Martinez-Fuerte,* we entertained Fourth Amendment challenges to stops at two permanent immigration checkpoints located on major United States highways less than 100 miles from the Mexican border. We ... found that the balance tipped in favor of the Government's interests in policing the Nation's borders. In so finding, we emphasized the difficulty of effectively containing illegal immigration at the border itself. We also stressed the impracticality of the particularized study of a given car to discern whether it was transporting illegal aliens, as well as the relatively modest degree of intrusion entailed by the stops. . . .

In *Sitz,* we evaluated the constitutionality of a Michigan highway sobriety checkpoint program. The *Sitz* checkpoint involved brief suspicionless stops of motorists so that police officers could detect signs of intoxication and remove impaired drivers from the road. Motorists who exhibited signs of intoxication were diverted for a license and registration check and, if warranted, further sobriety tests. This checkpoint program was clearly aimed at reducing the immediate hazard posed by the presence of drunk drivers on the highways, and there was an obvious connection between the imperative of highway safety and the law enforcement practice at issue. The gravity of the drunk driving problem and the magnitude of the State's interest in getting drunk drivers off the road weighed heavily in our determination that the program was constitutional.

In *Prouse,* we invalidated a discretionary, suspicionless stop for a spot check of a motorist's driver's license and vehicle registration. The officer's conduct in that case was unconstitutional primarily on account of his exercise of "standardless and unconstrained discretion." We nonetheless acknowledged the States' "vital interest in ensuring that only those qualified to do so are permitted to operate motor vehicles, that these vehicles are fit for safe operation, and hence that licensing, registration, and vehicle inspection requirements are being observed." Accordingly, we suggested that "questioning of all oncoming traffic at roadblock-type stops" would be a lawful means of serving this interest in highway safety.

We further indicated in *Prouse* that we considered the purposes of such a hypothetical roadblock to be distinct from a general purpose of investigating crime. [We considered the State's primary interest in this setting to be roadway safety.] Not only does the common thread of highway safety thus run through *Sitz* and *Prouse,* but *Prouse* itself reveals a difference in the Fourth Amendment significance of highway safety interests and the general interest in crime control.

It is well established that a vehicle stop at a highway checkpoint effectuates a seizure within the meaning of the Fourth Amendment. The fact that officers walk a narcotics-detection dog around the exterior of each car at the Indianapolis checkpoints does not transform the seizure into a search. See United States v. Place, 462 U.S. 696 (1983). Just as in *Place*, an exterior sniff of an automobile does not require entry into the car and is not designed to disclose any information other than the presence or absence of narcotics. . . . Rather, what principally distinguishes these checkpoints from those we have previously approved is their primary purpose.

As petitioners concede, the Indianapolis checkpoint program unquestionably has the primary purpose of interdicting illegal narcotics. In their stipulation of facts, the parties repeatedly refer to the checkpoints as "drug checkpoints" and describe them as "being operated by the City of Indianapolis in an effort to interdict unlawful drugs in Indianapolis." In addition, the first document attached to the parties' stipulation is entitled "DRUG CHECKPOINT CONTACT OFFICER DIRECTIVES BY ORDER OF THE CHIEF OF POLICE." These directives instruct officers to "advise the citizen that they are being stopped briefly at a drug checkpoint." . . .

We have never approved a checkpoint program whose primary purpose was to detect evidence of ordinary criminal wrongdoing. . . . Because the primary purpose of the Indianapolis narcotics checkpoint program is to uncover evidence of ordinary criminal wrongdoing, the program contravenes the Fourth Amendment.

Petitioners propose several ways in which the narcotics-detection purpose of the instant checkpoint program may instead resemble the primary purposes of the checkpoints in *Sitz* and *Martinez-Fuerte*. Petitioners state that the checkpoints in those cases had the same ultimate purpose of arresting those suspected of committing crimes. Securing the border and apprehending drunk drivers are, of course, law enforcement activities, and law enforcement officers employ arrests and criminal prosecutions in pursuit of these goals. If we were to rest the case at this high level of generality, there would be little check on the ability of the authorities to construct roadblocks for almost any conceivable law enforcement purpose. Without drawing the line at roadblocks designed primarily to serve the general interest in crime control, the Fourth Amendment would do little to prevent such intrusions from becoming a routine part of American life. . . .

Nor can the narcotics-interdiction purpose of the checkpoints be rationalized in terms of a highway safety concern similar to that present in *Sitz*. The detection and punishment of almost any criminal offense serves broadly the safety of the community, and our streets would no doubt be safer but for the scourge of illegal drugs. Only with respect to a smaller class of offenses, however, is society confronted with the type of immediate, vehicle-bound threat to life and limb that the sobriety checkpoint in *Sitz* was designed to eliminate. . . .

Of course, there are circumstances that may justify a law enforcement checkpoint where the primary purpose would otherwise, but for some emergency, relate to ordinary crime control. For example, as the Court of Appeals noted, the Fourth Amendment would almost certainly permit an appropriately tailored roadblock set up to thwart an imminent terrorist attack or to catch a dangerous criminal who is likely to flee by way of a particular route. The exigencies created by these scenarios are far removed from the circumstances under which authorities might simply stop cars as a matter of course to see if there just happens to be a felon leaving the jurisdiction. While we do not limit the purposes that may justify a checkpoint program to any rigid set of categories, we decline to approve a program whose primary purpose is ultimately indistinguishable from the general interest in crime control.

Petitioners argue that our prior cases preclude an inquiry into the purposes of the checkpoint program. For example, they cite Whren v. United States, 517 U.S. 806 (1996) . . . to support the proposition that "where the government articulates and pursues a legitimate interest for a suspicionless stop, courts should not look behind that interest to determine whether the government's 'primary purpose' is valid." These cases, however, do not control the instant situation.

In *Whren,* we held that an individual officer's subjective intentions are irrelevant to the Fourth Amendment validity of a traffic stop that is justified objectively by probable cause to believe that a traffic violation has occurred. . . . In so holding, we expressly distinguished cases where we had addressed the validity of searches conducted in the absence of probable cause. *Whren* therefore reinforces the principle that, while "subjective intentions play no role in ordinary, probable-cause Fourth Amendment analysis," programmatic purposes may be relevant to the validity of Fourth Amendment intrusions undertaken pursuant to a general scheme without individualized suspicion. . . .

Petitioners argue that the Indianapolis checkpoint program is justified by its lawful secondary purposes of keeping impaired motorists off the road and verifying licenses and registrations. If this were the case, however, law enforcement authorities would be able to establish checkpoints for virtually any purpose so long as they also included a license or sobriety check. For this reason, we examine the available evidence to determine the primary purpose of the checkpoint program. While we recognize the challenges inherent in a purpose inquiry, courts routinely engage in this enterprise in many areas of constitutional jurisprudence as a means of sifting abusive governmental conduct from that which is lawful. . . .

Because the primary purpose of the Indianapolis checkpoint program is ultimately indistinguishable from the general interest in crime control, the checkpoints violate the Fourth Amendment. . . .

REHNQUIST, C.J., dissenting.

The State's use of a drug-sniffing dog, according to the Court's holding, annuls what is otherwise plainly constitutional under our Fourth Amendment jurisprudence: brief, standardized, discretionless, roadblock seizures of automobiles, seizures which effectively serve a weighty state interest with only minimal intrusion on the privacy of their occupants. Because these seizures serve the State's accepted and significant interests of preventing drunken driving and checking for driver's licenses and vehicle registrations, and because there is nothing in the record to indicate that the addition of the dog sniff lengthens these otherwise legitimate seizures, I dissent. . . .

Petitioners acknowledge that the "primary purpose" of these roadblocks is to interdict illegal drugs, but this fact should not be controlling. Even accepting the Court's conclusion that the checkpoints at issue in *Martinez-Fuerte* and *Sitz* were not primarily related to criminal law enforcement, the question whether a law enforcement purpose could support a roadblock seizure is not presented in this case. The District Court found that another "purpose of the checkpoints is to check driver's licenses and vehicle registrations," and the written directives state that the police officers are to "look for signs of impairment.". . . That the roadblocks serve these legitimate state interests cannot be seriously disputed, as the 49 people arrested for offenses unrelated to drugs can attest. And it would be speculative to conclude—given the District Court's findings, the written directives, and the actual arrests—that petitioners would not have operated these roadblocks but for the State's interest in interdicting drugs.

Because of the valid reasons for conducting these roadblock seizures, it is constitutionally irrelevant that petitioners also hoped to interdict drugs. In Whren v. United States, we held that an officer's subjective intent would not invalidate an otherwise objectively justifiable stop of an automobile. The reasonableness of an officer's discretionary decision to stop an automobile, at issue in *Whren*, turns on whether there is probable cause to believe that a traffic violation has occurred. The reasonableness of highway checkpoints, at issue here, turns on whether they effectively serve a significant state interest with minimal intrusion on motorists. The stop in *Whren* was objectively reasonable because the police officers had witnessed traffic violations; so too the roadblocks here are objectively reasonable because they serve the substantial interests of preventing drunken driving and checking for driver's licenses and vehicle registrations with minimal intrusion on motorists.

Once the constitutional requirements for a particular seizure are satisfied, the subjective expectations of those responsible for it, be it police officers or members of a city council, are irrelevant. It is the objective effect of the State's actions on the privacy of the individual that animates the Fourth Amendment. Because the objective intrusion of a valid seizure does not turn upon anyone's subjective thoughts, neither should our constitutional analysis. . . .

The only difference between this case and *Sitz* is the presence of the dog. We have already held, however, that a "sniff test" by a trained narcotics dog is not a "search" within the meaning of the Fourth Amendment because it does not require physical intrusion of the object being sniffed and it does not expose anything other than the contraband items. And there is nothing in the record to indicate that the dog sniff lengthens the stop. Finally, the checkpoints' success rate—49 arrests for offenses unrelated to drugs [or 4.2% of the motorists stopped]—only confirms the State's legitimate interests in preventing drunken driving and ensuring the proper licensing of drivers and registration of their vehicles. These stops effectively serve the State's legitimate interests; they are executed in a regularized and neutral manner; and they only minimally intrude upon the privacy of the motorists. They should therefore be constitutional.

[W]hatever sense a non-law-enforcement primary purpose test may make in the search setting, it is ill suited to brief roadblock seizures, where we have consistently looked at the scope of the stop in assessing a program's constitutionality. [The reason] for not incorporating the "special needs" test in our roadblock seizure cases is that seizures of automobiles deal neither with searches nor with the sanctity of private dwellings, ordinarily afforded the most stringent Fourth Amendment protection. . . . One's expectation of privacy in an automobile and of freedom in its operation are significantly different from the traditional expectation of privacy and freedom in one's residence. This is because automobiles, unlike homes, are subjected to pervasive and continuing governmental regulation and controls. The lowered expectation of privacy in one's automobile is coupled with the limited nature of the intrusion: a brief, standardized, nonintrusive seizure. The brief seizure of an automobile can hardly be compared to the intrusive search of the body or the home.

Because of these extrinsic limitations upon roadblock seizures, the Court's newfound non-law-enforcement primary purpose test is both unnecessary to secure Fourth Amendment rights and bound to produce wide-ranging litigation over the "purpose" of any given seizure. Police designing highway roadblocks can never be sure of their validity, since a jury might later determine that a forbidden purpose exists. . . .

Page 99.   Add this material after the notes.

## Problem 2-4A.   Freezing the Situation

Tera McArthur asked police to "keep the peace" while she removed her belongings from the trailer she shared with her husband Charles. When she emerged from the trailer, she told Assistant Chief Love that "Chuck has dope in there," and that she had seen him "slide some dope under the couch." Charles McArthur refused to consent to a search of the trailer, so officers left the scene to get a warrant. Love told Charles that he could not reenter the trailer unless a police officer accompanied him. Charles reentered the trailer two or three times (to get cigarettes and to make phone calls) during the next two hours. Each time Love stood just inside the trailer door to observe. The later warranted search led to the discovery of marijuana. Charles moved to suppress the evidence on the ground that the temporary seizure of his trailer while the police sought the warrant violated the Fourth Amendment. How would you rule?

## NOTE

1. *Justifications for brief seizures: "freezing" the status quo.* In Illinois v. McArthur, 531 U.S. 326 (2001), the Supreme Court reversed the Illinois state courts and held that the two-hour detention of McArthur's trailer while a warrant was sought did not violate the Fourth Amendment. The Court explained:

> In the circumstances of the case before us, we cannot say that the warrantless seizure was *per se* unreasonable. It involves a plausible claim of specially pressing or urgent law enforcement need, i.e., "exigent circumstances." . . . We conclude that the restriction at issue was reasonable, and hence lawful. . . . First, the police had probable cause to believe that McArthur's trailer home contained evidence of a crime and contraband, namely, unlawful drugs. . . . Second, the police had good reason to fear that, unless restrained, McArthur would destroy the drugs before they could return with a warrant. . . . Third, the police made reasonable efforts to reconcile their law enforcement needs with the demands of personal privacy. They neither searched the trailer nor arrested McArthur before obtaining a warrant. Rather, they imposed a significantly less restrictive restraint, preventing McArthur only from entering the trailer unaccompanied. They left his home and his belongings intact – until a neutral Magistrate, finding probable cause, issued a warrant. Fourth, the police imposed the restraint for a limited period of time, namely, two hours. As far as the record reveals, this time period was no longer than reasonably necessary for the police, acting with diligence, to obtain the warrant. Given the nature of the intrusion and the law enforcement interest at stake, this brief seizure of the premises was permissible.

State courts have upheld short term actions by police to "freeze" situations or to "maintain the status quo" while police conduct a brief search or seek a warrant. For example, in City of Fargo v. Ovind, 575 N.W.2d 901 (N.D. 1998), a police officer responding at 1:45 A.M. to a report of a fight at the local Taco Bell observed only two vehicles in the parking lot and then saw "one car with a driver and two or three passengers backing out of a parking spot, and another car just exiting the lot onto First Avenue." The officer called for assistance and stopped both cars. The defendant challenged the stop on the grounds that the officer had no corroboration or individualized information, and therefore lacked reasonable suspicion to "freeze" the situation. The court responded:

While it may make sense to require an observation of illegality or impairment in corroborating tips regarding a specific impaired driver, this type of corroboration may not be practical in the prompt investigation of the scene of a reported recent crime. Some circumstances require a police officer to act quickly in order to preserve the status quo rather than to observe the situation further. Here, the officer is not trying to locate an individual driver and confirm a tip of impairment; but instead, the officer is attempting to investigate the scene of a reported fight. The issue in this case deals with the propriety of a limited investigative stop near the scene of a recent crime.

[An] investigative stop of a person present at the scene of a recently committed crime may be permissible without violating the Fourth Amendment. Such a stop is especially deemed permissible where only a limited number of persons are present at the scene of a violent crime. . . .

The officer's immediate purpose upon entering the lot was to investigate the reported fight. [The officer] testified that in his experience people involved in a fight tend to flee quickly afterward, especially if they find out the police have been called. . . .

## C.  Gathering Information Without Searching

### 1.  Plain View

**Page 107.   Add this material before the notes.**

### Steven Dewayne Bond v. United States
**529 U.S. 334 (2000)**

REHNQUIST, C.J.

This case presents the question whether a law enforcement officer's physical manipulation of a bus passenger's carry-on luggage violated the Fourth Amendment's proscription against unreasonable searches. We hold that it did.

Petitioner Steven Dewayne Bond was a passenger on a Greyhound bus that left California bound for Little Rock, Arkansas. The bus stopped [at a permanent Border Patrol checkpoint and] Border Patrol Agent Cesar Cantu boarded the bus to check the immigration status of its passengers. After reaching the back of the bus, having satisfied himself that the passengers were lawfully in the United States, Agent Cantu began walking toward the front. Along the way, he squeezed the soft luggage which passengers had placed in the overhead storage space above the seats. . . .

As Agent Cantu inspected the luggage in the compartment above petitioner's seat, he squeezed a green canvas bag and noticed that it contained a "brick-like" object. Petitioner admitted that the bag was his and agreed to allow Agent Cantu to open it. Upon opening the bag, Agent Cantu discovered a "brick" of methamphetamine. The brick had been wrapped in duct tape until it was oval-shaped and then rolled in a pair of pants.

Petitioner was indicted for conspiracy to possess, and possession with intent to distribute, methamphetamine. . . . He moved to suppress the drugs, [but the District Court denied the motion,] found him guilty on both counts and sentenced him to 57 months in prison.

[The] Government asserts that by exposing his bag to the public, petitioner lost a reasonable expectation that his bag would not be physically manipulated. The Government relies on our decisions in California v. Ciraolo, 476 U.S. 207 (1986), and Florida v. Riley, 488 U.S. 445 (1989), for the proposition that matters open to public observation are not protected by the Fourth Amendment. In *Ciraolo*, we held that police observation of a backyard from a plane flying at an altitude of 1,000 feet did not violate a reasonable expectation of privacy. Similarly, in *Riley*, we relied on *Ciraolo* to hold that police observation of a greenhouse in a home's curtilage from a helicopter passing at an altitude of 400 feet did not violate the Fourth Amendment. We reasoned that the property was "not necessarily protected from inspection that involves no physical invasion," and determined that because any member of the public could have lawfully observed the defendants' property by flying overhead, the defendants' expectation of privacy was "not reasonable and not one that society is prepared to honor."

But *Ciraolo* and *Riley* are different from this case because they involved only visual, as opposed to tactile, observation. Physically invasive inspection is simply more intrusive than purely visual inspection. For example, in Terry v. Ohio, 392 U.S. 1 (1968), we stated that a "careful [tactile] exploration of the outer surfaces of a person's clothing all over his or her body" is a "serious intrusion upon the sanctity of the person, which may inflict great indignity and arouse strong resentment, and is not to be undertaken lightly." Although Agent Cantu did not "frisk" petitioner's person, he did conduct a probing tactile examination of petitioner's carry-on luggage. Obviously, petitioner's bag was not part of his person. But travelers are particularly concerned about their carry-on luggage; they generally use it to transport personal items that, for whatever reason, they prefer to keep close at hand.

Here, petitioner concedes that, by placing his bag in the overhead compartment, he could expect that it would be exposed to certain kinds of touching and handling. But petitioner argues that Agent Cantu's physical manipulation of his luggage "far exceeded the casual contact [petitioner] could have expected from other passengers." . . .

Our Fourth Amendment analysis embraces two questions. First, we ask whether the individual, by his conduct, has exhibited an actual expectation of privacy; that is, whether he has shown that he sought to preserve something as private. Here, petitioner sought to preserve privacy by using an opaque bag and placing that bag directly above his seat. Second, we inquire whether the individual's expectation of privacy is "one that society is prepared to recognize as reasonable."[2] When a bus passenger places a bag in an overhead bin, he expects that other passengers or bus employees may move it for one reason or another. . . . He does not expect that other passengers or bus employees will, as a matter of course, feel the bag in an exploratory manner. But this is exactly what the agent did here. We therefore hold that the agent's physical manipulation of petitioner's bag violated the Fourth Amendment.

BREYER, J., dissenting.

Does a traveler who places a soft-sided bag in the shared overhead storage compartment of a bus have a "reasonable expectation" that strangers will not push, pull, prod, squeeze, or otherwise manipulate his luggage? Unlike the majority, I believe that he does not.

---

2. The parties properly agree that the subjective intent of the law enforcement officer is irrelevant in determining whether that officer's actions violate the Fourth Amendment. see Whren v. United States, 517 U.S. 806 (1996) (stating that "we have been unwilling to entertain Fourth Amendment challenges based on the actual motivations of individual officers"); California v. Ciraolo, 476 U.S. 207 (1986) (rejecting respondent's challenge to "the authority of government to observe his activity from any vantage point or place if the viewing is motivated by a law enforcement purpose, and not the result of a casual, accidental observation"). This principle applies to the agent's acts in this case as well; the issue is not his state of mind, but the objective effect of his actions.

Petitioner argues—and the majority points out—that, even if bags in overhead bins are subject to general "touching" and "handling," this case is special because Agent Cantu's physical manipulation of petitioner's luggage far exceeded the casual contact he could have expected from other passengers. But the record shows the contrary. Agent Cantu testified that border patrol officers (who routinely enter buses at designated checkpoints to run immigration checks) "conduct an inspection of the overhead luggage by squeezing the bags as we're going out." On the occasion at issue here, Agent Cantu "felt a green bag" which had "a brick-like object in it." He explained that he felt "the edges of the brick in the bag," and that it was a "[b]rick-like object . . . that, when squeezed, you could feel an outline of something of a different mass inside of it." Although the agent acknowledged that his practice was to "squeeze [bags] very hard," he testified that his touch ordinarily was not "[h]ard enough to break something inside that might be fragile." Petitioner also testified that Agent Cantu "reached for my bag, and he shook it a little, and squeezed it."

How does the "squeezing" just described differ from the treatment that overhead luggage is likely to receive from strangers in a world of travel that is somewhat less gentle than it used to be? I think not at all. Eagan, Familiar Anger Takes Flight with Airline Tussles, Boston Herald, Aug. 15, 1999, p. 8 ("It's dog-eat-dog trying to cram half your home into overhead compartments"). The trial court . . . viewed the agent's activity as "minimally intrusive touching." . . .

Privacy itself implies the exclusion of uninvited strangers, not just strangers who work for the Government. Hence, an individual cannot reasonably expect privacy in respect to objects or activities that he "knowingly exposes to the public." [The] fact that strangers may look down at fenced-in property from an aircraft or sift through garbage bags on a public street can justify a . . . police intrusion. The comparative likelihood that strangers will give bags in an overhead compartment a hard squeeze would seem far greater. Consider, too, the accepted police practice of using dogs to sniff for drugs hidden inside luggage. Surely it is less likely that nongovernmental strangers will sniff at other's bags (or, more to the point, permit their dogs to do so) than it is that such actors will touch or squeeze another person's belongings in the process of making room for their own.

Of course, the agent's purpose here—searching for drugs—differs dramatically from the intention of a driver or fellow passenger who squeezes a bag in the process of making more room for another parcel. But in determining whether an expectation of privacy is reasonable, it is the effect, not the purpose, that matters. Few individuals with something to hide wish to expose that something to the police, however careless or indifferent they may be in respect to discovery by other members of the public. Hence, a Fourth Amendment rule that turns on purpose could prevent police alone from intruding where other strangers freely tread. And the added privacy protection achieved by such an approach would not justify the harm worked to law enforcement—at least that is what this Court's previous cases suggest. . . .

If we are to depart from established legal principles, we should not begin here. At best, this decision will lead to a constitutional jurisprudence of "squeezes," thereby complicating further already complex Fourth Amendment law, increasing the difficulty of deciding ordinary criminal matters, and hindering the administrative guidance (with its potential for control of unreasonable police practices) that a less complicated jurisprudence might provide. At worst, this case will deter law enforcement officers searching for drugs near borders from using even the most nonintrusive touch to help investigate publicly exposed bags. At the same time, the ubiquity of nongovernmental pushes, prods, and squeezes (delivered by driver, attendant, passenger, or some other stranger) means that this decision cannot do much to protect true privacy. Rather, the traveler who wants to place a bag in a shared overhead bin and yet safeguard its contents from public touch should plan to pack those contents in a suitcase with hard sides, irrespective of the Court's decision today. For these reasons, I dissent.

## D.  Brief Searches of Individuals

### 2.  The Scope of a *Terry* Search

Page 131.   Add this material at the end of note 8.

One case discussing exit orders to passengers in cars, in light of controversies over racial discrimination in the selection of cars to stop for traffic violations, is Commonwealth v. Gonsalves, 711 N.E.2d 108

(Mass. 1999). The state court reaffirmed its earlier cases refusing to follow *Mimms* and held that the state constitution prevents police officers from ordering a driver *or* a passenger from a vehicle unless the officer has reasonable suspicion that the person presents a danger to the officer's safety or to the safety of others. One reason supporting this decision was the court's concern that the power to order drivers and passengers to exit a car during any traffic stop could be an "invitation to discriminatory enforcement." The court then cited evidence regarding evidence dealing with the disproportionate number of African-Americans stopped for traffic violations in New Jersey. A dissenting opinion stressed the need for officers to secure their safety during traffic stops and the minimal nature of the intrusion. The dissent also surveyed the decisions of other states on this question, concluding that 44 states have accepted *Mimms*, while only 2 other than Massachusetts (Oregon and Hawaii) have rejected it on constitutional grounds. About half the states have extended the *Mimms* rule to passengers, while only 3 (New Jersey, Tennessee, and Washington) have refused to do so at this point.

# Chapter 3

# Full Searches of People and Places: Basic Concepts

## B. Probable Cause

### 2. Sources of Information to Support Probable Cause

**Page 167.   Replace note 2 with this material.**

2. *Anonymous tips and reasonable suspicion.* In Chapter 2, we considered the "reasonable suspicion" necessary to justify a police stop of a person or vehicle. Sometimes anonymous tips give the police a reason to stop a person. Typically, courts require the officer to confirm some of the details that the anonymous tipster related before reasonable suspicion is present. In one common fact pattern, an anonymous tip identifies a driver who might be driving while intoxicated. If the officer stops a person on the basis of an anonymous tip without first developing some independent basis for reasonable suspicion, courts will frequently overturn the stop. Florida v. J.L., reprinted in Chapter 2 of this Supplement, is typical on this score. How often will this limitation prevent police officers from making a valid stop? Take, for example, these circumstances from State v. Miller, 510 N.W.2d 638 (N.D. 1994):

Shortly before midnight [the police dispatcher] notified Officer James Chase that a caller had reported a possible drunk driver in the Wendy's drive-up lane. The caller identified himself to the dispatcher as "Jody with Wendy's," but the dispatcher did not tell Chase the caller was identified, either by name or his employment. The dispatcher described the vehicle as a red pickup and gave its license plate number and location as second in line in the drive-up lane. The dispatcher also relayed the informant's statement that the driver "could barely hold his head up." Chase was about a mile away from Wendy's and arrived there in a matter of minutes. Chase saw an orange pickup coming out of the drive-up lane. The pickup pulled out of the Wendy's parking lot and drove east on Capitol. Chase followed the pickup as it drove north on the frontage road in front of Wendy's at about five to seven miles per hour, and then turned into the [opposite corner of the] Wendy's parking lot and parked. Chase verified that the pickup's license number matched the number reported by the dispatcher, but did not notice anything unusual about the pickup's driving. Chase pulled in behind the pickup and turned on his warning flashers. He then conducted field sobriety tests on [the driver] and arrested him.

The North Dakota Supreme Court held that the officer did not have reasonable suspicion to stop Miller's truck. Was this outcome consistent with Florida v. J.L.?

## C.  Warrants

### 3.   Execution of Warrants

Page 198.   Add this material at the end of note 3.

In United States v. Ramirez, 523 U.S. 65 (1998), the Court refused to impose any higher standards on "no knock" searches that cause property damage. Government agents searching for an escaped prisoner obtained a "no knock" warrant to enter Ramirez' home. Officers announced that they had a search warrant as they broke a window in the garage, while one officer pointed a gun through the opening to prevent occupants from picking up any of the weapons that the agents believed were in the garage. Ramirez was awakened by the noise and feared that his house was being burglarized, so he fired a pistol into the garage ceiling. He was convicted on weapons possession charges. The Supreme Court reaffirmed that a no-knock entry is justified if police have a reasonable suspicion that announcing their presence before entering would be dangerous or futile, or would inhibit the effective investigation of the crime. It also reiterated that a warrant must be executed in a "reasonable" manner, and "[e]xcessive or unnecessary property destruction during a search may violate the [Fourth] Amendment, even though the entry itself is lawful and the fruits of the search not subject to suppression." The no-knock search in this case, and the limited property damage involved, were both reasonable in the court's view.

**Page 199.    Add this material after note 4.**

5. *Ride-alongs and reasonableness.*    Many police departments allow members of the public or the media to ride along in their patrol cars and to observe the police at work. From time to time, the ride-along guest might observe the officers as they execute a search or arrest warrant in a home. Does the presence of media or other ride-along observers make a warranted search any less reasonable? What if the observers are taking pictures or filming the events for television viewers? The Supreme Court addressed these questions in Wilson v. Layne, 526 U.S. 603 (1999). Officers hoping to execute an arrest warrant for Dominic Wilson entered his parents' home in Rockville, Maryland, where they believed he was living. The team of federal marshals and county police officers entered the home at 6:45 A.M., accompanied by a reporter and a photographer from the *Washington Post.* Wilson's father awakened and ran into the living room to investigate the noise. He shouted angrily at the officers, and the officers (believing him to be Dominic) subdued him on the floor. When the officers learned that Dominic was not in the house, they left. The photographer took many pictures of these events, and the reporter also observed the confrontation in the living room. The newspaper never published its photographs.

The Supreme Court held that bringing the media into the home during the arrest was a violation of the Fourth Amendment, because it violated the "sanctity of the home" that is a central concern of the Amendment. Although officers may enter a suspect's home themselves to execute an arrest warrant, "it does not necessarily follow that they were entitled to bring a newspaper reporter and a photographer with them." Because the presence of the reporters inside the home was not "related to the objectives of the authorized intrusion" and did not "assist the police in their task" of arresting Wilson, it was improper for the reporter and photographer to enter. Although the court conceded that a ride-along policy could improve public support for the police in a general sense, and keep the public informed about police efforts, "that is not the same as furthering the purposes of the search." Officers might videotape home entries as part of a "quality control" effort that would minimize any abuse, and private photographers are not necessary for that purpose.

# D. *Consensual Searches*

## 1. Components of a Voluntary Choice

Page 220.    Add this material before the notes.

## United States v. Christopher Drayton
### 122 S. Ct. 2105 (2002)

KENNEDY, J.

The Fourth Amendment permits police officers to approach bus passengers at random to ask questions and to request their consent to searches, provided a reasonable person would understand that he or she is free to refuse. This case requires us to determine whether officers must advise bus passengers during these encounters of their right not to cooperate.

On February 4, 1999, respondents Christopher Drayton and Clifton Brown, Jr., were traveling on a Greyhound bus en route from Ft. Lauderdale, Florida, to Detroit, Michigan. The bus made a scheduled stop in Tallahassee, Florida. The passengers were required to disembark so the bus could be refueled and cleaned. As the passengers reboarded, the driver checked their tickets and then left to complete paperwork inside the terminal. As he left, the driver allowed three members of the Tallahassee Police Department to board the bus as part of a routine drug and weapons interdiction effort. The officers were dressed in plain clothes and carried concealed weapons and visible badges.

Once onboard Officer Hoover knelt on the driver's seat and faced the rear of the bus. He could observe the passengers and ensure the safety of the two other officers without blocking the aisle or otherwise obstructing the bus exit. Officers Lang and Blackburn went to the rear of the bus. Blackburn remained stationed there, facing forward. Lang worked his way toward the front of the bus, speaking with individual passengers as he went. He asked the passengers about their travel plans and sought to match passengers with luggage in the overhead racks. To avoid blocking the aisle, Lang stood next to or just behind each passenger with whom he spoke.

According to Lang's testimony, passengers who declined to cooperate with him or who chose to exit the bus at any time would have been allowed to do so without argument. In Lang's experience, however, most people are willing to cooperate. Some passengers go so far as to commend the police for their efforts to ensure the safety of their travel. Lang could recall five to six instances in the previous year in which passengers had declined to have their luggage searched.[*] It also was common for passengers to leave the bus for a cigarette or a snack while the officers were on board. Lang sometimes informed passengers of their right to refuse to cooperate. On the day in question, however, he did not.

Respondents were seated next to each other on the bus. Drayton was in the aisle seat, Brown in the seat next to the window. Lang approached respondents from the rear and leaned over Drayton's shoulder. He held up his badge long enough for respondents to identify him as a police officer. With his face 12- to-18 inches away from Drayton's, Lang spoke in a voice just loud enough for respondents to hear: "I'm Investigator Lang with the Tallahassee Police Department. We're conducting bus interdiction [*sic*], attempting to deter drugs and illegal weapons being transported on the bus. Do you have any bags on the bus?" Both respondents pointed to a single green bag in the overhead luggage rack. Lang asked, "Do you mind if I check it?," and Brown responded, "Go ahead." Lang handed the bag to Officer Blackburn to check. The bag contained no contraband.

Officer Lang noticed that both respondents were wearing heavy jackets and baggy pants despite the warm weather. In Lang's experience drug traffickers often use baggy clothing to conceal weapons or narcotics. The officer thus asked Brown if he had any weapons or drugs in his possession. And he asked Brown: "Do you mind if I check your person?" Brown answered, "Sure," and cooperated by leaning up in his

---

[*] The officer testified that he had conducted interdiction operations on over 800 buses during the previous year.—EDS.

seat, pulling a cell phone out of his pocket, and opening up his jacket. Lang reached across Drayton and patted down Brown's jacket and pockets, including his waist area, sides, and upper thighs. In both thigh areas, Lang detected hard objects similar to drug packages detected on other occasions. Lang arrested and handcuffed Brown. Officer Hoover escorted Brown from the bus.

Lang then asked Drayton, "Mind if I check you?" Drayton responded by lifting his hands about eight inches from his legs. Lang conducted a pat-down of Drayton's thighs and detected hard objects similar to those found on Brown. He arrested Drayton and escorted him from the bus. A further search revealed that respondents had duct-taped plastic bundles of powder cocaine between several pairs of their boxer shorts. Brown possessed three bundles containing 483 grams of cocaine. Drayton possessed two bundles containing 295 grams of cocaine.

Respondents were charged with conspiring to distribute cocaine . . . and with possessing cocaine with intent to distribute it. . . . They moved to suppress the cocaine, arguing that the consent to the pat-down search was invalid. [The trial court denied the motion and the defendants were convicted.] The Court of Appeals for the Eleventh Circuit reversed and remanded with instructions to grant respondents' motions to suppress. [We conclude that these defendants] were not seized and their consent to the search was voluntary; and we reverse.

Law enforcement officers do not violate the Fourth Amendment's prohibition of unreasonable seizures merely by approaching individuals on the street or in other public places and putting questions to them if they are willing to listen. Even when law enforcement officers have no basis for suspecting a particular individual, they may pose questions, ask for identification, and request consent to search luggage—provided they do not induce cooperation by coercive means. If a reasonable person would feel free to terminate the encounter, then he or she has not been seized.

The Court has addressed on a previous occasion the specific question of drug interdiction efforts on buses. In Florida v. Bostick, 501 U.S. 429 (1991), two police officers requested a bus passenger's consent to a search of his luggage. The passenger agreed, and the resulting search revealed cocaine in his suitcase. The Florida Supreme Court suppressed the cocaine. In doing so it adopted a *per se* rule that due to the cramped confines onboard a bus the act of questioning would deprive a person of his or her freedom of movement and so constitute a seizure under the Fourth Amendment.

This Court reversed. *Bostick* first made it clear that for the most part *per se* rules are inappropriate in the Fourth Amendment context. The proper inquiry necessitates a consideration of "all the circumstances surrounding the encounter." The Court noted next that the . . . proper inquiry "is whether a reasonable person would feel free to decline the officers' requests or otherwise terminate the encounter." Finally, the Court rejected Bostick's argument that he must have been seized because no reasonable person would consent to a search of luggage containing drugs. The reasonable person test, the Court explained, is objective and "presupposes an *innocent* person."

In light of the limited record, *Bostick* refrained from deciding whether a seizure occurred. The Court, however, identified two factors "particularly worth noting" on remand. First, although it was obvious that an officer was armed, he did not remove the gun from its pouch or use it in a threatening way. Second, the officer advised the passenger that he could refuse consent to the search.

Relying upon this latter factor, the Eleventh Circuit has adopted what is in effect a *per se* rule that evidence obtained during suspicionless drug interdiction efforts aboard buses must be suppressed unless the officers have advised passengers of their right not to cooperate and to refuse consent to a search. In United States v. Guapi, 144 F.3d 1393 (11th Cir. 1998), the Court of Appeals [stated that] "simple notification . . . is perhaps the most efficient and effective method to ensure compliance with the Constitution." The Court of Appeals then listed other factors that contributed to the coerciveness of the encounter: (1) the officer conducted the interdiction before the passengers disembarked from the bus at a scheduled stop; (2) the officer explained his presence in the form of a general announcement to the entire bus; (3) the officer wore a police uniform; and (4) the officer questioned passengers as he moved from the front to the rear of the bus, thus obstructing the path to the exit. . . .

Although the Court of Appeals has disavowed a *per se* requirement, the lack of an explicit warning to passengers is the only element common to all its cases. See United States v. Washington, 151 F.3d 1354, 1357 (11th Cir. 1998) ("It seems obvious to us that if police officers genuinely want to ensure that their encounters with bus passengers remain absolutely voluntary, they can simply say so. Without such notice in this case, we do not feel a reasonable person would have felt able to decline the agents' requests"). Under these cases, it appears that the Court of Appeals would suppress any evidence obtained during suspicionless drug interdiction efforts aboard buses in the absence of a warning that passengers may refuse to cooperate. The Court of Appeals erred in adopting this approach.

Applying the *Bostick* framework to the facts of this particular case, we conclude that the police did not seize respondents when they boarded the bus and began questioning passengers. The officers gave the passengers no reason to believe that they were required to answer the officers' questions. When Officer Lang approached respondents, he did not brandish a weapon or make any intimidating movements. He left the aisle free so that respondents could exit. He spoke to passengers one by one and in a polite, quiet voice. Nothing he said would suggest to a reasonable person that he or she was barred from leaving the bus or otherwise terminating the encounter. . . .

The fact that an encounter takes place on a bus does not on its own transform standard police questioning of citizens into an illegal seizure. Indeed, because many fellow passengers are present to witness officers' conduct, a reasonable person may feel even more secure in his or her decision not to cooperate with police on a bus than in other circumstances.

Respondents make much of the fact that Officer Lang displayed his badge. [However, officers] are often required to wear uniforms and in many circumstances this is cause for assurance, not discomfort. Much the same can be said for wearing sidearms. That most law enforcement officers are armed is a fact well known to the public. The presence of a holstered firearm thus is unlikely to contribute to the coerciveness of the encounter absent active brandishing of the weapon.

Officer Hoover's position at the front of the bus also does not tip the scale in respondents' favor. Hoover did nothing to intimidate passengers, and he said nothing to suggest that people could not exit and indeed he left the aisle clear. . . . Finally, the fact that in Officer Lang's experience only a few passengers have refused to cooperate does not suggest that a reasonable person would not feel free to terminate the bus encounter. In Lang's experience it was common for passengers to leave the bus for a cigarette or a snack while the officers were questioning passengers. And of more importance, bus passengers answer officers' questions and otherwise cooperate not because of coercion but because the passengers know that their participation enhances their own safety and the safety of those around them. . . .

Drayton contends that even if Brown's cooperation with the officers was consensual, Drayton was seized because no reasonable person would feel free to terminate the encounter with the officers after Brown had been arrested. . . . The arrest of one person does not mean that everyone around him has been seized by police. If anything, Brown's arrest should have put Drayton on notice of the consequences of continuing the encounter by answering the officers' questions. Even after arresting Brown, Lang addressed Drayton in a polite manner and provided him with no indication that he was required to answer Lang's questions.

We turn now from the question whether respondents were seized to whether they were subjected to an unreasonable search, *i.e.*, whether their consent to the suspicionless search was involuntary. In circumstances such as these, where the question of voluntariness pervades both the search and seizure inquiries, the respective analyses turn on very similar facts. And, as the facts above suggest, respondents' consent to the search of their luggage and their persons was voluntary. Nothing Officer Lang said indicated a command to consent to the search. Rather, when respondents informed Lang that they had a bag on the bus, he asked for their permission to check it. And when Lang requested to search Brown and Drayton's persons, he asked first if they objected, thus indicating to a reasonable person that he or she was free to refuse. Even after arresting Brown, Lang provided Drayton with no indication that he was required to consent to a search. To the contrary, Lang asked for Drayton's permission to search him ("Mind if I check you?"), and Drayton agreed.

The Court has rejected in specific terms the suggestion that police officers must always inform citizens of their right to refuse when seeking permission to conduct a warrantless consent search. See, *e.g.,* Ohio v. Robinette, 519 U.S. 33 (1996); Scheckloth v. Bustamonte, 412 U.S. 218 (1973). . . . Instead, the Court has repeated that the totality of the circumstances must control, without giving extra weight to the absence of this type of warning. Although Officer Lang did not inform respondents of their right to refuse the search, he did request permission to search, and the totality of the circumstances indicates that their consent was voluntary, so the searches were reasonable.

In a society based on law, the concept of agreement and consent should be given a weight and dignity of its own. Police officers act in full accord with the law when they ask citizens for consent. It reinforces the rule of law for the citizen to advise the police of his or her wishes and for the police to act in reliance on that understanding. When this exchange takes place, it dispels inferences of coercion. . . .

SOUTER, J., dissenting.

Anyone who travels by air today submits to searches of the person and luggage as a condition of boarding the aircraft. It is universally accepted that such intrusions are necessary to hedge against risks that, nowadays, even small children understand. The commonplace precautions of air travel have not, thus far, been justified for ground transportation, however, and no such conditions have been placed on passengers getting on trains or buses. There is therefore an air of unreality about the Court's explanation that bus passengers consent to searches of their luggage to "enhanc[e] their own safety and the safety of those around them." Nor are the other factual assessments underlying the Court's conclusion in favor of the Government more convincing.

The issue we took to review is whether the police's examination of the bus passengers, including respondents, amounted to a suspicionless seizure under the Fourth Amendment. If it did, any consent to search was plainly invalid as a product of the illegal seizure.

Florida v. Bostick, 501 U.S. 429 (1991), established the framework for determining whether the bus passengers were seized in the constitutional sense. In that case, we rejected the position that police questioning of bus passengers was a *per se* seizure, and held instead that the issue of seizure was to be resolved under an objective test considering all circumstances: whether a reasonable passenger would have felt "free to decline the officers' requests or otherwise terminate the encounter." . . .

Before applying the standard in this case, it may be worth getting some perspective from different sets of facts. A perfect example of police conduct that supports no colorable claim of seizure is the act of an officer who simply goes up to a pedestrian on the street and asks him a question. A pair of officers questioning a pedestrian, without more, would presumably support the same conclusion. Now consider three officers, one of whom stands behind the pedestrian, another at his side toward the open sidewalk, with the third addressing questions to the pedestrian a foot or two from his face. Finally, consider the same scene in a narrow alley. On such barebones facts, one may not be able to say a seizure occurred, even in the last case, but one can say without qualification that the atmosphere of the encounters differed significantly from the first to the last examples. [When] the attention of several officers is brought to bear on one civilian the imbalance of immediate power is unmistakable.

[In this case, the officers] addressed the passengers at very close range; the aisle was only fifteen inches wide, and each seat only eighteen. The quarters were cramped further by the overhead rack, nineteen inches above the top of the passenger seats. The passenger by the window could not have stood up straight, and the face of the nearest officer was only a foot or eighteen inches from the face of the nearest passenger being addressed. During the exchanges, the officers looked down, and the passengers had to look up if they were to face the police.

[The] officer said the police were "conducting bus interdiction," in the course of which they "would like . . . cooperation." The reasonable inference was that the "interdiction" was not a consensual exercise, but one the police would carry out whatever the circumstances; that they would prefer "cooperation" but would not let the lack of it stand in their way. There was no contrary indication that day, since no passenger had refused the cooperation requested, and there was no reason for any passenger to believe that the driver would return and the trip resume until the police were satisfied. The scene was set and an atmosphere of obligatory participation was established by this introduction. Later requests to search prefaced with "Do you mind . . ." would naturally have been understood in the terms with which the encounter began. . . .

While I am not prepared to say that no bus interrogation and search can pass the *Bostick* test without a warning that passengers are free to say no, the facts here surely required more from the officers than a quiet tone of voice. A police officer who is certain to get his way has no need to shout.

It is true of course that the police testified that a bus passenger sometimes says no, but that evidence does nothing to cast the facts here in a different light. We have no way of knowing the circumstances in which a passenger elsewhere refused a request; maybe that has happened only when the police have told passengers they had a right to refuse (as the officers sometimes advised them).

[The relevant question is] whether a passenger would reasonably have felt free to end his encounter with the three officers by saying no and ignoring them thereafter. In my view the answer is clear, . . . and I respectfully dissent.

# Chapter 4

# Searches in Recurring Contexts

## A. "Persons"

### 2. Intrusive Body Searches

**Page 251.    Add this material after note 4.**

5.    *Airport strip searches.* The Customs Service has the authority to order travelers entering the country to submit to searches of their bodies, including strip searches and body cavity searches, so long as officers have "reasonable suspicion" that the person might be hiding something illegal. Fewer than 2 percent of the 68 million fliers who passed through customs in 1997 had their luggage opened. Just under 50,000 travelers were personally searched. In 1997, customs officers ordered partial or full strip searches for 1,772 airline passengers, X-rays for 675 travelers, and body cavity searches for 19 travelers. They found drugs in 27 percent of these cases. Sixty percent of those pulled aside for body searches or X-rays were black or Hispanic. Thirty-three percent of Hispanics who were searched were found to have drugs compared with 31 percent of blacks and 26 percent of whites. Customs officials say that race is not a factor in their selection of travelers to undergo searches. Instead, travelers are chosen based on their flight and country of origin, the nature of their clothing, and their demeanor during interviews with

customs officers. See Stephen Barr, Aiming to Enforce Change at Customs; Shake-Up Underway; Scrutiny Looms, Washington Post, Feb. 17, 1999, at A15; Connie Cass, Searches Prompt Suits, Dayton Daily News, Dec. 2, 1998, at 18A.

## B. "Houses" and Other Places

### 1.   The Outer Boundaries of Houses

**Page 259.   Add this material after Problem 4-3.**

### Problem 4-3A. Scene of the Crime

Minister James Flippo and his wife Roseanne were vacationing at a cabin in a state park. One evening, Rev. Flippo called 911 to report that he and his wife had been attacked. The police arrived and found Rev. Flippo waiting outside the cabin, with injuries to his head and legs. An officer entered the building and found Mrs. Flippo's body, with fatal head wounds. The officers closed off the area, took Rev. Flippo to the hospital, and searched the exterior and environs of the cabin for footprints or signs of forced entry. When a police photographer arrived at about 5:30 A.M., the officers reentered the building and "processed the crime scene." For over 16 hours, they took photographs and searched the contents of the cabin. On a table in the cabin, they found a briefcase. The officers opened it and found inside some photographs taken of a man who appeared to be taking off his jeans. The man was later identified as Joel Boggess, a friend of Rev. Flippo and a member of his congregation.

Rev. Flippo was indicted for the murder of his wife. He moved to suppress the photographs and negatives discovered in an envelope in the closed briefcase during the search, arguing that the police had obtained no warrant, and that no exception to the warrant requirement justified the search and seizure. The government argued that, having secured the homicide scene, the officers could conduct a thorough investigation and examination of anything and everything found within the crime scene area, including the briefcase. How would you rule on the suppression motion?

called them in for H.
didn't necessarily give
consent but police are
supposed to protes crime
scene

## *NOTE*

1. *Crime scene searches.* Police often search crime scenes. Do they need to obtain warrants at any point? Officers can secure a crime scene without a warrant. Officers can also conduct an initial search in response to emergency situations such as assisting a victim or searching for an offender. Police may also seize evidence in plain view during their emergency search and while securing the crime scene. However, in Mincey v. Arizona, 437 U.S. 385 (1978), the U.S Supreme Court rejected a "crime scene exception" to the Fourth Amendment, and said that police should have obtained a warrant after they conducted a detailed four-day search of an apartment after a murder. Following *Mincey*, some state courts allowed warrantless crime scene searches when they were more immediate than the extended search in *Mincey*. See e.g., State v. Hatten, 315 S.E.2d 893 (Ga. 1984) (allowing six-hour crime scene search in homicide case). However, in Flippo v. West Virginia, 528 U.S. 11 (1999), the U.S. Supreme Court reaffirmed *Mincey* and rejected the warrantless search of the briefcase described above in Problem 4-3A. How often do defendants raise crime scene warrant issues? How do defendants and their lawyers know what police do at crime scenes, and when they do it? Are courts likely to issue search warrants for crime scenes that are more sweeping than for other kinds of investigations? See 22 Okl. St. Ann. §1230 (creating exception for daytime search warrant presumption for search of crime scenes).

## 3.   Schools and Prisons

Page 274.   Replace the *Vernonia* opinion with this material.

# Board of Education of Independent School District No. 92 of Pottawatomie County v. Lindsay Earls
122 S. Ct. 2559 (2002)

THOMAS, J.
The Student Activities Drug Testing Policy implemented by the Board of Education of Independent School District No. 92 of Pottawatomie County requires all students who participate in

competitive extracurricular activities to submit to drug testing. Because this Policy reasonably serves the School District's important interest in detecting and preventing drug use among its students, we hold that it is constitutional.

The city of Tecumseh, Oklahoma, is a rural community located approximately 40 miles southeast of Oklahoma City. . . . In the fall of 1998, the School District adopted the Student Activities Drug Testing Policy (Policy), which requires all middle and high school students to consent to drug testing in order to participate in any extracurricular activity. In practice, the Policy has been applied only to competitive extracurricular activities sanctioned by the Oklahoma Secondary Schools Activities Association, such as the Academic Team, Future Farmers of America, Future Homemakers of America, band, choir, pom pom, cheerleading, and athletics. Under the Policy, students are required to take a drug test before participating in an extracurricular activity, must submit to random drug testing while participating in that activity, and must agree to be tested at any time upon reasonable suspicion. The urinalysis tests are designed to detect only the use of illegal drugs, including amphetamines, marijuana, cocaine, opiates, and barbituates, not medical conditions or the presence of authorized prescription medications.

At the time of their suit, both respondents attended Tecumseh High School. Respondent Lindsay Earls was a member of the show choir, the marching band, the Academic Team, and the National Honor Society. Respondent Daniel James sought to participate in the Academic Team. Together with their parents, Earls and James brought a 42 U.S.C. § 1983 action against the School District, challenging the Policy both on its face and as applied to their participation in extracurricular activities. They alleged that the Policy violates the Fourth Amendment as incorporated by the Fourteenth Amendment and requested injunctive and declarative relief. They also argued that the School District failed to identify a special need for testing students who participate in extracurricular activities, and that the "Drug Testing Policy neither addresses a proven problem nor promises to bring any benefit to students or the school." [The District Court granted summary judgment to the School District, but the Tenth Circuit reversed.]

Searches by public school officials, such as the collection of urine samples, implicate Fourth Amendment interests. We must therefore review the School District's Policy for "reasonableness," which is the touchstone of the constitutionality of a governmental search. In the criminal context, reasonableness usually requires a showing of probable cause. The probable-cause standard, however, is peculiarly related to criminal investigations and may be unsuited to determining the reasonableness of administrative searches where the Government seeks to *prevent* the development of hazardous conditions. The Court has also held that a warrant and finding of probable cause are unnecessary in the public school context because such requirements "would unduly interfere with the maintenance of the swift and informal disciplinary procedures [that are] needed." New Jersey v. T.L.O., 469 U.S. 325, 340-341 (1985).

Given that the School District's Policy is not in any way related to the conduct of criminal investigations, respondents do not contend that the School District requires probable cause before testing students for drug use. Respondents instead argue that drug testing must be based at least on some level of individualized suspicion. It is true that we generally determine the reasonableness of a search by balancing the nature of the intrusion on the individual's privacy against the promotion of legitimate governmental interests. But we have long held that the Fourth Amendment imposes no irreducible requirement of individualized suspicion. In certain limited circumstances, the Government's need to discover such latent or hidden conditions, or to prevent their development, is sufficiently compelling to justify the intrusion on privacy entailed by conducting such searches without any measure of individualized suspicion. Treasury Employees v. Von Raab, 489 U.S. 656 (1989) [allowing drug testing of customs employees in drug enforcement positions]; Skinner v. Railway Labor Executives' Assn., 489 U.S. 602 (1989) [allowing drug testing of railway employees after train accidents]. Therefore, in the context of safety and administrative regulations, a search unsupported by probable cause may be reasonable when "special needs, beyond the normal need for law enforcement, make the warrant and probable-cause requirement impracticable." *T.L.O.* at 351.

Significantly, this Court has previously held that "special needs" inhere in the public school context. While schoolchildren do not shed their constitutional rights when they enter the schoolhouse, "Fourth Amendment rights . . . are different in public schools than elsewhere; the 'reasonableness' inquiry cannot disregard the schools' custodial and tutelary responsibility for children." Vernonia School Dist. 47J v. Acton, 515 U.S. 646, 656 (1995). In particular, a finding of individualized suspicion may not be necessary when a school conducts drug testing.

In *Vernonia*, this Court held that the suspicionless drug testing of athletes was constitutional. The Court, however, did not simply authorize all school drug testing, but rather conducted a fact-specific balancing of the intrusion on the children's Fourth Amendment rights against the promotion of legitimate governmental interests. Applying the principles of *Vernonia* to the somewhat different facts of this case, we conclude that Tecumseh's Policy is also constitutional.

We first consider the nature of the privacy interest allegedly compromised by the drug testing. As in *Vernonia*, the context of the public school environment serves as the backdrop for the analysis of the privacy interest at stake and the reasonableness of the drug testing policy in general. See *ibid.* ("Central . . . is the fact that the subjects of the Policy are (1) children, who (2) have been committed to the temporary custody of the State as schoolmaster"). A student's privacy interest is limited in a public school environment where the State is responsible for maintaining discipline, health, and safety. Schoolchildren are routinely required to submit to physical examinations and vaccinations against disease. Securing order in the school environment sometimes requires that students be subjected to greater controls than those appropriate for adults.

Respondents argue that because children participating in nonathletic extracurricular activities are not subject to regular physicals and communal undress, they have a stronger expectation of privacy than the athletes tested in *Vernonia*. This distinction, however, was not essential to our decision in *Vernonia*, which depended primarily upon the school's custodial responsibility and authority.

In any event, students who participate in competitive extracurricular activities voluntarily subject themselves to many of the same intrusions on their privacy as do athletes. Some of these clubs and activities require occasional off-campus travel and communal undress. All of them have their own rules and requirements for participating students that do not apply to the student body as a whole. For example, each of the competitive extracurricular activities governed by the Policy must abide by the rules of the Oklahoma Secondary Schools Activities Association, and a faculty sponsor monitors the students for compliance with the various rules dictated by the clubs and activities. . . . We therefore conclude that the students affected by this Policy have a limited expectation of privacy.

Next, we consider the character of the intrusion imposed by the Policy. Urination is an excretory function traditionally shielded by great privacy. But the degree of intrusion on one's privacy caused by collecting a urine sample depends upon the manner in which production of the urine sample is monitored. Under the Policy, a faculty monitor waits outside the closed restroom stall for the student to produce a sample and must "listen for the normal sounds of urination in order to guard against tampered specimens and to insure an accurate chain of custody." The monitor then pours the sample into two bottles that are sealed and placed into a mailing pouch along with a consent form signed by the student. This procedure is virtually identical to that reviewed in *Vernonia*, except that it additionally protects privacy by allowing male students to produce their samples behind a closed stall. Given that we considered the method of collection in *Vernonia* a "negligible" intrusion, the method here is even less problematic.

In addition, the Policy clearly requires that the test results be kept in confidential files separate from a student's other educational records and released to school personnel only on a "need to know" basis. Respondents nonetheless contend that the intrusion on students' privacy is significant because the Policy fails to protect effectively against the disclosure of confidential information and, specifically, that the school "has been careless in protecting that information: for example, the Choir teacher looked at students' prescription drug lists and left them where other students could see them." But the choir teacher is someone with a "need to know," because during off-campus trips she needs to know what medications are taken by her students. . . . This one example of alleged carelessness hardly increases the character of the intrusion.

Moreover, the test results are not turned over to any law enforcement authority. Nor do the test results here lead to the imposition of discipline or have any academic consequences. Rather, the only consequence of a failed drug test is to limit the student's privilege of participating in extracurricular activities. Indeed, a student may test positive for drugs twice and still be allowed to participate in extracurricular activities. After the first positive test, the school contacts the student's parent or guardian for a meeting. The student may continue to participate in the activity if within five days of the meeting the student shows proof of receiving drug counseling and submits to a second drug test in two weeks. For the second positive test, the student is suspended from participation in all extracurricular activities for 14 days, must complete four hours of substance abuse counseling, and must submit to monthly drug tests. Only after a third positive test will the student be suspended from participating in any extracurricular activity for the remainder of the school year, or 88 school days, whichever is longer.

Given the minimally intrusive nature of the sample collection and the limited uses to which the test results are put, we conclude that the invasion of students' privacy is not significant.

Finally, this Court must consider the nature and immediacy of the government's concerns and the efficacy of the Policy in meeting them. This Court has already articulated in detail the importance of the governmental concern in preventing drug use by schoolchildren. The drug abuse problem among our Nation's youth has hardly abated since *Vernonia* was decided in 1995. In fact, evidence suggests that it has only grown worse.[5] As in *Vernonia*, "the necessity for the State to act is magnified by the fact that this evil is being visited not just upon individuals at large, but upon children for whom it has undertaken a special responsibility of care and direction." The health and safety risks identified in *Vernonia* apply with equal force to Tecumseh's children. Indeed, the nationwide drug epidemic makes the war against drugs a pressing concern in every school.

Additionally, the School District in this case has presented specific evidence of drug use at Tecumseh schools. Teachers testified that they had seen students who appeared to be under the influence of drugs and that they had heard students speaking openly about using drugs. A drug dog found marijuana cigarettes near the school parking lot. Police officers once found drugs or drug paraphernalia in a car driven by a Future Farmers of America member. And the school board president reported that people in the community were calling the board to discuss

---

5. For instance, the number of 12th graders using any illicit drug increased from 48.4 percent in 1995 to 53.9 percent in 2001. The number of 12th graders reporting they had used marijuana jumped from 41.7 percent to 49.0 percent during that same period. See Department of Health and Human Services, Monitoring the Future: National Results on Adolescent Drug Use, Overview of Key Findings (2001) (Table 1).

the "drug situation." We decline to second-guess the finding of the District Court that "viewing the evidence as a whole, it cannot be reasonably disputed that the School District was faced with a 'drug problem' when it adopted the Policy." . . .

Given the nationwide epidemic of drug use, and the evidence of increased drug use in Tecumseh schools, it was entirely reasonable for the School District to enact this particular drug testing policy. [We] refuse to fashion what would in effect be a constitutional quantum of drug use necessary to show a "drug problem." . . .

We also reject respondents' argument that drug testing must presumptively be based upon an individualized reasonable suspicion of wrongdoing because such a testing regime would be less intrusive. [We] question whether testing based on individualized suspicion in fact would be less intrusive. Such a regime would place an additional burden on public school teachers who are already tasked with the difficult job of maintaining order and discipline. A program of individualized suspicion might unfairly target members of unpopular groups. The fear of lawsuits resulting from such targeted searches may chill enforcement of the program, rendering it ineffective in combating drug use. In any case, this Court has repeatedly stated that reasonableness under the Fourth Amendment does not require employing the least intrusive means, because the logic of such elaborate less-restrictive-alternative arguments could raise insuperable barriers to the exercise of virtually all search-and-seizure powers. . . .

Within the limits of the Fourth Amendment, local school boards must assess the desirability of drug testing schoolchildren. In upholding the constitutionality of the Policy, we express no opinion as to its wisdom. Rather, we hold only that Tecumseh's Policy is a reasonable means of furthering the School District's important interest in preventing and deterring drug use among its schoolchildren. . . .

BREYER, J., concurring.
. . . When trying to resolve this kind of close question involving the interpretation of constitutional values, I believe it important that the school board provided an opportunity for the airing of these differences at public meetings designed to give the entire community the opportunity to be able to participate in developing the drug policy. The board used this democratic, participatory process to uncover and to resolve

differences, giving weight to the fact that the process, in this instance, revealed little, if any, objection to the proposed testing program.

[A] contrary reading of the Constitution, as requiring "individualized suspicion" in this public school context, could well lead schools to push the boundaries of "individualized suspicion" to its outer limits, using subjective criteria that may "unfairly target members of unpopular groups," or leave those whose behavior is slightly abnormal stigmatized in the minds of others. If so, direct application of the Fourth Amendment's prohibition against "unreasonable searches and seizures" will further that Amendment's liberty-protecting objectives at least to the same extent as application of the mediating "individualized suspicion" test, where, as here, the testing program is neither criminal nor disciplinary in nature. . . .

GINSBURG, J., dissenting.

Seven years ago, in Vernonia School Dist. 47J v. Acton, 515 U.S. 646 (1995), this Court determined that a school district's policy of randomly testing the urine of its student athletes for illicit drugs did not violate the Fourth Amendment. In so ruling, the Court emphasized that drug use "increased the risk of sports-related injury" and that Vernonia's athletes were the "leaders" of an aggressive local "drug culture" that had reached "epidemic proportions." Today, the Court relies upon *Vernonia* to permit a school district with a drug problem its superintendent repeatedly described as "not major" to test the urine of an academic team member solely by reason of her participation in a nonathletic, competitive extracurricular activity—participation associated with neither special dangers from, nor particular predilections for, drug use. . . . The particular testing program upheld today is not reasonable, it is capricious, even perverse: Petitioners' policy targets for testing a student population least likely to be at risk from illicit drugs and their damaging effects. I therefore dissent.

This case presents circumstances dispositively different from those of *Vernonia*. True, as the Court stresses, Tecumseh students participating in competitive extracurricular activities other than athletics share two relevant characteristics with the athletes of *Vernonia*. First, both groups attend public schools. . . . Concern for student health and safety is basic to the school's caretaking, and it is undeniable that drug use carries a variety of health risks for children, including death from overdose.

Those risks, however, are present for *all* schoolchildren. *Vernonia* cannot be read to endorse invasive and suspicionless drug testing of all students upon any evidence of drug use, solely because drugs jeopardize the life and health of those who use them. Many children, like many adults, engage in dangerous activities on their own time; that the children are enrolled in school scarcely allows government to monitor all such activities. . . .

The second commonality to which the Court points is the voluntary character of both interscholastic athletics and other competitive extracurricular activities. . . . The comparison is enlightening. While extracurricular activities are "voluntary" in the sense that they are not required for graduation, they are part of the school's educational program; for that reason, the petitioner . . . is justified in expending public resources to make them available. Participation in such activities is a key component of school life, essential in reality for students applying to college, and, for all participants, a significant contributor to the breadth and quality of the educational experience. Students "volunteer" for extracurricular pursuits in the same way they might volunteer for honors classes: They subject themselves to additional requirements, but they do so in order to take full advantage of the education offered them.

Voluntary participation in athletics has a distinctly different dimension: Schools regulate student athletes discretely because competitive school sports by their nature require communal undress and, more important, expose students to physical risks that schools have a duty to mitigate. . . . Competitive extracurricular activities other than athletics, however, serve students of all manner: the modest and shy along with the bold and uninhibited. Activities of the kind plaintiff-respondent Lindsay Earls pursued—choir, show choir, marching band, and academic team—afford opportunities to gain self-assurance. . . . On "occasional out-of-town trips," students like Lindsay Earls must sleep together in communal settings and use communal bathrooms. But those situations are hardly equivalent to the routine communal undress associated with athletics; the School District itself admits that when such trips occur, "public-like restroom facilities," which presumably include enclosed stalls, are ordinarily available for changing, and that "more modest students" find other ways to maintain their privacy. . . .

Finally, the nature and immediacy of the governmental concern faced by the Vernonia School District dwarfed that confronting Tecumseh administrators. Vernonia initiated its drug testing policy in response to an alarming situation: "[A] large segment of the student body, particularly those involved in interscholastic athletics, was in a state of rebellion . . . fueled by alcohol and drug abuse as well as the students' misperceptions about the drug culture." Tecumseh, by contrast, repeatedly reported to the Federal Government during the period leading up to the adoption of the policy that "types of drugs [other than alcohol and tobacco] including controlled dangerous substances, are present [in the schools] but have not identified themselves as major problems at this time." 1998-1999 Tecumseh School's Application for Funds under the Safe and Drug-Free Schools and Communities Program. . . .

Nationwide, students who participate in extracurricular activities are significantly less likely to develop substance abuse problems than are their less-involved peers. See, e.g., N. Zill, C. Nord, & L. Loomis, Adolescent Time Use, Risky Behavior, and Outcomes 52 (1995) (tenth graders "who reported spending no time in school-sponsored activities were . . . 49 percent more likely to have used drugs" than those who spent 1-4 hours per week in such activities). Even if students might be deterred from drug use in order to preserve their extracurricular eligibility, it is at least as likely that other students might forgo their extracurricular involvement in order to avoid detection of their drug use. Tecumseh's policy thus falls short doubly if deterrence is its aim: It invades the privacy of students who need deterrence least, and risks steering students at greatest risk for substance abuse away from extracurricular involvement that potentially may palliate drug problems.

To summarize, this case resembles *Vernonia* only in that the School Districts in both cases conditioned engagement in activities outside the obligatory curriculum on random subjection to urinalysis. The defining characteristics of the two programs, however, are entirely dissimilar. The Vernonia district sought to test a subpopulation of students distinguished by their reduced expectation of privacy, their special susceptibility to drug-related injury, and their heavy involvement with drug use. The Tecumseh district seeks to test a much larger population associated with none of these factors. It does so, moreover, without carefully safeguarding student confidentiality and without regard to the program's untoward effects. A program so sweeping is not sheltered by *Vernonia*;

its unreasonable reach renders it impermissible under the Fourth Amendment.

[Schools'] tutelary obligations to their students require them to "teach by example" by avoiding symbolic measures that diminish constitutional protections. "That [schools] are educating the young for citizenship is reason for scrupulous protection of Constitutional freedoms of the individual, if we are not to strangle the free mind at its source and teach youth to discount important principles of our government as mere platitudes." West Virginia Bd. of Ed. v. Barnette, 319 U.S. 624, 637 (1943). . . .

**Page 282.   Add this material at the end of the notes.**

In Ferguson v. City of Charleston, 532 U.S. 67 (2001), the Supreme Court returned to the question of drug testing in special institutional settings. A state hospital instructed its staff to identify pregnant patients suspected of drug abuse, to test those patients for drug abuse, and to report positive tests to the police. Patients who tested positive for cocaine use were arrested and prosecuted for child abuse.

The Court held that this testing was an unreasonable search. Given the amount of cooperation between the hospital and criminal prosecutors in this program, the tests served no "special needs" apart from the State's "general law enforcement interest." The central purpose of the program was the use of criminal law enforcement to coerce patients into substance abuse treatment. Drug testing in these circumstances was a search that was not accomplished through consent and not supported by probable cause.

# D.   "Effects"

## 2.   Cars and Containers

**Page 317.   Add this material to the end of note 6.**

The Supreme Court returned to the persistent question of searching containers in cars in Wyoming v. Houghton, 526 U.S. 295 (1999). During a routine traffic stop, a Wyoming Highway Patrol officer noticed a hypodermic syringe in the shirt pocket of the male driver, and the driver admitted using the syringe to take drugs. The officer then searched the passenger compartment for contraband, including the female passenger's purse. He found drug paraphernalia in the purse and arrested both parties.

The Wyoming Supreme Court required probable cause and a warrant to justify a search of "passenger property" in an automobile. However, the U.S. Supreme Court declared that police officers with probable cause to search a car may inspect passengers' belongings inside the car if they are capable of concealing the object of the search. Passengers, just like drivers, possess a reduced expectation of privacy when it comes to property inside cars. Balanced against the passenger's reduced privacy expectations, the governmental interest in effective law enforcement is especially strong here, since property inside a mobile automobile could be lost while a warrant is obtained. In addition, requiring a warrant in this setting might encourage drivers to hide contraband in containers belonging to passengers. What would be the effects of a warrant requirement for "passenger property" in cars? Would this rule prove more difficult to administer than the rule that the Vermont court adopted in *Savva*?

# Chapter 5

# Arrests

## C. Police Discretion in the Arrest Decision

**Page 352.  Add this material after the notes.**

    7.  *Arrest quotas.* Police department policies *other* than those calling for automatic or presumed arrests in some situations can have a powerful effect on individual officers' arrest decisions. How will officers respond to a departmental policy that evaluates and rewards officers based on the number of arrests they make? See Howie Carr, Arresting Memo Puts State Cops in a Pinch, Boston Herald, Oct. 21, 1998, at 1 (quoting internal memorandum of Massachusetts State Police, reviewing arrest journal and calling for "corrective action" to "increase the level of activity" because arrests are a "valid indicator" but not the only indicator of good performance); Larry Celona and Linda Massarella, "Collar" Shortage Puts Queens Cops in Doghouse, New York Post, June 11, 1998, at 12 (describing memorandum from precinct commander, saying officers who do not make enough arrests will not receive days off). Is there a plausible legal basis for challenging a system of "arrest quotas" in court? Disputes over these policies more often arise during labor negotiations between police officer unions and department administrators. See Thomas Ott, Police Sergeants, Lieutenants Say Mentor Unfair, Cleveland Plain Dealer, Feb. 25, 1999, at 4B (describing a labor dispute centering on a system of arrest and ticket quotas).

**Page 354.   Add this material at the end of note 1.**

For more recent studies describing the impact of extralegal factors (such as a suspect's demeanor) that shape police arrest decisions, see Richard Lundman, Demeanor or Crime? The Midwest City Police-Citizen Encounters Study, 32 Criminology 631 (1994); Robert Worden, Situational and Attitudinal Explanations of Police Behaviors: A Theoretical Reappraisal and Empirical Assessment, 23 L. & Socy. Rev. 667 (1989) (arrests after traffic stops and disputes).

## D.  Paper Arrests: Citations

**Page 363.   Add this material to the end of note 1.**

Some foreign jurisdictions make extensive use of devices such as citations to give police officers an alternative to custodial arrest. For instance, in Queensland, Australia, police can issue a "notice to appear" (NTA) for any criminal offense. The NTA can be issued in the field or after taking the person into custody. It is used most frequently for traffic violations, prostitution, drugs, and weapons charges. If police officers in the United States had similarly broad powers to use citations, do you believe they would use it in similar categories of cases? Would citation in the field or at the station prove more popular? See Criminal Justice Commission, Police Powers in Queensland: Notices to Appear, Research Paper, Vol. 5, No. 2, May 1999, available at http://www.cjc.qld.gov.au/.

**Page 363.   Replace notes 3 and 4 with the following material.**

## Patrick Knowles v. Iowa
### 525 U.S. 113 (1998)

REHNQUIST, C.J.

An Iowa police officer stopped petitioner Knowles for speeding, but issued him a citation rather than arresting him. The question presented is whether such a procedure authorizes the officer, consistently with the Fourth Amendment, to conduct a full search of the car. We answer this question "no."

Knowles was stopped in Newton, Iowa, after having been clocked driving 43 miles per hour on a road where the speed limit was 25 miles per hour. The police officer issued a citation to Knowles, although under Iowa law he might have arrested him. The officer then conducted a full search of the car, and under the driver's seat he found a bag of marijuana and a "pot pipe." Knowles was then arrested and charged with violation of state laws dealing with controlled substances.

Before trial, Knowles moved to suppress the evidence so obtained. He argued that the search could not be sustained under the "search incident to arrest" exception recognized in United States v. Robinson, 414 U.S. 218 (1973), because he had not been placed under arrest. At the hearing on the motion to suppress, the police officer conceded that he had neither Knowles' consent nor probable cause to conduct the search. He relied on Iowa law dealing with such searches.

Iowa Code Ann. §321.485(1)(a) provides that Iowa peace officers having cause to believe that a person has violated any traffic or motor vehicle equipment law may arrest the person and immediately take the person before a magistrate. Iowa law also authorizes the far more usual practice of issuing a citation in lieu of arrest or in lieu of continued custody after an initial arrest.[1] Section 805.1(4) provides that the issuance of a citation in lieu of an arrest "does not affect the officer's authority to conduct an otherwise lawful search." The Iowa Supreme Court has interpreted this provision as providing authority to officers to conduct a full-blown search of an automobile and driver in those cases where police elect not to make a custodial arrest and instead issue a citation — that is, a search incident to citation. See State v. Meyer, 543 N.W.2d 876, 879 (Iowa 1996). Based on this authority, the trial court denied the motion to suppress and found Knowles guilty. . . .

In *Robinson*, we noted the two historical rationales for the "search incident to arrest" exception: (1) the need to disarm the suspect in order to take him into custody, and (2) the need to preserve evidence for later

---

1.   Iowa law permits the issuance of a citation in lieu of arrest for most offenses for which an accused person would be "eligible for bail." See Iowa Code Ann. §805.1(1). In addition to traffic and motor vehicle equipment violations, this would permit the issuance of a citation in lieu of arrest for such serious felonies as second-degree burglary and first-degree theft, both bailable offenses under Iowa law. The practice in Iowa of permitting citation in lieu of arrest is consistent with law reform efforts. See 3 W. LaFave, Search and Seizure §5.2(h), p. 99, and n. 151 (3d ed. 1996).

use at trial. But neither of these underlying rationales for the search incident to arrest exception is sufficient to justify the search in the present case.

We have recognized that the first rationale—officer safety—is both legitimate and weighty. The threat to officer safety from issuing a traffic citation, however, is a good deal less than in the case of a custodial arrest. In *Robinson*, we stated that a custodial arrest involves "danger to an officer" because of "the extended exposure which follows the taking of a suspect into custody and transporting him to the police station." 414 U.S., at 234-235. . . . A routine traffic stop, on the other hand, is a relatively brief encounter and is more analogous to a so-called *Terry* stop than to a formal arrest.

This is not to say that the concern for officer safety is absent in the case of a routine traffic stop. It plainly is not. But while the concern for officer safety in this context may justify the "minimal" additional intrusion of ordering a driver and passengers out of the car, it does not by itself justify the often considerably greater intrusion attending a full field-type search. Even without the search authority Iowa urges, officers have other, independent bases to search for weapons and protect themselves from danger. For example, they may order out of a vehicle both the driver, Pennsylvania v. Mimms, 434 U.S. 106, 111 (1977) (per curiam), and any passengers, Maryland v. Wilson, 519 U.S. 408, 414 (1997); perform a "patdown" of a driver and any passengers upon reasonable suspicion that they may be armed and dangerous, Terry v. Ohio, 392 U.S. 1 (1968); conduct a *"Terry* patdown" of the passenger compartment of a vehicle upon reasonable suspicion that an occupant is dangerous and may gain immediate control of a weapon, Michigan v. Long, 463 U.S. 1032 (1983); and even conduct a full search of the passenger compartment, including any containers therein, pursuant to a custodial arrest, New York v. Belton, 453 U.S. 454, 460 (1981).

Nor has Iowa shown the second justification for the authority to search incident to arrest—the need to discover and preserve evidence. Once Knowles was stopped for speeding and issued a citation, all the evidence necessary to prosecute that offense had been obtained. No further evidence of excessive speed was going to be found either on the person of the offender or in the passenger compartment of the car.

Iowa nevertheless argues that a "search incident to citation" is justified because a suspect who is subject to a routine traffic stop may attempt to hide or destroy evidence related to his identity (e.g., a driver's license or vehicle registration), or destroy evidence of another, as yet undetected crime. As for the destruction of evidence relating to identity, if a police officer is not satisfied with the identification furnished by the driver, this may be a basis for arresting him rather than merely issuing a citation. As for destroying evidence of other crimes, the possibility that an officer would stumble onto evidence wholly unrelated to the speeding offense seems remote.

In *Robinson*, we held that the authority to conduct a full field search as incident to an arrest was a "bright-line rule," which was based on the concern for officer safety and destruction or loss of evidence, but which did not depend in every case upon the existence of either concern. Here we are asked to extend that "bright-line rule" to a situation where the concern for officer safety is not present to the same extent and the concern for destruction or loss of evidence is not present at all. We decline to do so. . . .

## Gail Atwater v. City of Lago Vista
### 532 U.S. 318 (2001)

SOUTER, J.

The question is whether the Fourth Amendment forbids a warrantless arrest for a minor criminal offense, such as a misdemeanor seatbelt violation punishable only by a fine. We hold that it does not.

In Texas, if a car is equipped with safety belts, a front-seat passenger must wear one, and the driver must secure any small child riding in front. Violation of either provision is a misdemeanor punishable by a fine not less than $25 or more than $50. Texas law expressly authorizes "any peace officer [to] arrest without warrant a person found committing a violation" of these seatbelt laws, Transp. Code §543.001, although it permits police to issue citations in lieu of arrest.

In March 1997, Petitioner Gail Atwater was driving her pickup truck in Lago Vista, Texas, with her 3-year-old son and 5-year-old daughter in the front seat. None of them was wearing a seatbelt. Respondent Bart Turek, a Lago Vista police officer at the time, observed the seatbelt violations and pulled Atwater over. According to Atwater's complaint (the allegations of which we assume to be true for present purposes),

Turek approached the truck and "yelled" something to the effect of "we've met before" and "you're going to jail."[1] He then called for backup and asked to see Atwater's driver's license and insurance documentation, which state law required her to carry. When Atwater told Turek that she did not have the papers because her purse had been stolen the day before, Turek said that he had "heard that story two hundred times."

Atwater asked to take her frightened, upset, and crying children to a friend's house nearby, but Turek told her, "you're not going anywhere." As it turned out, Atwater's friend learned what was going on and soon arrived to take charge of the children. Turek then handcuffed Atwater, placed her in his squad car, and drove her to the local police station, where booking officers had her remove her shoes, jewelry, and eyeglasses, and empty her pockets. Officers took Atwater's "mug shot" and placed her, alone, in a jail cell for about one hour, after which she was taken before a magistrate and released on $310 bond.

Atwater was charged with driving without her seatbelt fastened, failing to secure her children in seatbelts, driving without a license, and failing to provide proof of insurance. She ultimately pleaded no contest to the misdemeanor seatbelt offenses and paid a $50 fine; the other charges were dismissed.

Atwater and her husband, petitioner Michael Haas, filed suit in a Texas state court under 42 U.S.C. §1983, [alleging that the City] had violated Atwater's Fourth Amendment "right to be free from unreasonable seizure," and sought compensatory and punitive damages.

[A]n examination of the common-law understanding of an officer's authority to arrest sheds light on the obviously relevant, if not entirely dispositive, consideration of what the Framers of the Amendment might have thought to be reasonable. Thus, the first step here is to assess Atwater's claim that peace officers' authority to make warrantless arrests for misdemeanors was restricted at common law. . . . Atwater's specific contention is that "founding-era common-law rules" forbade peace officers to make warrantless misdemeanor arrests except in cases of "breach of the peace," a category she claims was then understood

---

1. Turek had previously stopped Atwater for what he had thought was a seatbelt violation, but had realized that Atwater's son, although seated on the vehicle's armrest, was in fact belted in. Atwater acknowledged that her son's seating position was unsafe, and Turek issued a verbal warning.

narrowly as covering only those nonfelony offenses "involving or tending toward violence." Although her historical argument is by no means insubstantial, it ultimately fails.

We [find that] the common-law commentators (as well as the sparsely reported cases) reached divergent conclusions with respect to officers' warrantless misdemeanor arrest power. Moreover, in the years leading up to American independence, Parliament repeatedly extended express warrantless arrest authority to cover misdemeanor-level offenses not amounting to or involving any violent breach of the peace. . . .

On one side of the divide there are certainly eminent authorities supporting Atwater's position. . . . James Fitzjames Stephen and Glanville Williams both seemed to indicate that the common law confined warrantless misdemeanor arrests to actual breaches of the peace. See 1 J. Stephen, A History of the Criminal Law of England 193 (1883) ("The common law did not authorise the arrest of persons guilty or suspected of misdemeanours, except in cases of an actual breach of the peace either by an affray or by violence to an individual"); G. Williams, Arrest for Breach of the Peace, *1954 Crim. L. Rev. 578, 578* ("Apart from arrest for felony . . . , the only power of arrest at common law is in respect of breach of the peace"). . . .

The great commentators were not unanimous, however, and there is also considerable evidence of a broader conception of common-law misdemeanor arrest authority unlimited by any breach-of-the-peace condition. Sir Matthew Hale, Chief Justice of King's Bench from 1671 to 1676, wrote in his History of the Pleas of the Crown that, by his "original and inherent power," a constable could arrest without a warrant "for breach of the peace and some misdemeanors, less than felony." 2 M. Hale, The History of the Pleas of the Crown 88 (1736). . . .

A second, and equally serious, problem for Atwater's historical argument is posed by the "divers Statutes," M. Dalton, Country Justice ch. 170, §4, p. 582 (1727), enacted by Parliament well before this Republic's founding that authorized warrantless misdemeanor arrests without reference to violence or turmoil. [T]he legal background of any conception of reasonableness the Fourth Amendment's Framers might have entertained would have included English statutes, some centuries old, authorizing peace officers (and even private persons) to make warrantless arrests for all sorts of relatively minor offenses unaccompanied by violence. The so-called "nightwalker" statutes are perhaps the most notable examples. From the enactment of the Statute of Winchester in 1285, through its various readoptions and until its repeal in 1827, night watchmen were authorized and charged "as . . . in Times past" to "watch the Town continually all Night, from the Sun-setting unto the Sun-rising" and were directed that "if any Stranger do pass by them, he shall be arrested until Morning. . . ." 13 Edw. I, ch. 4, §§5-6, 1 Statutes at Large 232-233.

[T]hroughout the period leading up to the framing, Parliament repeatedly extended warrantless arrest power to cover misdemeanor-level offenses not involving any breach of the peace. One 16th-century statute, for instance, authorized peace officers to arrest persons playing "unlawful games" like bowling, tennis, dice, and cards, and for good measure extended the authority beyond players to include persons "haunting" the "houses, places and alleys where such games shall be suspected to be holden, exercised, used or occupied." 33 Hen. VIII, ch. 9, §§11-16, 5 Statutes at Large 84-85 (1541). . . .

An examination of specifically American evidence is to the same effect. Neither the history of the framing era nor subsequent legal development indicates that the Fourth Amendment was originally understood, or has traditionally been read, to embrace Atwater's position. . . .

During the period leading up to and surrounding the framing of the Bill of Rights, colonial and state legislatures, like Parliament before them, regularly authorized local peace officers to make warrantless misdemeanor arrests without conditioning statutory authority on breach of the peace. See, e.g., First Laws of the State of Connecticut 214-215 (Cushing ed. 1982) (1784 compilation; exact date of Act unknown) (authorizing warrantless arrests of "all Persons unnecessarily travelling on the Sabbath or Lord's Day"). . . .

A number of state constitutional search-and-seizure provisions served as models for the Fourth Amendment, and the fact that many of the original States with such constitutional limitations continued to grant their own peace officers broad warrantless misdemeanor arrest authority undermines Atwater's contention that the founding generation meant to bar federal law enforcement officers from exercising the same authority.

. . . Nor does Atwater's argument from tradition pick up any steam from the historical record as it has unfolded since the framing, there being no indication that her claimed rule has ever become woven into the fabric of American law. The story, on the contrary, is of two centuries of uninterrupted (and largely unchallenged) state and federal practice permitting warrantless arrests for misdemeanors not amounting to or involving breach of the peace.

First, there is no support for Atwater's position in this Court's cases. . . . Although the Court has not had much to say about warrantless misdemeanor arrest authority, what little we have said tends to cut against Atwater's argument. In discussing this authority, we have focused on the circumstance that an offense was committed in an officer's presence, to the omission of any reference to a breach-of-the-peace limitation. See Bad Elk v. United States, 177 U.S. 529, 534 (1900) (noting common-law pedigree of state statute permitting warrantless arrest "for a public offense committed or attempted in [officer's] presence").

Second, [there are] numerous early- and mid-19th-century decisions expressly sustaining (often against constitutional challenge) state and local laws authorizing peace officers to make warrantless arrests for misdemeanors not involving any breach of the peace. See, e.g., Mayo v. Wilson, 1 N.H. 53 (1817) (upholding statute authorizing warrantless arrests of those unnecessarily traveling on Sunday against challenge based on state due process and search-and-seizure provisions). . . .

Small wonder, then, that today statutes in all 50 States and the District of Columbia permit warrantless misdemeanor arrests by at least some (if not all) peace officers without requiring any breach of the peace, as do a host of congressional enactments.

[But] Atwater does not wager all on history. Instead, she asks us to mint a new rule of constitutional law on the understanding that when historical practice fails to speak conclusively to a claim grounded on the Fourth Amendment, courts are left to strike a current balance between individual and societal interests by subjecting particular contemporary circumstances to traditional standards of reasonableness. . . .

If we were to derive a rule exclusively to address the uncontested facts of this case, Atwater might well prevail. She was a known and established resident of Lago Vista with no place to hide and no incentive to flee, and common sense says she would almost certainly have buckled up as a condition of driving off with a citation. In her case, the physical incidents of arrest were merely gratuitous humiliations imposed by a police officer who was (at best) exercising extremely poor judgment.

Atwater's claim to live free of pointless indignity and confinement clearly outweighs anything the City can raise against it specific to her case.

But we have traditionally recognized that a responsible Fourth Amendment balance is not well served by standards requiring sensitive, case-by-case determinations of government need, lest every discretionary judgment in the field be converted into an occasion for constitutional review. Often enough, the Fourth Amendment has to be applied on the spur (and in the heat) of the moment, and the object in implementing its command of reasonableness is to draw standards sufficiently clear and simple to be applied with a fair prospect of surviving judicial second-guessing months and years after an arrest or search is made. . . .

At first glance, Atwater's argument may seem to respect the values of clarity and simplicity, so far as she claims that the Fourth Amendment generally forbids warrantless arrests for minor crimes not accompanied by violence or some demonstrable threat of it (whether "minor crime" be defined as a fine-only traffic offense, a fine-only offense more generally, or a misdemeanor). But the claim is not ultimately so simple, nor could it be, for complications arise the moment we begin to think about the possible applications of the several criteria Atwater proposes for drawing a line between minor crimes with limited arrest authority and others not so restricted.

One line, she suggests, might be between "jailable" and "fine-only" offenses, between those for which conviction could result in commitment and those for which it could not. The trouble with this distinction, of course, is that an officer on the street might not be able to tell. It is not merely that we cannot expect every police officer to know the details of frequently complex penalty schemes, but that penalties for ostensibly identical conduct can vary on account of facts difficult (if not impossible) to know at the scene of an arrest. Is this the first offense or is the suspect a repeat offender? Is the weight of the marijuana a gram above or a gram below the fine-only line? Where conduct could implicate more than one criminal prohibition, which one will the district attorney ultimately decide to charge? And so on.

But Atwater's refinements would not end there. She represents that if the line were drawn at nonjailable traffic offenses, her proposed limitation should be qualified by a proviso authorizing warrantless arrests where "necessary for enforcement of the traffic laws or when [an] offense would otherwise continue and pose a danger to others on the road." (Were the line drawn at misdemeanors generally, a comparable qualification would presumably apply.) The proviso only compounds the difficulties. Would, for instance, either exception apply to speeding? At oral argument, Atwater's counsel said that "it would not be reasonable to arrest a driver for speeding unless the speeding rose to the level of reckless driving." But is it not fair to expect that the chronic speeder will speed again despite a citation in his pocket, and should that not qualify as showing that the "offense would . . . continue" under Atwater's rule? And why, as a constitutional matter, should we assume that only reckless driving will "pose a danger to others on the road" while speeding will not? . . . Atwater's rule therefore would not only place police in an almost impossible spot but would guarantee increased litigation over many of the arrests that would occur. . . .

An officer not quite sure that the drugs weighed enough to warrant jail time or not quite certain about a suspect's risk of flight would not arrest, even though it could perfectly well turn out that, in fact, the offense called for incarceration and the defendant was long gone on the day of trial. Multiplied many times over, the costs to society of such underenforcement could easily outweigh the costs to defendants of being needlessly arrested and booked, as Atwater herself acknowledges.

Just how easily the costs could outweigh the benefits may be shown by asking, as one Member of this Court did at oral argument, "how bad the problem is out there." The very fact that the law has never jelled the way Atwater would have it leads one to wonder whether warrantless misdemeanor arrests need constitutional attention, and there is cause to think the answer is no. [A]nyone arrested for a crime without formal process, whether for felony or misdemeanor, is entitled to a magistrate's review of probable cause within 48 hours. . . . Many jurisdictions, moreover, have chosen to impose more restrictive safeguards through statutes limiting warrantless arrests for minor offenses. [The Court cited statutes from Alabama, California, Kentucky, Louisiana, Maryland, South Dakota, Tennessee, and Virginia.] It is of course easier to devise a minor-offense limitation by statute than to derive one through the Constitution, simply because the statute can let the arrest power turn on any sort of practical consideration without having to subsume it under a broader principle. It is, in fact, only natural that States should resort to this sort of legislative regulation, for, as Atwater's own *amici* emphasize, it is in the interest of the police to limit petty-offense arrests, which carry costs that are simply too great to incur without good reason.

. . . The upshot of all these influences, combined with the good sense (and, failing that, the political accountability) of most local lawmakers and law-enforcement officials, is a dearth of horribles demanding redress. [T]he country is not confronting anything like an epidemic of unnecessary minor-offense arrests. That fact caps the reasons for rejecting Atwater's request for the development of a new and distinct body of constitutional law.

Accordingly, we confirm today what our prior cases have intimated. . . . If an officer has probable cause to believe that an individual has committed even a very minor criminal offense in his presence, he may, without violating the Fourth Amendment, arrest the offender.

O'CONNOR, J., dissenting.

[H]istory is just one of the tools we use in conducting the reasonableness inquiry. And when history is inconclusive, as the majority amply demonstrates it is in this case, we will evaluate the search or seizure under traditional standards of reasonableness by assessing, on the one hand, the degree to which it intrudes upon an individual's privacy and, on the other, the degree to which it is needed for the promotion of legitimate governmental interests. In other words, in determining reasonableness, each case is to be decided on its own facts and circumstances.

The majority gives a brief nod to this bedrock principle of our Fourth Amendment jurisprudence, and even acknowledges that "Atwater's claim to live free of pointless indignity and confinement clearly outweighs anything the City can raise against it specific to her case." But instead of remedying this imbalance, the majority allows itself to be swayed by the worry that "every discretionary judgment in the field [will] be converted into an occasion for constitutional review." It therefore mints a new rule that "if an officer has probable cause to believe that an individual has committed even a very minor criminal offense in his presence, he may, without violating the Fourth Amendment, arrest the offender." This rule is not only unsupported by our precedent, but runs contrary to the principles that lie at the core of the Fourth Amendment.

As the majority tacitly acknowledges, we have never considered the precise question presented here, namely, the constitutionality of a warrantless arrest for an offense punishable only by fine. . . . A custodial arrest exacts an obvious toll on an individual's liberty and privacy, even when the period of custody is relatively brief. The arrestee is subject to a full search of her person and confiscation of her possessions. If the arrestee is the occupant of a car, the entire passenger compartment of the car, including packages therein, is subject to search as well. The arrestee may be detained for up to 48 hours without having a magistrate determine whether there in fact was probable cause for the arrest. Because people arrested for all types of violent and nonviolent offenses may be housed together awaiting such review, this detention period is potentially dangerous. And once the period of custody is over, the fact of the arrest is a permanent part of the public record. . . .

Because a full custodial arrest is such a severe intrusion on an individual's liberty, its reasonableness hinges on the degree to which it is needed for the promotion of legitimate governmental interests. In light of the availability of citations to promote a State's interests when a fine-only offense has been committed, I cannot concur in a rule which deems a full custodial arrest to be reasonable in every circumstance. . . . Instead, I would require that when there is probable cause to believe that a fine-only offense has been committed, the police officer should issue a citation unless the officer is able to point to specific and articulable facts which, taken together with rational inferences from those facts, reasonably warrant the additional intrusion of a full custodial arrest.

The majority insists that a bright-line rule focused on probable cause is necessary to vindicate the State's interest in easily administrable law enforcement rules. Probable cause itself, however, is not a model of precision.... The rule I propose—which merely requires a legitimate reason for the decision to escalate the seizure into a full custodial arrest—thus does not undermine an otherwise "clear and simple" rule....

At bottom, the majority offers two related reasons why a bright-line rule is necessary: the fear that officers who arrest for fine-only offenses will be subject to personal 42 U.S.C. §1983 liability for the misapplication of a constitutional standard, and the resulting systematic disincentive to arrest where arresting would serve an important societal interest. These concerns are certainly valid, but they are more than adequately resolved by the doctrine of qualified immunity.

If, for example, an officer reasonably thinks that a suspect poses a flight risk or might be a danger to the community if released, he may arrest without fear of the legal consequences. Similarly, if an officer reasonably concludes that a suspect may possess more than four ounces of marijuana and thus might be guilty of a felony, the officer will be insulated from liability for arresting the suspect even if the initial assessment turns out to be factually incorrect. . . .

The record in this case makes it abundantly clear that Ms. Atwater's arrest was constitutionally unreasonable. . . . The Court's error, however, does not merely affect the disposition of this case. The *per se* rule that the Court creates has potentially serious consequences for the everyday lives of Americans. A broad range of conduct falls into the category of fine-only misdemeanors. In Texas alone, for example, disobeying any sort of traffic warning sign is a misdemeanor punishable only by fine, as is failing to pay a highway toll, and driving with expired license plates. Nor are fine-only crimes limited to the traffic context. In several States, for example, littering is a criminal offense punishable only by fine. To be sure, such laws are valid and wise exercises of the States' power to protect the public health and welfare. My concern lies not with the decision to enact or enforce these laws, but rather with the manner in which they may be enforced. Under today's holding, when a police officer has probable cause to believe that a fine-only misdemeanor offense has occurred, that officer may stop the suspect, issue a citation, and let the person continue on her way. Or, if a traffic violation, the officer may stop the car, arrest the driver, search the driver, search the entire passenger compartment of the car including any purse or package inside, and impound the car and inventory all of its contents. Although the Fourth Amendment expressly requires that the latter course be a reasonable and proportional response to the circumstances of the offense, the majority gives officers unfettered discretion to choose that course without articulating a single reason why such action is appropriate.

Such unbounded discretion carries with it grave potential for abuse. The majority takes comfort in the lack of evidence of "an epidemic of unnecessary minor-offense arrests." But the relatively small number of published cases dealing with such arrests proves little and should provide little solace. Indeed, as the recent debate over racial profiling demonstrates all too clearly, a relatively minor traffic infraction may often serve as an excuse for stopping and harassing an individual. After today, the arsenal available to any officer extends to a full arrest and the searches permissible concomitant to that arrest. An officer's subjective motivations for making a traffic stop are not relevant considerations in determining the reasonableness of the stop. But it is precisely because these motivations are beyond our purview that we must vigilantly ensure that officers' poststop actions—which are properly within our reach—comport with the Fourth Amendment's guarantee of reasonableness. . . .

## NOTES

1. *Search incident to citation: majority position.* Prior to the Supreme Court's 1998 ruling in *Knowles*, a small group of courts had concluded that the issuance of a desk appearance ticket gives a police officer the right to conduct a "search incident to citation." They sometimes used a "lesser includes the greater" form of argument: If the officer could search incident to an arrest and chooses not to arrest but instead to issue an appearance ticket, the officer can still conduct a search. See People v. Hazelwood, 429 N.Y.S.2d 1012 (Crim. Ct. 1980). However, very few courts had addressed the question at all before *Knowles*. Why did state courts develop so little case law on this subject? Was the practice of "search incident to citation" simply too rare to generate much litigation? Or was the practice common but unchallenged because prosecutors used other techniques to avoid appellate rulings on the subject? Here, as with many issues surrounding arrest and detention, police department policies often supplement statutes and judicial doctrine. See Phoenix Police Manual Order No. B-5(5)(D) (prohibiting search incident to issuance of a citation).

2. *Pretextual arrest.* Recall the discussion from Chapter 2 about pretextual stops. Are courts any more or less likely to place controls on pretextual arrests—arrests motivated by some factor other than a desire to enforce some law that the officer has probable cause to believe the suspect has violated? Courts have given comparable treatment to claims about pretextual stops and arrests. See State v. Hofmann, 537 N.W.2d 767 (Iowa 1995) (motive of arresting officer in conducting search not relevant if probable cause to arrest was present).

3.  *Fingerprint incident to citation.* In May 1998, New York City Police Commissioner Howard Safir announced a new policy for desk appearance tickets. When officers detain a person to issue the DAT, the person must now remain in police custody until a computerized fingerprint check is complete. The department issues about 80,000 DATs each year. The change in policy was designed to prevent the erroneous release of parole violators and fugitives from justice who present false identification to an officer making a stop. One such parole violator, Jose Serrano, presented false identification when arrested on a drug charge and killed a police officer soon after his release. Under the old policy, officers had discretion to release a suspect before the results of fingerprint and criminal records checks were available. The new policy removes that discretion. In many cases, it takes up to eight hours to complete a check of a person's fingerprints and criminal record. See David Kocieniewski and Michael Cooper, Police to Tighten the Scrutiny of All Suspects Under Arrest, New York Times, May 28, 1998, at A1. Imagine that you are a legal advisor to the chief of police in another jurisdiction who is contemplating a similar change in policy. What are the legal and policy consequences of this change? How will the officers in the department react to it? How will prosecutors react? Should the chief expect any particular public reaction?

## E.  Use of Force in Making Arrests

**Page 375.    Add this material after note 6.**

7.  *Extent of the use of force.* The Department of Justice has now begun collecting statistics regarding use of "excessive force by law enforcement officers," as required by §210402 of the Violent Crime Control and Law Enforcement Act of 1994. In 1996, an estimated 44.6 million persons had a face-to-face contact with a police officer. Of those 44.6 million, an estimated 500,000 persons (0.2 percent of the population age 12 or older) were hit, pushed, choked, threatened with a flashlight, restrained by a police dog, threatened or actually sprayed with chemical or pepper spray, threatened with a gun, or experienced some other form of force. See Lawrence Greenfeld, Patrick Langan, and

Steven Smith, Police Use of Force: Collection of National Data (January 1998, NCJ-165040).


**Page 379.   Add this material after note 2.**

Federal law is not hospitable to constitutional tort claims based on high-speed chases. In Sacramento County, California v. Lewis, 523 U.S. 833 (1998), the court affirmed the lower court's dismissal of a suit brought by the estate of a passenger on a motorcycle who was killed after the police and the driver of the motorcycle engaged in a high-speed chase. The court held that the high-speed police chase here did not amount to a Fourth Amendment "seizure" because the chase did not terminate the passenger's "freedom of movement through means intentionally applied." An allegation that the officers gave chase with "deliberate indifference" to the passenger's survival was insufficient to state a substantive due process claim. Instead, a plaintiff must show an "intent to harm suspects physically."

3.   *Public scrutiny of use of force.* Public scrutiny of police departments often centers on the use of force. Newspapers routinely publish articles about high visibility cases, especially those resulting in the payment of tort damages by the city; they also periodically review the department's use of force policies more generally. For instance, a 1998 series of articles in the Washington Post reviewed the use of force by officers in the District of Columbia. Over a five-year period, "D.C. officers shot and killed 57 people—three more than police reported in Chicago, which has three times the police force and five times the population. During that period, D.C. officers were involved in 640 shooting incidents—40 more than the Los Angeles Police Department, which has more than double the officers and serves six times the population." Jeff Leen, Jo Craven, David Jackson, and Sari Horwitz, D.C. Police Lead Nation in Shootings; Lack of Training, Supervision Implicated as Key Factors, Washington Post, Nov. 15, 1998, at A1.


**Page 381.   Add this material after Problem 5-3.**

In the aftermath of the Ruby Ridge incident, Randy Weaver brought a civil suit against the government and settled the case for $3.1 million.

Kevin Harris also filed a civil action against the government and its agents. See Harris v. Roderick, 126 F.3d 1189 (9th Cir. 1997). The state of Idaho filed involuntary manslaughter charges against one of the government sharpshooters, but those charges were removed to federal court and dismissed because the Supremacy Clause protected the agent from criminal charges based on his reasonable belief that deadly force was necessary. See Idaho v. Horiuchi, 2000 U.S. App. Lexis 13920 (June 14, 2000).

Civil process often provides a forum to review government use of force where criminal proceedings do not. In the federal government's deadly effort to seize the Branch Davidian compound in Waco, Texas, congressional review and civil suits have been the avenue for testing the government's actions.

# Chapter 6

# Remedies for Unreasonable Searches and Seizures

## A. Origins of the Exclusionary Rule

**Page 400.   Add this material to note 2.**

An ambitious empirical study, based on a 1997 survey of law enforcement officers in Ventura County, California, offers more equivocal evidence about the deterrent effects of the exclusionary rule. About 20 percent of the officers responding to the survey said they were primarily concerned with the risk of exclusion of evidence, while nearly 60 percent considered suppression to be an "important" concern. The officers who had "lost" evidence were no more likely than other officers to give correct answers to hypothetical search and seizure questions. See Timothy Perrin, H. Mitchell Caldwell, Carol Chase and Ronald Fagan, If It's Broken, Fix It: Moving Beyond The Exclusionary Rule — A New and Extensive Empirical Study of the Exclusionary Rule and a Call for a Civil Administrative Remedy to Partially Replace the Rule, 83 Iowa L. Rev. 669 (1998).

**Page 400.   Add this material to note 3.**

We might consider the purpose of the exclusionary rule in more traditional remedial terms: The exclusionary rule returns all parties to the positions they would hold if there had been no violation of the Constitution. Like tort damages, it restores the status quo ante. Does this rationale add anything to the "judicial integrity" rationale? See Jerry Norton, The Exclusionary Rule Reconsidered: Restoring the Status Quo Ante, 33 Wake Forest L. Rev. 261 (1998).

**Page 401.   Add this material after note 5.**

6. *International adoption of exclusionary rule.* Although judges in the United States sometimes claim that no other country in the world uses an exclusionary rule, the claim is not true. See Bivens v. Six Unknown Named Agents, 403 U.S. 388, 415 (1971) (Burger, C.J., dissenting). For instance, in Germany, judges must consider whether admission of evidence obtained illegally would violate the constitutionally protected privacy interests of the defendant. German judges "balance, on a case-by-case basis, the defendant's interests in privacy against the importance of the evidence and the seriousness of the offense charged." Craig Bradley, The Exclusionary Rule in Germany, 96 Harv. L. Rev. 1032 (1983). England uses an attenuated case-by-case form of the exclusionary rule as a remedy for improper searches or seizures. The common law rule was that evidence was admissible no matter how it was obtained. This rule is now codified in §78 of the Police and Criminal Evidence Act of 1984. Exclusion is available to English judges as a remedy today, but they are reluctant to withhold strong evidence of guilt from the jury. In Canada, the constitutionally based Charter of Rights and Freedoms gives the accused a basis for excluding evidence that was obtained improperly. Evidence is excluded only if a breach of a Charter right or freedom is demonstrated and if the admission of the evidence in the trial would tend to bring the administration of justice "into disrepute."

The basis for the exclusionary rule in these and other countries focuses more on judicial integrity than deterrence of police misconduct. If courts in the United States were to emphasize once again the "imperative of judicial integrity," would that open the way to an exclusionary rule that is applied less consistently than it is today?

# B.  Limitations on the Exclusionary Rule

## 1.  Evidence Obtained in "Good Faith"

**Page 414.  Add this material at the end of note 1.**

If police officers have special training in how to conduct searches at crime scenes, will courts in jurisdictions that otherwise allow a "good faith" exception to the exclusionary rule be less likely to forgive a failure to obtain a warrant for a crime scene? Consider Minn. Stat. §626.8462 (requiring part-time peace officers to be trained in "general principles of criminal investigations; crime scene search and investigation, and preservation and collection of crime scene evidence").

**Page 415.  Add this material at the end of note 2.**

In Pennsylvania Board of Probation and Parole v. Scott, 524 U.S. 357 (1998), the court held that parole boards are not required by federal law to exclude evidence obtained in violation of the Fourth Amendment. In *Scott*, parole officers improperly entered a parolee's home to search for weapons; they found firearms, a bow, and arrows. The government introduced this evidence at his parole violation hearing. Because the exclusionary rule is designed only to deter constitutional violations, the court declared that the prospect of exclusion during the prosecution's case in a criminal trial would provide enough deterrent power.

## 2.  Causation Limits: Inevitable Discovery and Independent Source

**Page 422.  Add this material to note 1.**

Smith v. State, 948 P.2d 473 (Alaska 1997) (adopts inevitable discovery doctrine under state constitution, but requires prosecution to prove inevitability by clear and convincing evidence; lists Hawaii and Massachusetts as other states adopting clear and convincing standard).

## 3.   Standing to Challenge Illegal Searches and Seizures

Page 429.   The following material replaces notes 1 and 2.

## Minnesota v. Wayne Thomas Carter
525 U.S. 83 (1998)

REHNQUIST, C.J.

Respondents and the lessee of an apartment were sitting in one of its rooms, bagging cocaine. While so engaged they were observed by a police officer, who looked through a drawn window blind. The Supreme Court of Minnesota held that the officer's viewing was a search which violated respondents' Fourth Amendment rights. We hold that no such violation occurred.

James Thielen, a police officer in the Twin Cities' suburb of Eagan, Minnesota, went to an apartment building to investigate a tip from a confidential informant. The informant said that he had walked by the window of a ground-floor apartment and had seen people putting a white powder into bags. The officer looked in the same window through a gap in the closed blind and observed the bagging operation for several minutes. He then notified headquarters, which began preparing affidavits for a search warrant while he returned to the apartment building. When two men left the building in a previously identified Cadillac, the police stopped the car. Inside were respondents Carter and Johns. As the police opened the door of the car to let Johns out, they observed a black zippered pouch and a handgun, later determined to be loaded, on the vehicle's floor. Carter and Johns were arrested, and a later police search of the vehicle the next day discovered pagers, a scale, and 47 grams of cocaine in plastic sandwich bags.

After seizing the car, the police returned to Apartment 103 and arrested the occupant, Kimberly Thompson, who is not a party to this appeal. A search of the apartment pursuant to a warrant revealed cocaine residue on the kitchen table and plastic baggies similar to those found in the Cadillac. Thielen identified Carter, Johns, and Thompson as the three people he had observed placing the powder into baggies. The police later learned that while Thompson was the lessee of the apartment, Carter and Johns lived in Chicago and had come to the apartment for the sole purpose of packaging the cocaine. Carter and Johns had never been to the apartment before and were only in the apartment for approximately 2 1/2 hours. In return for the use of the apartment, Carter and Johns had given Thompson one-eighth of an ounce of the cocaine.

Carter and Johns were charged with conspiracy to commit controlled substance crime in the first degree and aiding and abetting in a controlled substance crime in the first degree. . . . They moved to suppress all evidence obtained from the apartment and the Cadillac, as well as to suppress several post-arrest incriminating statements they had made. [The trial court denied the motion. Because] Carter and Johns were not overnight social guests but temporary out-of-state visitors, they were not entitled to claim the protection of the Fourth Amendment against the government intrusion into the apartment. . . . After a trial, Carter and Johns were each convicted of both offenses. . . .

The Minnesota [appellate] courts analyzed whether respondents had a legitimate expectation of privacy under the rubric of "standing" doctrine, an analysis which this Court expressly rejected 20 years ago in Rakas v. Illinois, 439 U.S. 128 (1978). In that case, we held that automobile passengers could not assert the protection of the Fourth Amendment against the seizure of incriminating evidence from a vehicle where they owned neither the vehicle nor the evidence. Central to our analysis was the idea that in determining whether a defendant is able to show the violation of his (and not someone else's) Fourth Amendment rights, the "definition of those rights is more properly placed within the purview of substantive Fourth Amendment law than within that of standing." Thus, we held that in order to claim the protection of the Fourth Amendment, a defendant must demonstrate that he personally has an expectation of privacy in the place searched, and that his expectation is reasonable; i.e., one which has "a source outside of the Fourth Amendment, either by reference to concepts of real or personal property law or to understandings that are recognized and permitted by society."

The Fourth Amendment . . . protects persons against unreasonable searches of "their persons [and] houses" and thus [the text] indicates that the Fourth Amendment is a personal right that must be invoked by an individual. But the extent to which the Fourth Amendment protects people may depend upon where those people are. We have held that "capacity to claim the protection of the Fourth Amendment depends . . .

upon whether the person who claims the protection of the Amendment has a legitimate expectation of privacy in the invaded place." *Rakas*, 439 U.S. at 143.

The text of the Amendment suggests that its protections extend only to people in "their" houses. But we have held that in some circumstances a person may have a legitimate expectation of privacy in the house of someone else. In Minnesota v. Olson, 495 U.S. 91 (1990), for example, we decided that an overnight guest in a house had the sort of expectation of privacy that the Fourth Amendment protects. We said:

> To hold that an overnight guest has a legitimate expectation of privacy in his host's home merely recognizes the every day expectations of privacy that we all share. Staying overnight in another's home is a long-standing social custom that serves functions recognized as valuable by society. . . . From the overnight guest's perspective, he seeks shelter in another's home precisely because it provides him with privacy, a place where he and his possessions will not be disturbed by anyone but his host and those his host allows inside. We are at our most vulnerable when we are asleep because we cannot monitor our own safety or the security of our belongings. . . .

In Jones v. United States, 362 U.S. 257, 259 (1960), the defendant seeking to exclude evidence resulting from a search of an apartment had been given the use of the apartment by a friend. He had clothing in the apartment, had slept there "maybe a night," and at the time was the sole occupant of the apartment. But while the holding of *Jones*—that a search of the apartment violated the defendant's Fourth Amendment rights—is still valid, its statement that "anyone legitimately on the premises where a search occurs may challenge its legality" was expressly repudiated in Rakas v. Illinois. Thus an overnight guest in a home may claim the protection of the Fourth Amendment, but one who is merely present with the consent of the householder may not.

Respondents here were obviously not overnight guests, but were essentially present for a business transaction and were only in the home a matter of hours. There is no suggestion that they had a previous relationship with Thompson, or that there was any other purpose to their visit. Nor was there anything similar to the overnight guest relationship in *Olson* to suggest a degree of acceptance into the household. While the apartment was a dwelling place for Thompson, it was for these respondents simply a place to do business.

Property used for commercial purposes is treated differently for Fourth Amendment purposes than residential property. [T]he Court has held that in some circumstances a worker can claim Fourth Amendment protection over his own workplace. See, e.g., O'Connor v. Ortega, 480 U.S. 709, 716-17 (1987). But there is no indication that respondents in this case had nearly as significant a connection to Thompson's apartment as the worker in *O'Connor* had to his own private office.

If we regard the overnight guest in Minnesota v. Olson as typifying those who may claim the protection of the Fourth Amendment in the home of another, and one merely "legitimately on the premises" as typifying those who may not do so, the present case is obviously somewhere in between. But the purely commercial nature of the transaction engaged in here, the relatively short period of time on the premises, and the lack of any previous connection between respondents and the householder, all lead us to conclude that respondents' situation is closer to that of one simply permitted on the premises. We therefore hold that any search which may have occurred did not violate their Fourth Amendment rights. . . .

SCALIA, J., concurring.

. . . I write separately to express my view that [the] case law—like the submissions of the parties in this case—gives short shrift to the text of the Fourth Amendment, and to the well and long understood meaning of that text. . . . The Fourth Amendment protects "[t]he right of the people to be secure in their persons, houses, papers, and effects, against unreasonable searches and seizures. . . ." It must be acknowledged that the phrase "their . . . houses" in this provision is, in isolation, ambiguous. It could mean "their respective houses," so that the protection extends to each person only in his own house. But it could also mean "their respective and each other's houses," so that each person would be protected even when visiting the house of someone else. As today's opinion for the Court suggests, however, it is not linguistically possible to give the provision the latter, expansive interpretation with respect to "houses" without giving it the same interpretation with respect to the nouns that are parallel to "houses" — "persons, . . . papers, and effects" — which would give me a constitutional right not to have your person unreasonably searched. This is so absurd that it has to my knowledge never been contemplated. The obvious meaning of the

115

provision is that each person has the right to be secure against unreasonable searches and seizures in his own person, house, papers, and effects.

The Founding-era materials that I have examined confirm that this was the understood meaning. . . . Like most of the provisions of the Bill of Rights, the Fourth Amendment was derived from provisions already existing in state constitutions. Of the four of those provisions that contained language similar to that of the Fourth Amendment, two used the same ambiguous "their" terminology. The other two, however, avoided the ambiguity by using the singular instead of the plural. See Mass. Const., pt. I, Art. XIV (1780) ("Every subject has a right to be secure from all unreasonable searches, and seizures of his person, his houses, his papers, and all his possessions"); N.H. Const. §XIX (1784) ("Every subject hath a right to be secure from all unreasonable searches and seizures of his person, his houses, his papers, and all his possessions"). . . .

That "their . . . houses" was understood to mean "their respective houses" would have been clear to anyone who knew the English and early American law of arrest and trespass that underlay the Fourth Amendment. The people's protection against unreasonable search and seizure in their "houses" was drawn from the English common-law maxim, "A man's home is his castle." As far back as Semayne's Case of 1604, the leading English case for that proposition . . . the King's Bench proclaimed that "the house of any one is not a castle or privilege but for himself, and shall not extend to protect any person who flies to his house." Semayne v. Gresham, 77 Eng. Rep. 194, 198 (K.B. 1604). . . .

Thus, in deciding the question presented today we write upon a slate that is far from clean. The text of the Fourth Amendment, the common-law background against which it was adopted, and the understandings consistently displayed after its adoption make the answer clear. We were right to hold in Chapman v. United States, 365 U.S. 610 (1961), that the Fourth Amendment protects an apartment tenant against an unreasonable search of his dwelling, even though he is only a leaseholder. And we were right to hold in Bumper v. North Carolina, 391 U.S. 543 (1968), that an unreasonable search of a grandmother's house violated her resident grandson's Fourth Amendment rights because the area searched "was his home." We went to the absolute limit of what text and tradition permit in Minnesota v. Olson, 495 U.S. 91

(1990), when we protected a mere overnight guest against an unreasonable search of his hosts' apartment. But whereas it is plausible to regard a person's overnight lodging as at least his "temporary" residence, it is entirely impossible to give that characterization to an apartment that he uses to package cocaine. Respondents here were not searched in "their . . . hous[e]" under any interpretation of the phrase that bears the remotest relationship to the well understood meaning of the Fourth Amendment. . . .

KENNEDY, J., concurring.

I join the Court's opinion, for its reasoning is consistent with my view that almost all social guests have a legitimate expectation of privacy, and hence protection against unreasonable searches, in their host's home.

[I]t is beyond dispute that the home is entitled to special protection as the center of the private lives of our people. Security of the home must be guarded by the law in a world where privacy is diminished by enhanced surveillance and sophisticated communication systems. As is well established, however, Fourth Amendment protection, though dependent upon spatial definition, is in essence a personal right. Thus, as the Court held in Rakas v. Illinois, there are limits on who may assert it.

The dissent, as I interpret it, does not question *Rakas* or the principle that not all persons in the company of the property owner have the owner's right to assert the spatial protection. *Rakas*, it is true, involved automobiles, where the necessities of law enforcement permit more latitude to the police than ought to be extended to houses. The analysis in *Rakas* was not conceived, however, as a utilitarian exception to accommodate the needs of law enforcement. The Court's premise was a more fundamental one. Fourth Amendment rights are personal, and when a person objects to the search of a place and invokes the exclusionary rule, he or she must have the requisite connection to that place.

[R]espondents have no independent privacy right, the violation of which results in exclusion of evidence against them, unless they can establish a meaningful connection to Thompson's apartment. The settled rule is that the requisite connection is an expectation of privacy that society recognizes as reasonable. The application of that rule involves consideration of the kind of place in which the individual claims the privacy interest and what expectations of privacy are traditional and well recognized. I would expect that most, if not all, social guests legitimately expect that, in accordance with social custom, the homeowner will exercise her discretion to include or exclude others for the guests' benefit. As we recognized in Minnesota v. Olson, where these social expectations exist—as in the case of an overnight guest—they are sufficient to create a legitimate expectation of privacy, even in the absence of any property right to exclude others. In this respect, the dissent must be correct that reasonable expectations of the owner are shared, to some extent, by the guest. This analysis suggests that, as a general rule, social guests will have an expectation of privacy in their host's home. That is not the case before us, however.

In this case respondents have established nothing more than a fleeting and insubstantial connection with Thompson's home. For all that appears in the record, respondents used Thompson's house simply as a convenient processing station, their purpose involving nothing more than the mechanical act of chopping and packing a substance for distribution. There is no suggestion that respondents engaged in confidential communications with Thompson about their transaction. Respondents had not been to Thompson's apartment before, and they left it even before their arrest. . . .

If respondents here had been visiting twenty homes, each for a minute or two, to drop off a bag of cocaine and were apprehended by a policeman wrongfully present in the nineteenth home; or if they had left the goods at a home where they were not staying and the police had seized the goods in their absence, we would have said that *Rakas* compels rejection of any privacy interest respondents might assert. So it does here, given that respondents have established no meaningful tie or connection to the owner, the owner's home, or the owner's expectation of privacy. . . .

GINSBURG, J., dissenting.

The Court's decision undermines not only the security of short-term guests, but also the security of the home resident herself. In my view, when a homeowner or lessor personally invites a guest into her home to share in a common endeavor, whether it be for conversation, to engage in leisure activities, or for business purposes licit or illicit, that guest should share his host's shelter against unreasonable searches and seizures. . . .

My concern centers on an individual's choice to share her home and her associations there with persons she selects. Our decisions indicate that people have a reasonable expectation of privacy in their homes in part because they have the prerogative to exclude others. The power to exclude implies the power to include. Our Fourth Amendment decisions should reflect these complementary prerogatives.

A homedweller places her own privacy at risk, the Court's approach indicates, when she opens her home to others, uncertain whether the duration of their stay, their purpose, and their "acceptance into the household" will earn protection. . . . Human frailty suggests that today's decision will tempt police to pry into private dwellings without warrant, to find evidence incriminating guests who do not rest there through the night. . . . As I see it, people are not genuinely "secure in their . . . houses . . . against unreasonable searches and seizures," if their invitations to others increase the risk of unwarranted governmental peering and prying into their dwelling places. . . .

As the Solicitor General acknowledged, the illegality of the host-guest conduct, the fact that they were partners in crime, would not alter the analysis. In *Olson*, for example, the guest whose security this Court's decision shielded stayed overnight while the police searched for him. The Court held that the guest had Fourth Amendment protection against a warrantless arrest in his host's home despite the guest's involvement in grave crimes (first-degree murder, armed robbery, and assault). Other decisions have similarly sustained Fourth Amendment pleas despite the criminality of the defendants' activities. Indeed, it must be this way. If the illegality of the activity made constitutional an otherwise unconstitutional search, such Fourth Amendment protection, reserved for the innocent only, would have little force in regulating police behavior toward either the innocent or the guilty.

Our leading decision in Katz v. United States, 389 U.S. 347 (1967), is key to my view of this case. There, we ruled that the Government violated the petitioner's Fourth Amendment rights when it electronically recorded him transmitting wagering information while he was inside a public telephone booth. We were mindful that "the Fourth Amendment protects people, not places," and held that this electronic monitoring of a business call "violated the privacy upon which [the caller] justifiably relied while using the telephone booth." . . .

The Court's decision in this case veers sharply from the path marked in *Katz*. I do not agree that we have a more reasonable expectation of privacy when we place a business call to a person's home from a public telephone booth on the side of the street, than when we actually enter that person's premises to engage in a common endeavor. For the reasons stated, I dissent from the Court's judgment, and would retain judicial surveillance over the warrantless searches today's decision allows.

## NOTES

1. *Standing: majority position.* A slight majority of states follow the federal "legitimate expectation of privacy" approach when they determine who may invoke the exclusionary rule to remedy an illegal search or seizure. Others, like the Vermont court in *Wood,* use some form of the older "legitimately on the premises" test for standing. Often, these courts say that a defendant challenging an illegal search or seizure must demonstrate a "proprietary, possessory, or participatory interest" in the premises searched or the property seized. Try to imagine situations in which the federal test and the "legitimately on the premises" test produce different results.

The Supreme Court attempted, in Rakas v. Illinois, 439 U.S. 128 (1978), to eliminate any distinction between a person's "standing" to challenge an illegal search and the "extent of a particular defendant's rights" under the Fourth Amendment. Rights against unreasonable searches and seizures, said the Court, are personal rights and third parties may not assert them. See Roger Kirst, Constitutional Rights of Bystanders in the War on Crime, 28 N.M. L. Rev. 59 (1998). What would be the consequences of allowing a criminal defendant to challenge an allegedly improper search of a third party's property? Why require standing *at all* for a litigant who hopes to challenge governmental misconduct?

2. *Standing for searches of residences, business premises, and cars.* Even though a defendant, under the federal (and majority) rule, must show a "legitimate" expectation of privacy in the premises searched or the property seized, this does not preclude challenges by

those who do not own or lease property. The easier cases to decide involve the search of a residence, where the defendant lives full time even though another person owns or leases the residence. Courts in that setting have no trouble in concluding that the person living in the house has standing to challenge a search of any common area in the house or any area within the special control of the defendant. How might these residential cases apply to business premises?

More difficult cases involve guests and others who are present in a residence for shorter periods. In Minnesota v. Olson, 495 U.S. 91 (1990), the Court recognized standing for an overnight guest at an apartment: "[s]taying overnight in another's home is a longstanding social custom that serves functions recognized as valuable by society." On the other hand, the Court in the 1998 *Carter* case concluded that defendants present in an apartment only for a few hours did not have a "legitimate expectation of privacy" in the premises. What does the future hold for the standing of nonresidents in a home or nonemployees in a place of business? What could be said in favor of allowing dinner guests to challenge the admission of evidence obtained when the police make a warrantless entry of a home to arrest the guest or search her possessions? What if the police illegally search the purse of one person and find inside some contraband belonging to another person? See Rawlings v. Kentucky, 448 U.S. 98 (1980) (denying standing in such a setting).

Should it matter whether a challenged search takes place after a traffic stop rather than in a residence? See State v. Bowers, 976 S.W.2d 379 (Ark. 1998) (passenger has standing to challenge search of car after illegal stop, even though passenger has no possessory interest in the car).

## C. Additions and Alternatives to the Exclusionary Rule

### 1. Administrative Remedies

Page 434.    Add this material at the end of note 1.

For a comparison of "internal," "external," and "hybrid" forms of police review based on survey research of police attitudes and citizen complaints, see Douglas Perez, Common Sense About Police Review (1996).


## 2.   Tort Actions and Criminal Prosecutions

**Page 445.   Add this material at the end of note 9.**

Criminal sanctions for illegal police behavior have again become a high profile public issue with prominent incidents in New York City including the brutal beating of Abner Louima and the shooting of Amadou Diallo. New York City police officers in both cases were prosecuted, for federal civil rights violations in the Louima case and for second-degree murder in the Diallo case. Officers involved in the Louima matter were convicted on the federal criminal charges; officers in the Diallo matter were acquitted on state criminal charges.

Would criminal charges occur more frequently if persons complaining about police brutality or other search and seizure violations could present their complaints directly to a grand jury? See Peter Davis, Rodney King and the Decriminalization of Police Brutality in America: Direct and Judicial Access to the Grand Jury as Remedies for Victims of Police Brutality When the Prosecutor Declines to Prosecute, 53 Md. L. Rev. 271 (1994).


**Page 448.   Add this material at the end of note 1.**

One limitation on the availability of injunctions (at least in federal court) is the standing doctrine. Who has standing to challenge a police policy or practice? When a plaintiff seeks injunctive relief rather than damages, the Supreme Court has held that the plaintiff must show a likelihood of future harm. In City of Los Angeles v. Lyons, 461 U.S. 95 (1983), a plaintiff who was challenging the use of "chokeholds" by the police department had no standing to obtain injunctive or declaratory relief (as opposed to damages). Although the police had used the chokehold on Adolph Lyons in a situation where the officers faced no threat of injury, Lyons could not demonstrate a "substantial likelihood" that he personally would be choked again in the future. Is this standing limitation applicable mostly to use of force policies? Is it possible to identify the likely future victim of any type of illegal police policies (say, the use of sobriety checkpoints near bars)?

**Page 449.   Add this material after Problem 6-5.**

## Problem 6-6. Rampart Crash

In 1998, eight pounds of cocaine were found missing from a police evidence locker in the Los Angeles Police Department's Rampart division. Investigations led to officer Raphael Perez, a member of Rampart's elite anti-gang unit known as CRASH, for Community Resources Against Street Hoodlums. The Rampart CRASH unit was one of many throughout the city, with a citywide total of 240 CRASH officers. Like criminals everywhere, Officer Perez told prosecutors that he had information on other officers that he would provide in exchange for a reduced sentence of five years. The information from Officer Perez, much of which has since been confirmed from independent sources, has revealed one of the largest police abuse situations in U.S. history.

Officer Perez told investigators a wild tale of police run rampant: conspiring to frame innocent suspects, beating suspects, and covering up unjustified shootings. In other words, the "abuses" extended from lies to murder. Already, Rampart has changed some of the basic assumptions about U.S. criminal procedure. There is wide agreement, for example, that innocent suspects pled guilty in a number of cases. The widely held belief that wholly innocent individuals will refuse plea bargains (or that careful prosecutors would never make such offers) has been shattered.

Almost every governmental institutional that might respond to police abuse has done so, including the police department, the Los Angeles District Attorney, city and state political bodies, and federal civil rights representatives. As of May 2000, 99 felony cases were found to be tainted by alleged police misconduct, and hundreds of additional cases are under investigation. Since September 1999, when the scandal broke, at least 29 officers have been relieved of duty, suspended, quit or been fired. More than 70 officers are being examined. Estimates of civil damages run from $125 million on the low end, to $200-300 million or more on the high end.

A 362-page internal LAPD Board of Inquiry report, released on March 1, 2000, blamed poor hiring, the isolation of the special CRASH unit, and "rogue cops" for the calamity. L.A. Police Chief Bernard C. Parks explained:

> [T]he Board of Inquiry report . . . points out in graphic detail [that] people with troubling backgrounds have been hired as police officers. We need to tighten up that hiring process. Individuals with criminal records or with histories of violent behavior or narcotics involvement have no place in this department. We need to make sure that field officers are supervised closely and that supervisors have the courage to take corrective action when necessary. I recognize there is a fine line between smothering officers under a stifling bureaucratic blanket and beefing up supervision. The Board of Inquiry report tells us how to walk that fine line and how to do it effectively. We need to make sure specialized entities like the anti-gang CRASH unit are home to senior, seasoned officers as well as relative newcomers. We need to make sure they are not run as independent fiefdoms but as responsive law enforcement programs. . . .
>
> As the members of the Board of Inquiry have emphasized, we do not need to reinvent the wheel, introduce a flock of new programs or institute revolutionary approaches to police work. What we do need to do is emphasize a scrupulous adherence to existing policies and standards. . . .

Chief Parks offered a promise—or perhaps it was a plea, or a prayer: "May it never happen again." Chief Parks issued an 18-page order detailing his response to Rampart, including abolition of the CRASH name in favor of generic "gang details," a limited three-year tour of duty with the new special anti-gang units, and new requirements for members and supervisors of the units.

Promises and prayers may obscure some of the base brutality of the actions by Los Angeles Officers. For example, Officer Perez said that two officers in particular—Brian Hewitt and Daniel Lujan—were well known among a group of Rampart's rogue cops for administering street justice. Perez told investigators:

> [Hewitt's] biggest forte was thumping people. He just had this thing about beating people up while they were handcuffed. That's what he did. He was just a brutal guy. . . . I'll give you a little story. [I was sitting in the hallway talking to another gang member, looking into the room where Hewitt was conducting his interview.] And all of a sudden Hewitt is choking a guy with his hands, making him talk. Choking him, just choking him. The guy's looking like he's about to pass out—just with one hand—he's just choking the guy. [The suspect's hands were cuffed behind his back]. I saw Officer

Hewitt hit this guy so hard in the neck that the guy flipped backward and onto the floor. . . . Let's say [Hewitt] catches you dirty, he would rather beat you up, beat you to a pulp, and then say, "OK, we're even now, right?" I've seen Hewitt beat up more people by himself than I've seen probably by the entire department put together.

Lujan and Hewitt are suspected of teaming up in another alleged beating on Feb. 21, 1996, when they arrested Rene Alfredo Canales on drug charges. Canales' injuries were explained in a police report as occurring when the suspect "attempted to dive out the [third-]floor window, hitting the right side of his head [and] forehead on the window frame . . . got up and again lost his balance and fell forward while [attempting] to escape and hit his head numerous times against the metal balcony, arm rail and steps." Canales claims he was sitting on a milk crate outside a third-floor apartment room, waiting for a friend, when officers converged on him. Canales alleges that the officers, for no apparent reason, handcuffed him, threw him to the floor and started kicking him in the head, face and back. He said that the officers stopped beating him when a sergeant approached.

Hewitt was fired by the LAPD for the alleged beating of Ismael Jimenez. Jimenez, an 18th Street gang member, was allegedly beaten because the mother of another 18th Streeter filed a complaint against the officers who allegedly beat her son.

Police initiated an immediate and thorough investigation of the station-house attack and Chief Parks fired Hewitt, acting on the recommendation of the Board of Rights, a panel of officers who hear disciplinary cases. Evidence compiled by LAPD detectives against Hewitt includes samples of blood splattered on the walls of the Rampart Station, which were matched to the victim's DNA; testimony from an emergency room doctor detailing the victim's injuries; testimony from several citizens and law enforcement personnel; and a piece of carpet from the Rampart Station that was soaked with the victim's bloody vomit.

But prosecutors, citing a lack of evidence, have twice declined to file charges against Hewitt. The county prosecutors concluded that there was "insufficient evidence" to prove in court that Hewitt assaulted Jimenez. The office argued there were no witnesses, except possibly another gang member, and no photographs of his injuries. The case

125

remains under investigation and Jimenez has been subpoenaed to testify before a grand jury investigating alleged crimes by LAPD officers.

The federal government has entered the scene, with an extensive civil rights investigation of the LAPD now under way. Among other questions, the federal officials want to know whether Los Angeles ever implemented the recommendations of the 1991 Christopher Commission report, issued following the Rodney King beating and the trials of the officers who beat him. Los Angeles has received federal funds to implement those prior recommendations. Bill Lann Lee, acting assistant attorney general in the Civil Rights Division of the U.S. Department of Justice, wrote in a letter addressed to City Attorney James K. Hahn that "Serious deficiencies in city and LAPD policies and procedures for training, supervising and investigating and disciplining officers foster and perpetuate officer misconduct. [The LAPD has] failed to supervise officers properly by failing to identify and respond to patterns of at-risk officer behavior."

The reaction in Los Angeles has been mixed. Many citizens call for an outside, but local review of the LAPD. A number of officials expressed relief at possible federal involvement. However, L.A. Mayor Richard Riordan issued a statement following discussions with federal officials: "In these discussions and meetings on police issues, I wanted to make clear to them that we know what the problems are. We know what must be done to correct those problems." The Los Angeles Times editorial board wrote:

> For their part, city and police officials will have little choice but to comply with federal demands, and quickly. There are indications now that the liability costs that Los Angeles faces for those who were falsely imprisoned on trumped-up charges will greatly exceed current expectations. The last thing that the city and its taxpayers need is the burden of fighting a federal lawsuit. . . . It's a damning indictment of the people who claim to run this city that the federal government had to come in and threaten the LAPD as it once did small-town Southern sheriffs.

What responses might the "system" have to such outrageous behavior? Consult the list of remedial options below. Each of these has been suggested or pursued as a proper response to the Rampart scandal. Which of these actions are likely to produce the greatest justice? The fairest outcome for the citizens and officers in this case? The outcomes most likely to prevent such behavior in the future?  How might we measure the effectiveness of the responses?

### Legal remedies
a.  state criminal prosecutions
b.  grand jury investigation
c.  state civil actions
d.  federal prosecution
e.  federal civil actions

### Administrative Remedies
a.  firing, demotion & other sanctions for individual officers
b.  disbanding CRASH units, new supervisory structures, new reporting requirements
c.  internal affairs
d.  Police Board review
e.  cameras in interrogations and on police cars

### Political Remedies
a.  review of police by City Council
b.  review of police by state legislature
c.  new crime of presenting falsified evidence
d.  External review of Rampart by an independent panel (like the "Christopher Commission" in 1991)
e.  Permanent citizen review board

### NOTES

1.  *Rampart: renegade cops or renegade police culture?* No one defends the brutality of the individual Rampart officers. But is the problem, as the police department and its defenders suggest, with bad cops and weak supervision, or is there a wider problem with the culture of policing? How can isolated and collective problems be distinguished? What different responses are called for by the two kinds of problems? Consider William Shakespeare's perspective, from Julius Caesar, Act I, scene ii, where Cassius says to Brutus:

Why, man, he doth bestride the narrow world
Like a Colossus, and we petty men
Walk under his huge legs and peep about
To find ourselves dishonourable graves.
Men at some time are masters of their fates:
The fault, dear Brutus, is not in our stars,
But in ourselves, that we are underlings.

2. *Local, state and federal involvement in police review.* Local prosecutors are charged with the duty of prosecuting crimes, whether they are committed by citizens or officers. But do prosecutors aggressively prosecute police officers, with whom they work on a daily basis? Evidence from Los Angeles suggests a hesitation to prosecute officers spanning many decades. For example, according to news reports, from 1977–87, LAPD officers were involved in 571 shootings; many victims were unarmed civilians. But only one officer was indicted. Special units have been created in the district attorney's office, only to be underfunded, and eventually disbanded. In a bizarre twist to the Rampart scandal, at one point Chief Parks ordered his detectives to deny county prosecutors access to information regarding the ongoing Rampart corruption investigation on the grounds that District Attorney Gil Garcetti had mishandled the six-month probe, and had given the LAPD bad legal advice and could no longer be trusted. Garcetti's response: "We have a department out of control—or trying to control everything. This is not permissible in our system of government. This chief is accountable to the justice system. If [Parks] wants to test this in court, we are going to win."

Over the past several years, the U.S. Department of Justice has entered into a series of consent decrees with local and state police departments around the country, focusing on issues including racial bias in stops, use of deadly force, and mistreatment of citizens. See James Turner, Police Accountability in the Federal System, 30 McGeorge L. Rev. 991 (1999).

### Problem 6-7.  Clear As A Post

Prison guards twice handcuffed inmate Larry Hope to a "hitching post," once for two hours, and the other time for seven hours. On the second occasion, Hope was given water only once or twice and was given no bathroom breaks. A guard taunted Hope about his thirst. He first gave water to some dogs, then brought the water cooler closer to Hope, removed its lid, and kicked the cooler over, spilling the water onto the ground. Hope filed a civil claim under 42 U.S.C. §1983 against three guards who had either ordered or actually hitched him to the post. The district court entered judgment for the guards, finding they were entitled to qualified immunity.

The doctrine of qualified immunity protects state actors from suit despite their participation in constitutionally impermissible conduct, if their actions did not violate "clearly established statutory or constitutional rights of which a reasonable person would have known." Harlow v. Fitzgerald, 457 U.S. 800, 818 (1982). In Hope's case, the U.S. Supreme Court held that a situation could be factually novel, and yet violate "clearly established" rights:

> As we have explained, qualified immunity operates to ensure that before they are subjected to suit, officers are on notice their conduct is unlawful. For a constitutional right to be clearly established, its contours must be sufficiently clear that a reasonable official would understand that what he is doing violates that right. This is not to say that an official action is protected by qualified immunity unless the very action in question has previously been held unlawful, but it is to say that in the light of pre-existing law the unlawfulness must be apparent.

Hope v. Pelzer, 122 S. Ct. 2508 (2002). The high court found that several sources of law—including Eleventh Circuit precedent, Alabama Department of Corrections (ADOC) regulations from 1993, and a 1994 U.S. Department of Justice report—put the prison guards on notice that their actions were unconstitutional. Also relevant, perhaps, was that in 1995 Alabama was the only State that chained inmates to one another in work squads. It was also the only State that handcuffed prisoners to hitching posts if they either refused to work or disrupted other work squads. Perhaps notice of the unconstitutionality of the act also came from the cruelty of the act itself:

> The obvious cruelty inherent in this practice should have provided respondents with some notice that their alleged conduct violated Hope's constitutional protection against cruel and unusual punishment. Hope was treated in a way antithetical to human dignity—he was hitched to a post for an extended period of time in a position that was painful, and under circumstances that were both degrading and dangerous.

The Supreme Court remanded two other cases for reconsideration in light of *Hope*. Both of the remanded cases involved police actions.

In Vaughn v. Cox, 264 F.3d 1027 (11th Cir. 2001), Jerry Vaughn filed suit under §1983, claiming that Deputy Fred Cox and Sheriff Mike Yeager of Coweta County, Georgia, used excessive force during a police chase. In the early morning of January 5, 1998, the Sheriff's Department received a report that a red pickup truck with a silver tool box in its bed had been stolen from a service station along the interstate highway near Atlanta. The report included the information that the suspect, a white male wearing a white T-shirt, was believed to be heading north on the interstate.

Deputy Cox joined the pursuit. In an attempt to determine whether the vehicle was indeed the stolen truck, Deputy Cox sped up and passed the truck, which was traveling near the speed limit. He observed two men in the cab. The man in the passenger's seat, Vaughan, matched the description of the suspect. Cox's suspicions confirmed, he and a fellow deputy in another car decided to use a "rolling roadblock" to stop the vehicle. In a rolling roadblock, officers surround a suspect's vehicle with their police cars and reduce speed, in the hope that the suspect will slow down as well. Deputy Cox moved in front of the truck and applied his brakes. The truck rammed into the back of Cox's cruiser.

The driver of the truck, Freddy Rayson, did not pull over following the collision, but instead accelerated while staying in the same lane of traffic. Deputy Cox decided to reposition his vehicle behind the truck. He unholstered his sidearm and rolled down the passenger side window, in case Rayson made aggressive moves in his direction. Cox then shifted his cruiser one lane to the left and slowed to allow the truck to pass by him. As soon as his cruiser was even with the pickup, Deputy Cox turned on his rooftop lights. Rayson responded by accelerating to eighty-five miles per hour. Cox then fired three rounds into the truck. It is undisputed that Deputy Cox did not warn the truck's occupants before he used his weapon. Cox later testified that he fired because the pickup swerved as if to smash into his cruiser. Vaughan disagreed, maintaining that the truck made no motion in the direction of Cox's vehicle.

Deputy Cox's plan was to disable either the truck or Rayson so that he could force the truck off the road. However, the third bullet fired from Cox's weapon punctured Vaughan's spine, paralyzing him below the chest. Rayson's reaction to the shooting was to drive faster and more recklessly. As the chase continued into more heavily congested sections of the highway, Cox made several more attempts to stop the vehicle, firing his weapon once more. After an extended chase, the pickup struck a cement median and came to a stop.

The Eleventh Circuit held that Deputy Cox should be shielded from suit based on qualified immunity since "a reasonable officer in Deputy Cox's position could have believed that he had sufficient probable cause to apply deadly force." A reasonable officer in Cox's position could have concluded that the suspects, who were fleeing down a major highway at eighty-five miles per hour in a pickup and apparently were not about to stop, posed a serious threat of harm to other motorists.

The Eleventh Circuit also found "that the law was not sufficiently established on the day of the shooting that Deputy Cox knew that he needed to warn the occupants of the truck before firing his weapon." The Eleventh Circuit noted that the U.S. Supreme Court had found in Tennessee v. Garner, 471 U.S. 1 (1985), that a police officer must warn a suspect of the potential application of deadly force "where feasible," but the *Garner* Court made no effort to define under what factual situations such a warning would be necessary. No Eleventh Circuit decisions or decisions of the Supreme Court of Georgia held that a warning was necessary in similar factual circumstances.

What will be the result on remand as the court applies the *Hope* decision to the facts of *Vaughn*? What else would you need to know to predict the outcome of these cases? A second case remanded after *Hope* involved a finding of qualified immunity for a teacher, county policy officer, and principals who allowed an unconstitutional strip search of school children. See Thomas v. Roberts, 261 F.3d 1160 (11th Cir. 2001).

# Chapter 7

# The Impact of Technology and Politics

## A. *Technology*

### 1. Enhancement of the Senses

**Page 460.  Delete Problem 7-1.**

**Page 462.  Substitute the following for note 2.**

2. *Technological enhancements of the human senses: majority position.* Courts often find that use of devices more sophisticated than flashlights, binoculars and mirrors constitute searches. This is especially true for searches that provide information not readily gathered by normal senses, searches that are very expensive, or techniques that are not familiar to the public. Whether a particular device is merely an aid to an almost-plain view, or crosses the not-so-plain line and becomes a search, is an especially difficult question for high-powered versions of familiar tools, such as high-powered binoculars.

Page 463.    Add the following case and notes before Problem 7-2.

### c.    *Technological Information Gathering Beyond the Human Senses*

Courts and legislatures divide sharply on whether technological enhancements that provide information that normal human senses could not provide constitute a search, and if so, under what standards such searches should be evaluated. One familiar and early test of high technology searches arose over the use of wiretaps, considered in the next section. In Olmstead v. United States, 277 U.S. 438 (1928), the court refused to extend the Fourth Amendment to the "new" technology of the telephone, over the famous dissent of Justice Brandeis. In Katz v. United States, 389 U.S. 347 (1967), the court applied the Fourth Amendment to prevent electronic bugging of a public telephone booth. Federal and state courts have wrestled with a variety of investigative technologies over the past forty years, often on a technology-by-technology basis. One new technology that has been used increasingly over the past fifteen years is thermal imaging or "infra-red radar," used to assess the heat being produced in homes as a basis for obtaining warrants to find drug labs. This issue was addressed for the first time by the U.S. Supreme Court in the following decision.  Consider whether this decision provides a useful framework for assessing high technology searches in other contexts.

## Danny Lee Kyllo v. United States
### 533 U.S. 27 (2001)

SCALIA, J.

This case presents the question whether the use of a thermal-imaging device aimed at a private home from a public street to detect relative amounts of heat within the home constitutes a "search" within the meaning of the Fourth Amendment.

In 1991 Agent William Elliott of the United States Department of the Interior came to suspect that marijuana was being grown in the home belonging to petitioner Danny Kyllo, part of a triplex on Rhododendron Drive in Florence, Oregon. Indoor marijuana growth typically requires high-intensity lamps. In order to determine whether an amount of heat was emanating from petitioner's home consistent with the use of such lamps, at 3:20 a.m. on January 16, 1992, Agent Elliott and Dan Haas used an Agema Thermovision 210 thermal imager to scan the triplex. Thermal imagers detect infrared radiation, which virtually all objects emit but which is not visible to the naked eye. The imager converts radiation into images based on relative warmth—black is cool, white is hot, shades of gray connote relative differences; in that respect, it operates somewhat like a video camera showing heat images. The scan of Kyllo's home took only a few minutes and was performed from the passenger seat of Agent Elliott's vehicle across the street from the front of the house and also from the street in back of the house. The scan showed that the roof over the garage and a side wall of petitioner's home were relatively hot compared to the rest of the home and substantially warmer than neighboring homes in the triplex. Agent Elliott concluded that petitioner was using halide lights to grow marijuana in his house, which indeed he was. Based on tips from informants, utility bills, and the thermal imaging, a Federal Magistrate Judge issued a warrant authorizing a search of petitioner's home, and the agents found an indoor growing operation involving more than 100 plants. Petitioner was indicted on one count of manufacturing marijuana. . . . He unsuccessfully moved to suppress the evidence seized from his home and then entered a conditional guilty plea.

[T]he District Court found that the Agema 210 "is a non-intrusive device which emits no rays or beams and shows a crude visual image of the heat being radiated from the outside of the house"; it "did not show any people or activity within the walls of the structure"; "[t]he device used cannot penetrate walls or windows to reveal conversations or human activities"; and "[n]o intimate details of the home were observed." Based on these findings, the District Court upheld the validity of the warrant that relied in part upon the thermal imaging. . . .

At the very core of the Fourth Amendment stands the right of a man to retreat into his own home and there be free from unreasonable governmental intrusion. With few exceptions, the question whether a warrantless search of a home is reasonable and hence constitutional must be answered no.

On the other hand, the antecedent question of whether or not a Fourth Amendment "search" has occurred is not so simple under our precedent. The permissibility of ordinary visual surveillance of a home

135

used to be clear because, well into the 20th century, our Fourth Amendment jurisprudence was tied to common-law trespass. See, e.g., Olmstead v. United States, 277 U.S. 438 (1928). Visual surveillance was unquestionably lawful because "the eye cannot by the laws of England be guilty of a trespass." Boyd v. United States, 116 U.S. 616 (1886) (quoting Entick v. Carrington, (K.B.1765)). We have since decoupled violation of a person's Fourth Amendment rights from trespassory violation of his property, but the lawfulness of warrantless visual surveillance of a home has still been preserved. As we observed in California v. Ciraolo, 476 U.S. 207 (1986), "[t]he Fourth Amendment protection of the home has never been extended to require law enforcement officers to shield their eyes when passing by a home on public thoroughfares."

One might think that the . . . validating rationale would be that examining the portion of a house that is in plain public view, while it is a "search" despite the absence of trespass, is not an "unreasonable" one under the Fourth Amendment. But in fact we have held that visual observation is no "search" at all—perhaps in order to preserve somewhat more intact our doctrine that warrantless searches are presumptively unconstitutional. In assessing when a search is not a search, we have applied somewhat in reverse the principle first enunciated in Katz v. United States, 389 U.S. 347 (1967). *Katz* involved eavesdropping by means of an electronic listening device placed on the outside of a telephone booth—a location not within the catalog ("persons, houses, papers, and effects") that the Fourth Amendment protects against unreasonable searches. We held that the Fourth Amendment nonetheless protected Katz from the warrantless eavesdropping because he "justifiably relied" upon the privacy of the telephone booth. As Justice Harlan's oft-quoted concurrence described it, a Fourth Amendment search occurs when the government violates a subjective expectation of privacy that society recognizes as reasonable. We have subsequently applied this principle to hold that a Fourth Amendment search does *not* occur—even when the explicitly protected location of a *house* is concerned—unless "the individual manifested a subjective expectation of privacy in the object of the challenged search," and "society [is] willing to recognize that expectation as reasonable." We have applied this test in holding that it is not a search for the police to use a pen register at the phone company to determine what numbers were dialed in a private home, Smith v. Maryland, 442 U.S. 735 (1979), and we have applied the test on two different occasions in holding that aerial surveillance of private homes and surrounding areas does not constitute a search, *Ciraolo*; Florida v. Riley, 488 U.S. 445 (1989).

The present case involves officers on a public street engaged in more than naked-eye surveillance of a home. We have previously reserved judgment as to how much technological enhancement of ordinary perception from such a vantage point, if any, is too much. While we upheld enhanced aerial photography of an industrial complex in Dow Chemical v. United States, 476 U.S. 227 (1986), we noted that we found "it important that this is *not* an area immediately adjacent to a private home, where privacy expectations are most heightened."

It would be foolish to contend that the degree of privacy secured to citizens by the Fourth Amendment has been entirely unaffected by the advance of technology. For example, as the cases discussed above make clear, the technology enabling human flight has exposed to public view (and hence, we have said, to official observation) uncovered portions of the house and its curtilage that once were private. The question we confront today is what limits there are upon this power of technology to shrink the realm of guaranteed privacy.

The *Katz* test—whether the individual has an expectation of privacy that society is prepared to recognize as reasonable—has often been criticized as circular, and hence subjective and unpredictable. See Posner, The Uncertain Protection of Privacy by the Supreme Court, 1979 S. Ct. Rev. 173. While it may be difficult to refine *Katz* when the search of areas such as telephone booths, automobiles, or even the curtilage and uncovered portions of residences are at issue, in the case of the search of the interior of homes—the prototypical and hence most commonly litigated area of protected privacy—there is a ready criterion, with roots deep in the common law, of the minimal expectation of privacy that *exists,* and that is acknowledged to be *reasonable.* To withdraw protection of this minimum expectation would be to permit police technology to erode the privacy guaranteed by the Fourth Amendment. We think that obtaining by sense-enhancing technology any information regarding the interior of the home that could not otherwise have been obtained without physical "intrusion into a constitutionally protected area," constitutes a search—at least where (as here) the technology in question is not in general public use. This assures preservation of that degree of privacy against government that existed when the Fourth Amendment was adopted. On the basis of this criterion, the information obtained by the thermal imager in this case was the product of a search.

The Government maintains, however, that the thermal imaging must be upheld because it detected "only heat radiating from the external surface of the house." The dissent makes this its leading point, contending that there is a fundamental difference between what it calls "off-the-wall" observations and "through-the-wall surveillance." But just as a thermal imager captures only heat emanating from a house, so also a powerful directional microphone picks up only sound emanating from a house—and a satellite capable of scanning from many miles away would pick up only visible light emanating from a house. We rejected such a mechanical interpretation of the Fourth Amendment in *Katz,* where the eavesdropping device picked up only sound waves that reached the exterior of the phone booth. Reversing that approach would leave the homeowner at the mercy of advancing technology—including imaging technology that could discern all human activity in the home. While the technology used in the present case was relatively crude, the rule we adopt must take account of more sophisticated systems that are already in use or in development.[3] . . .

The Government also contends that the thermal imaging was constitutional because it did not "detect private activities occurring in private areas." It points out that in *Dow Chemical* we observed that the enhanced aerial photography did not reveal any "intimate details." *Dow Chemical,* however, involved enhanced aerial photography of an industrial complex, which does not share the Fourth Amendment sanctity of the home. The Fourth Amendment's protection of the home has never been tied to measurement of the quality or quantity of

---

3. The ability to "see" through walls and other opaque barriers is a clear, and scientifically feasible, goal of law enforcement research and development. The National Law Enforcement and Corrections Technology Center, a program within the United States Department of Justice, features on its Internet Website projects that include a "Radar-Based Through-the-Wall Surveillance System," "Handheld Ultrasound Through the Wall Surveillance," and a "Radar Flashlight" that "will enable law officers to detect individuals through interior building walls." www.nlectc.org/techproj/ (visited May 3, 2001). Some devices may emit low levels of radiation that travel "through-the-wall," but others, such as more sophisticated thermal imaging devices, are entirely passive, or "off-the-wall" as the dissent puts it.

information obtained. . . . In the home, our cases show, *all* details are intimate details, because the entire area is held safe from prying government eyes. Thus, in United States v. Karo, 468 U. S. 705 (1984), the only thing detected was a can of ether in the home; and in Arizona v. Hicks, 480 U.S. 321 (1987), the only thing detected by a physical search that went beyond what officers lawfully present could observe in "plain view" was the registration number of a phonograph turntable. These were intimate details because they were details of the home, just as was the detail of how warm—or even how relatively warm—Kyllo was heating his residence.

Limiting the prohibition of thermal imaging to "intimate details" would not only be wrong in principle; it would be impractical in application, failing to provide a workable accommodation between the needs of law enforcement and the interests protected by the Fourth Amendment. To begin with, there is no necessary connection between the sophistication of the surveillance equipment and the "intimacy" of the details that it observes—which means that one cannot say (and the police cannot be assured) that use of the relatively crude equipment at issue here will always be lawful. The Agema Thermovision 210 might disclose, for example, at what hour each night the lady of the house takes her daily sauna and bath—a detail that many would consider "intimate"; and a much more sophisticated system might detect nothing more intimate than the fact that someone left a closet light on. We could not, in other words, develop a rule approving only that through-the-wall surveillance which identifies objects no smaller than 36 by 36 inches, but would have to develop a jurisprudence specifying which home activities are "intimate" and which are not. And even when (if ever) that jurisprudence were fully developed, no police officer would be able to know *in advance* whether his through-the-wall surveillance picks up "intimate" details—and thus would be unable to know in advance whether it is constitutional. . . .

We have said that the Fourth Amendment draws "a firm line at tʰ entrance to the house." That line, we think, must be not only firm also bright—which requires clear specification of those metho surveillance that require a warrant. While it is certainly posᶜ conclude from the videotape of the thermal imaging that occurr case that no "significant" compromise of the homeowner's ʳ occurred, we must take the long view, from the original mʸ

*¹⁴₀*

Fourth Amendment forward.

> The Fourth Amendment is to be construed in the light of what was deemed an unreasonable search and seizure when it was adopted, and in a manner which will conserve public interests as well as the interests and rights of individual citizens. Carroll v. United States, 267 U.S. 132 (1925).

Where, as here, the Government uses a device that is not in general public use, to explore details of the home that would previously have been unknowable without physical intrusion, the surveillance is a "search" and is presumptively unreasonable without a warrant.

Since we hold the Thermovision imaging to have been an unlawful search, it will remain for the District Court to determine whether, without the evidence it provided, the search warrant issued in this case was supported by probable cause—and if not, whether there is any other basis for supporting admission of the evidence that the search pursuant to the warrant produced. . . .

STEVENS, J., dissenting.

There is, in my judgment, a distinction of constitutional magnitude between "through-the-wall surveillance" that gives the observer or listener direct access to information in a private area, on the one hand, and the thought processes used to draw inferences from information in the public domain, on the other hand. The Court has crafted a rule that purports to deal with direct observations of the inside of the home, but the case before us merely involves indirect deductions from "off-the-wall" surveillance, that is, observations of the exterior of the home. Those observations were made with a fairly primitive thermal imager that gathered data exposed on the outside of petitioner's home but did not invade any constitutionally protected interest in privacy.

[It is well settled] that searches and seizures of property in plain view are presumptively reasonable. Whether that property is residential or commercial, the basic principle is the same: What a person knowingly exposes to the public, even in his own home or office, is not a subject of Fourth Amendment protection. That is the principle implicated here.

While the Court "take[s] the long view" and decides this case based largely on the potential of yet-to-be-developed technology that might allow "through-the-wall surveillance," this case involves nothing more ian off-the-wall surveillance by law enforcement officers to gather information exposed to the general public from the outside of petitioner's home. All that the infrared camera did in this case was passively measure heat emitted from the exterior surfaces of petitioner's home; all that those measurements showed were relative differences in emission levels, vaguely indicating that some areas of the roof and outside walls were warmer than others. [No] details regarding the interior of petitioner's home were revealed. . . .

Indeed, the ordinary use of the senses might enable a neighbor or passerby to notice the heat emanating from a building, particularly if it is vented, as was the case here. Additionally, any member of the public might notice that one part of a house is warmer than another part or a nearby building if, for example, rainwater evaporates or snow melts at different rates across its surfaces. Such use of the senses would not convert into an unreasonable search if, instead, an adjoining neighbor allowed an officer onto her property to verify her perceptions with a sensitive thermometer. Nor, in my view, does such observation become an unreasonable search if made from a distance with the aid of a device that merely discloses that the exterior of one house, or one area of the house, is much warmer than another. Nothing more occurred in this case.

Thus, the notion that heat emissions from the outside of a dwelling is a private matter [covered under] the Fourth Amendment (the text of which guarantees the right of people "to be secure *in* their . . . houses" against unreasonable searches and seizures (emphasis added)) is not only unprecedented but also quite difficult to take seriously. Heat waves, like aromas that are generated in a kitchen, or in a laboratory or opium den, enter the public domain if and when they leave a building. A subjective expectation that they would remain private is not only implausible but also surely not one that society is prepared to recognize as reasonable....

In the Court's own words, based on what the thermal imager showed regarding the outside of petitioner's home, the officers concluded that petitioner was engaging in illegal activity inside the home. It would be quite absurd to characterize their thought processes as "searches," regardless of whether they inferred (rightly) that petitioner was growing marijuana in his house, or (wrongly) that "the lady of the house [was taking] her daily sauna and bath." . . . For the first time in its history, the Court assumes that an inference can amount to a Fourth Amendment violation.

Notwithstanding the implications of today's decision, there is a strong public interest in avoiding constitutional litigation over the monitoring of emissions from homes, and over the inferences drawn from such monitoring. Just as "the police cannot reasonably be expected to avert their eyes from evidence of criminal activity that could have been observed by any member of the public," so too public officials should not have to avert their senses or their equipment from detecting emissions in the public domain such as excessive heat, traces of smoke, suspicious odors, odorless gases, airborne particulates, or radioactive emissions, any of which could identify hazards to the community. In my judgment, monitoring such emissions with sense-enhancing technology, and drawing useful conclusions from such monitoring, is an entirely reasonable public service.

On the other hand, the countervailing privacy interest is at best trivial. After all, homes generally are insulated to keep heat in, rather than to prevent the detection of heat going out, and it does not seem to me that society will suffer from a rule requiring the rare homeowner who both intends to engage in uncommon activities that produce extraordinary amounts of heat, and wishes to conceal that production from outsiders, to make sure that the surrounding area is well insulated.

. . . Despite the Court's attempt to draw a line that is "not only firm but also bright," the contours of its new rule are uncertain because its protection apparently dissipates as soon as the relevant technology is "in general public use." Yet how much use is general public use is not even hinted at by the Court's opinion, which makes the somewhat doubtful assumption that the thermal imager used in this case does not satisfy that criterion.[5] In any event, putting aside its lack of clarity, this criterion is somewhat perverse because it seems likely that the threat to privacy will grow, rather than recede, as the use of intrusive equipment becomes more readily available.

It is clear, however, that the category of "sense-enhancing

---

5. The record describes a device that numbers close to a thousand manufactured units; that has a predecessor numbering in the neighborhood of 4,000 to 5,000 units; that competes with a similar product numbering from 5,000 to 6,000 units; and that is "readily available to the public" for commercial, personal, or law enforcement purposes, and is just an 800-number away from being rented from "half a dozen national companies" by anyone who wants one. Since, by virtue of the Court's new rule, the issue is one of first impression, perhaps it should order an evidentiary hearing to determine whether these facts suffice to establish "general public use."

technology" covered by the new rule, is far too broad. It would, for example, embrace potential mechanical substitutes for dogs trained to react when they sniff narcotics. But in United States v. Place, 462 U.S. 696 (1983), we held that a dog sniff that "discloses only the presence or absence of narcotics" does not constitute a search within the meaning of the Fourth Amendment, and it must follow that sense-enhancing equipment that identifies nothing but illegal activity is not a search either. Nevertheless, the use of such a device would be unconstitutional under the Court's rule, as would the use of other new devices that might detect the odor of deadly bacteria or chemicals for making a new type of high explosive, even if the devices (like the dog sniffs) are so limited in both the manner in which they obtain information and in the content of the information they reveal. . . .

If it takes sensitive equipment to detect an odor that identifies criminal conduct and nothing else, the fact that the odor emanates from the interior of a home should not provide it with constitutional protection. . . .

Although the Court is properly and commendably concerned about the threats to privacy that may flow from advances in the technology available to the law enforcement profession, it has unfortunately failed to heed the tried and true counsel of judicial restraint. Instead of concentrating on the rather mundane issue that is actually presented by the case before it, the Court has endeavored to craft an all-encompassing rule for the future. It would be far wiser to give legislators an unimpeded opportunity to grapple with these emerging issues rather than to shackle them with prematurely devised constitutional constraints.

## NOTES

1. *Thermal imaging: majority position.* State and federal law enforcement authorities started using thermal imaging—also commonly referred to as forward-looking infra-red radar or "FLIR"—in the late 1980s. In 1991, the U.S. District Court for the District of Hawaii upheld the constitutionality of thermal imaging without a warrant, analogizing the examination of the heat emitted from the house to examination of garbage left at the curb allowed under federal law by the U.S. Supreme Court in *Greenwood*, and to the molecules sniffed by a dog during the warrantless external examination of a bag, approved by the Supreme

Court in *Place*. See United States v. Penny-Feeney, 773 F. Supp. 220 (D. Haw. 1991). Federal circuit courts of appeal before *Kyllo* largely followed this analysis. In contrast, three of the four state supreme courts that addressed the constitutionality of thermal imaging deemed it unconstitutional, with Washington State and Montana resting their decisions on state grounds. See Commonwealth v. Gindlesperger, 743 A.2d 898 (Pa. 1999); State v. Young, 867 P.2d 593 (Wash. 1994); State v. Siegal, 934 P.2d 176 (Mont. 1997); but see LaFollette v. Commonwealth, 915 S.W.2d 747 (Ky. 1996) (not a search under Fourth Amendment). In *Kyllo*, decided 10 years after the first of the thermal imaging cases appeared in federal courts, the Supreme Court held that thermal imaging of a home is a search under the Fourth Amendment. The decision surprised many observers, who saw many doctrinal avenues in the court's existing doctrine for the court to find that thermal imaging was a not a search at all.

2.   *New doctrine for new technology?* Both the majority and dissent in *Kyllo* recognize that the *Katz* test, based on individual and societal expectations of privacy, created an inherent tension with new technologies for observation and investigation. First, as a technology becomes widespread it might become unreasonable for an individual to hold a subjective expectation of privacy. If humans develop Superman's X-ray vision, we will all subjectively need to recognize that our walls (and perhaps our clothes) no longer create an barrier to observation. Second, as technology becomes more widespread, members of society might be less and less willing to recognize individual subjective preferences as reasonable. Is either element of the *Katz* test modified by *Kyllo*, or does the court simply apply *Katz* to find that thermal imaging is a search? Will *Kyllo* lead federal or state courts to reconsider the use of helicopters, planes, and high magnification cameras to gather information? Does *Kyllo* provide a doctrinal framework that will help courts, legislatures and executive agencies to resolve questions about the use of other search technologies in the future?

3.   *Home sweet home.* The majority in *Kyllo* finds thermal imaging inappropriate for the home, which it calls the "prototypical" area of protected privacy. Will the holding be read to apply only to technological searches of the home? The majority also qualifies its holding by observing that the image here provided information "that would previously have been unknowable without physical intrusion."

Could an observer know about heat emanating from a home without physical intrusion? Will *Kyllo* be limited only to devices that provide information that would have required "physical intrusion"?

4. *Cheap technology and cheap doctrine.* The majority in *Kyllo* limited its holding to devices that are "not in general public use." But it does not define "general public use." Is this language part of the holding, or merely dicta? Will this limitation pose the same kind of continual erosion as the original "expectation" doctrine of *Katz*, since technology often becomes cheaper and more widespread over time?

## 2. Wiretapping

### b. Statutory Wiretapping Procedures

**Page 488. Add the following material at the end of the notes.**

8. *Wiretap statutes vs. First Amendment.* Title III and many state laws prohibit the intentional disclosure of illegally intercepted communications. Under 18 U.S.C. §2511(1)(c), a person commits a crime or may be subject to civil suit if he or she "intentionally discloses" the contents of an illegally intercepted communication, "knowing or having reason to know" that the information was obtained through illegal interception. In Bartnicki v. Vopper, 532 U.S. 514 (2001), the Supreme Court held that the First Amendment protected the right of the press to publish "truthful information of public concern" even though the information had originally been intercepted illegally by a third party. In *Bartnicki*, a radio commentator, Frederick Vopper, played an illegally recorded tape of a cell phone conversation between the president of a local teachers' union and its chief negotiator, Gloria Bartnicki. Bartnicki sued Vopper under Title III and state law. The Supreme Court held that on these facts, "privacy concerns give way when balanced against the interest in publishing matters of public importance."

**Page 504.    Add this material at the end of note 6.**

Looking at the number of wiretaps makes wiretapping seem like a fairly modest mode of investigation, and therefore (whatever its wisdom) a fairly modest practical concern. Another perspective, however, is to consider the number of conversations reached by court-ordered wiretaps. According to the Department of Justice, while there were 1,186 wiretap requests approved by judges in 1997 — an increase of 3 percent over 1996 — these wiretaps reached 2 million conversations, the highest number ever. Of the 1,186 requests, the three leading states were New York (304), New Jersey (70), and Florida (57). In 1998 there were 1,329 wiretap requests approved. 1998 Sourcebook of Criminal Justice Statistics Online, Table 5.2 http://www.albany.edu/ sourcebook/1995/ pdf/t52.pdf; Administrative Office of the U.S. Courts, 1998 Wiretap Report.

## 3.    Searching Electronic Records

### a.    Electronic Records in the Hands of Third Parties

**Page 523.    Add this material to note 3.**

Are Internet service providers (ISPs) required to provide the government with records of usage by its users? If the records being requested by the government involve e-mail and communications, they might be covered by the Electronic Communications Privacy Act. But what if the materials sought by the government are not communications, but stored files and documents? Is the delivery of such information by the service provider a matter covered solely by the contractual relationship between the user and the provider? Should it be? See Tom Onyshko and Lesia Stangret, Privacy and the Internet: Recent Developments in Canada, The U.S. and Europe, 4 no. 2 Cyberspace Lawyer 2 (Apr. 1999).

*b.    Computerized Government Databases*

**Page 529.    Add this material after note 2.**

3.  *Noncriminal government use of personal information.* The government may obtain some of its information from private sources, such as banks and businesses. The government's power to use this information later for noncriminal as opposed to criminal enforcement purposes may not always be clear. In 1995, the European Community issued a long "Directive on the protection of individuals with regard to the processing of personal data and on the free movement of such data." European Community Directive 95/46 (24 Oct. 1995). That Directive provides in its preamble that "data which are capable by their nature of infringing fundamental freedoms or privacy should not be processed unless the data subject gives his explicit consent." The detailed Directive provides in part:

Article 6
1. Member States shall provide that personal data must be:
    (a) processed fairly and lawfully;
    (b) collected for specified, explicit and legitimate purposes and not further processed in a way incompatible with those purposes. Further processing of data for historical, statistical or scientific purposes shall not be considered as incompatible provided that Member States provide appropriate safeguards;
    (c) adequate, relevant and not excessive in relation to the purposes for which they are collected and/or further processed;
    (d) accurate and, where necessary, kept up to date; every reasonable step must be taken to ensure that data which are inaccurate or incomplete, having regard to the purposes for which they were collected or for which they are further processed, are erased or rectified;
    (e) kept in a form which permits identification of data subjects for no longer than is necessary for the purposes for which the data were collected or for which they are further processed. Member States shall lay down appropriate safeguards for personal data stored for longer periods for historical, statistical or scientific use. . . .

Article 7
Member States shall provide that personal data may be processed only if:
    (a) the data subject has unambiguously given his consent; or
    (b) processing is necessary for the performance of a contract to which the data subject is party or in order to take steps at the request of the data subject prior to entering into a contract; or

(c) processing is necessary for compliance with a legal obligation to which the [person or agency holding the data] is subject; or

(d) processing is necessary in order to protect the vital interests of the data subject; or

(e) processing is necessary for the performance of a task carried out in the public interest or in the exercise of official authority vested in the controller or in a third party to whom the data are disclosed; or

(f) processing is necessary for the purposes of the legitimate interests pursued by the [person or agency holding the data] or by the third party or parties to whom the data are disclosed, except where such interests are overridden by the interests for fundamental rights and freedoms of the data subject which require protection under Article 1 (1).

Article 8
Member States shall prohibit the processing of personal data revealing racial or ethnic origin, political opinions, religious or philosophical beliefs, trade-union membership, and the processing of data concerning health or sex life.

The Directive specifically does not apply "to processing operations concerning public security, defence, State security (including the economic well-being of the State when the processing operation relates to State security matters) and the activities of the State in areas of criminal law." Article 3. Are these cold words nonetheless comforting in terms of the protection they would provide against collection and use of personal data by government? If not, why not? See generally James Harvey, An Overview of the European Union's Personal Data Directive, 15 No. 10 Computer Lawyer 19 (Oct. 1998). See also Robert Gellman, Can Privacy Be Regulated Effectively on a National Level? Thoughts on the Possible Need for International Privacy Rules, 41 Vill. L. Rev. 129 (1996).

4.  *DNA databases.*  The kinds of data held by the government increasingly extend beyond financial records. Such nonfinancial information includes citizenship and birth records, often linked to an individual's Social Security number. The kinds of information that might be kept about individuals are virtually limitless. One especially powerful class of information is genetic information, revealed through chemical patterns in an individual's DNA.

DNA information has seen increasing use in criminal and civil cases throughout the country over the past decade. Most states have now firmly established the validity, as an evidentiary matter, of at least some types of DNA evidence. Beyond the evidentiary and technical aspects of DNA evidence, its use can be quite dramatic. DNA evidence has proven the innocence of some people wrongly convicted. The "Innocence Project" directed by Professor Barry Scheck of Cardozo Law School and attorney Peter Neufeld relies on DNA evidence to reexamine convictions.

But individual use of DNA to establish whether a known individual was (or was not) the likely offender is very different from having a broad database that allows the government to match any genetic material to a particular person. A database containing genetic information about many individuals, and perhaps an entire population, might allow investigators who find hairs, blood, semen or mucus to identify quickly the most likely suspects.

What only a few years ago sounded like science fiction increasingly sounds like science fact. Every state in the country has now passed legislation authorizing a DNA database made up of information concerning various categories of citizens, most often groups of offenders or suspects. The military obtains genetic information from every member of the armed services. Some states have begun to collect identifying information, such as fingerprints, as part of providing basic services, such as a driver's license. It may not be long until the basic elements of citizenship and commerce obligate individuals to provide a sample of their DNA.

The development of genetic databases raises a huge range of issues. Those issues focus on how the information is obtained, how it may be used, and who will have access to it. Both government and private uses of this information raise the possibility of a profoundly different relationship between individuals and the government, and individuals and commercial entities, than has been true before.

Take Massachusetts as an example. The legislature passed in 1997 a statute authorizing collection and analysis of DNA samples from defendants convicted of any of the thirty-three enumerated felonies. The law applied retroactively to those currently incarcerated, on probation, or on parole as a result of such a conviction. If a conviction is later dismissed, relevant DNA records may be expunged by court order. Law enforcement officers and correction personnel are authorized to use "reasonable force" to collect the DNA samples.

Once samples are collected, the state crime laboratory performs "DNA typing tests" to generate numerical identification information. This numerical identifier becomes part of the state DNA database, and is also forwarded to the Federal Bureau of Investigation for storage and maintenance in a national index system.

The Massachusetts Act limits access to the information obtained from DNA samples. The crime lab forwards a DNA record to local police departments, to the Department of Correction, to a sheriff's department, to the parole board, or to prosecuting officers on written or electronic request. The crime lab also must disclose DNA records to "local, state and federal criminal justice and law enforcement agencies, including forensic laboratories serving such agencies, for identification purposes in order to further official criminal investigations or prosecutions." Defendants who are charged with crimes as a result of a DNA database search are provided with a copy of their own DNA record. The director of the crime lab also has discretion to release DNA records for identifying victims of mass disasters or for "advancing other humanitarian purposes."

If you, as an attorney in Massachusetts, hoped to challenge the constitutionality of this law, who would be your ideal client? What situations would present the strongest settings for challenging the law? What constitutional texts and doctrines would you invoke? As Director of the state crime laboratory, what regulations would you issue to address any potential constitutional difficulties? What situations create the greatest risk of a political backlash that might lead to a repeal or amendment of the statute?

The Massachusetts statute has survived an initial constitutional challenge. Landry v. Attorney General, 709 N.E. 2d 1085 (Mass. 1999); see also State v. Olivas, 856 P.2d 1076 (Wash. 1993) (en banc).

5. *Voluntary DNA testing.* When is it appropriate for police or victims to encourage voluntary DNA testing to help solve a crime? In one nationally reported case, a comatose woman was raped while hospitalized in a Massachusetts nursing home. Police asked family, friends, and hospital workers to submit DNA samples. Should hospitals and nursing homes set up a private DNA database? Could provision of genetic material be made a requirement of employment?

6. *Compensating the innocent imprisoned.* The Innocence Project at Cardozo Law School has in its first years built an impressive record of overturned convictions. Though little careful analytic work has yet been published examining these cases, two important lessons from these cases (and from cases of wrongful convictions discovered through means other

than DNA evidence) seem to emerge. First, the most common source of wrongful convictions is erroneous identification evidence, especially in cases where the identifications formed a central part of the case. Second, wrongful convictions seem far more likely to be uncovered when some advocate is investigating the case: These cases do not uncover themselves. When a person is freed after years of imprisonment for a crime they did not commit, should they be compensated? By whom? See Michael Higgins, Tough Luck for the Innocent Man: As Scientific Breakthroughs Help Overturn More Convictions of Wrongly Imprisoned People, the New Crime Is How Little Their Lost Lives Are Worth, 85 A.B.A. J. 46 (Mar. 1999).

## 4.  Nongovernmental Infringement of Privacy

**Page 537.    Add this note after note 4.**

5.  *Voluntary privacy limits in commerce.* News stories in 1998 described efforts by the National Retail Federation, which represents a wide range of companies including various department stores and discount warehouses, to voluntarily set policies regarding the use of information gathered about customers. Will businesses develop privacy policies as strong or stronger than those that a legislature or agency might develop? Will consumers be able to negotiate for higher levels of privacy?

# B.  *Politics*

## 2.   Effects on Judicial Doctrine

**Page 545.    Add this note after note 4.**

5.  *Electing justice.* A long-standing issue among the states is whether elected judges retain an appropriate degree of judicial independence in deciding difficult questions, especially in systems that allow lawyers to contribute to judges' campaigns. Is the greater concern that judges are elected, and therefore might be influenced by the voters'

will, or that lawyers and other interest groups may contribute money to judges' campaigns? See Daniel Pinello, The Impact of Judicial Selection Method on State Supreme Court Policy (1995); Jason Levien and Stacie Fatka, Cleaning Up Judicial Elections: Examining the First Amendment Limitations on Judicial Campaign Regulation, 2 Mich. L. & Poly. Rev. 71 (1997). The American Bar Association has expressed concern that contributions by lawyers to judges are undermining public confidence in the judiciary. See James Podgers, Taking a Second Look at Giving: Committee Hones Proposals on Judicial Campaign Contributions, 85 A.B.A. J. 87 (Apr. 1999).

# Chapter 8

# Interrogations

**Page 550.    Add this material at the end of the introduction.**

Richard Leo and Richard Ofshe have surveyed a collection of 60 cases in which the government arrested and prosecuted a suspect based entirely on a confession that was probably false. They conclude that such confessions have a powerful influence on the later decisions of investigators, prosecutors, and triers of fact. See Leo and Ofshe, The Consequences of False Confessions: Deprivations of Liberty and Miscarriages of Justice in the Age of Psychological Interrogation, 88 J. Crim. L. & Criminology 429 (1998); but see Paul Cassell, The Guilty and the "Innocent": An Examination of Alleged Cases of Wrongful Conviction from False Confessions, 22 Harv. J.L. & Pub. Poly. 523 (1999) (analyzing cases of alleged false confessions and concluding that virtually all defendants were indeed guilty of the crime charged). See also Saul Kassin and Katherine Neumann, On the Power of Confession Evidence: An Experimental Test of the Fundamental Difference Hypothesis, 21 Law & Hum. Behav. 469 (1997).

# A.  Voluntariness of Confessions

## 1.  Physical Abuse and Deprivations

**Page 556.   Add this material to the end of note 4.**

The legitimacy of the limited use of physical torture is still a live issue in some places. In 1999, the Israeli Supreme Court banned the use of physical force by General Security Service interrogators. For decades, their methods included violently shaking the suspects' upper torsos, forcing them to crouch, handcuffing them in painful positions, placing filthy sacks over their heads, and depriving them of sleep.

Critics advocated new legislation to reauthorize some forms of physical force in interrogations. Reuven Rivlin, a leading legislator of the Likud Party, said the law "was intended to protect the victims, not the murderers." Rivlin said he would introduce legislation giving the attorney general the right to authorize the use of force ahead of time. Critics of the Supreme Court's decision argued that force is necessary in a "ticking bomb situation," when the General Security Service suspects that a terror attack is about to take place, but does not know where, and has to find out in order to prevent loss of life. The Supreme Court's decision noted that in such a case, a court might accept the argument that physical force was necessary. Deborah Sontag, Israel Court Bans Most Use of Force in Interrogations, N.Y. Times, Sept. 7, 1999 at A1.

**Page 556.   Add this material to the end of note 5.**

Some states have special rules (embodied in statutes, court rules, or constitutional due process rulings) requiring prompt presentation of juveniles to a judicial officer. See W. Va. Code, §49-5-8(d); In re Steven William T., 499 S.E.2d 876 (W. Va. 1997) (when a juvenile is taken into custody, he must immediately be taken before a referee, circuit judge, or magistrate; confession obtained as a result of the delay will be invalid where it appears that the primary purpose of the delay was to obtain a confession from the juvenile).

## 2.   Promises and Threats

**Page 563.    Add this material at the end of note 3.**

The availability of videotapes and other recordings of many interrogations in recent years has created a rich field for psychological and sociological research. Richard Ofshe and Richard Leo have used these materials to develop a model of true and false confessions that emphasizes the misuse of standard interrogation techniques as a major cause of false confessions. They pay particular attention to the "post-admission" portion of an interrogation, when a suspect provides the details that can corroborate or repudiate the suspect's admission of guilt. See Ofshe and Leo, The Decision to Confess Falsely: Rational Choice and Irrational Action, 74 Denv. U. L. Rev. 979 (1997).

4.   *Frequency of false confessions.* How often do suspects confess to crimes they did not commit, and how often do such false confessions lead to an erroneous conviction? Paul Cassell has attempted to estimate the number of wrongful convictions based on false confessions. He concludes that the estimated frequency of wrongful convictions is "somewhere between 1 in 2,400 convictions and 1 in 90,000 convictions, depending on what assumptions one makes." Cassell, Protecting the Innocent from False Confessions and Lost Confessions — And from *Miranda*, 88 J. Crim. L. & Criminology 497, 502 (1998). For a discussion of the uncertainties involved in this sort of estimate, see Richard Leo and Richard Ofshe, Using the Innocent to Scapegoat *Miranda*: Another Reply to Paul Cassell, 88 J. Crim. L. & Criminology 557 (1998).

## 3.   Police Lies

**Page 570.    Add this material to note 5.**

Christopher Slobogin has applied the work of moral philosopher Sissela Bok to the ethics of police lies during interrogations. He concludes that many lies told to "publicly-targeted suspects" are ethically justifiable, especially in cases where police begin the interrogation with strong independent grounds to suspect the target's guilt. Slobogin, Deceit, Pretext, and Trickery: Investigative Lies by the Police, 76 Or. L. Rev. 775 (1997); but see Margaret Paris, Lying to Ourselves, 76 Or. L. Rev. 817 (1997) (applying Bok's framework to conclude that almost all police lies during interrogations are ethically unjustified because investigators have alternatives to lying); Robert Mosteller, Moderating Investigative Lies by Disclosure and Documentation, 76 Or. L. Rev. 833 (1997).

## B.  Miranda *Warnings*

### 3.   Form of Warnings

**Page 623.    Add this material to note 1.**

See also Ajabu v. State, 693 N.E.2d 921 (Ind. 1998) (adopts *Moran* under state constitution; reviews cases from other states).

## D.  Miranda: *Cures, Impacts, and Alternatives*

### 1.   Cures and Remedies for *Miranda* Violations

**Page 659.    Add this material at the end of note 3.**

In California and other states, some training materials for prosecutors and police officers explicitly advocate that investigators continue an interrogation even after a suspect invokes *Miranda* rights. As Assistant District Attorney Devallis Rutledge of Orange County, California, puts it in a training video, "Can you [question a guy 'outside *Miranda*']? Sure you can. All of these cases have said there's legitimate uses that a *Miranda*-violative statement can be put to. The only use it can't be put to is to prove the person's guilt at trial." The California Peace Officers Legal Sourcebook, issued by the State Attorney General's office, makes the same point. See Jan Hoffman, Police Are Skirting Restraints to Get Confessions, New York Times, Mar. 29, 1998, at 1, 21; Charles Weisselberg, Saving *Miranda*, 84 Cornell L. Rev. 109

(1998) (collecting evidence of training that encourages interrogations outside *Miranda*).

Does the fact that investigators intentionally obtain "*Miranda*-violative statements" on a department-wide basis change the remedy that is constitutionally required? See People v. Peevy, 953 P.2d 1212 (Cal. 1998) (government can use statements for impeachment even if police intentionally questioned defendant in violation of *Miranda*).

Both federal and state law allow criminal suspects to sue police officers for the use of illegal interrogation techniques. Although there are some important barriers to recovery in both state and federal courts (as we saw in Chapter 6), plaintiffs sometimes can recover damages after they have been subjected to illegal interrogations, including *Miranda* violations and the use of physical deprivations. Would an intentional violation of *Miranda* make recovery easier in a civil suit? Is it possible that courts would allow the government to use a *Miranda*-violative statement for impeachment of a defendant during a criminal trial, while allowing the suspect to recover damages in a civil suit? See Cooper v. Dupnik, 963 F.2d 1220 (9th Cir. 1992) (en banc); California Attorneys for Criminal Justice v. Butts, 195 F.3d 1039 (9th Cir. 1999); Susan Klein, *Miranda* Deconstitutionalized: When the Self-Incrimination Clause and the Civil Rights Act Collide, 143 U. Pa. L. Rev. 417 (1994).

## 2.   Systemwide Impacts

**Page 669.   Add this material at the end of note 3.**

Another difficulty in measuring the effects of *Miranda* on the confession rate is that the warnings and a request for waiving the rights might simultaneously discourage and encourage confessions. Some suspects will refuse to talk once they hear the warnings, while the process of explaining the *Miranda* rights and obtaining a waiver may create a more cooperative atmosphere and lead to more (or more damaging) admissions. George Thomas reviewed the available empirical studies and concluded that they are inconclusive, but still consistent with the view that *Miranda* helps as much as it hurts. Thomas, Plain Talk About the *Miranda* Empirical Debate: A "Steady-State" Theory of Confessions, 43 UCLA L. Rev. 933 (1986).

**Page 670.   Add this material at the end of note 6.**

7.   *Clearance rates.* An ideal measurement of *Miranda*'s costs over time (such as a reliable account of confession rates before *Miranda* and during the years since then) is not available. One indirect measurement of the effects is the "clearance rate," that is, the percentage of reported crimes that the police declare "solved." Those rates, which have been collected and reported since at least 1950, declined just after the *Miranda* decision and have remained at the lower levels since that time. Paul Cassell and Richard Fowles have analyzed this data. After attempting to control for other possible explanations for the lower clearance rates, they conclude that "without *Miranda*, the number of crimes cleared would be substantially higher—by as much as 6.6 to 29.7% for robbery, 6.2 to 28.9% for burglary, 0.4 to 11.9% for larceny, and 12.8 to 45.4% for vehicle theft." Cassell and Fowles, Handcuffing the Cops? A Thirty-Year Perspective on *Miranda*'s Harmful Effects on Law Enforcement, 50 Stan. L. Rev. 1055, 1126 (1998). For what crimes would you expect *Miranda* to have the largest effect? Would you expect clearance rates to show more or less of an impact than confession rates? See John Donohue, Did *Miranda* Diminish Police Effectiveness?, 50 Stan. L. Rev. 1147 (1998).

## 3.   Alternatives to *Miranda*

**Page 671.   The following material replaces the first paragraph immediately following the text of 18 U.S.C. §3501.**

In one of the odder puzzles in modern federal criminal procedure, federal prosecutors and investigators have not taken up the invitation in §3501. They rarely rely on §3501 when *Miranda* errors occur. See 124 A.L.R. 263 (1995) (examining all cases discussing §3501). Only recently has the Supreme Court addressed the constitutionality of the statute.

## Charles Thomas Dickerson v. United States
### 530 U.S. 428 (2000)

REHNQUIST, C.J.

In Miranda v. Arizona, 384 U.S. 436 (1966), we held that certain warnings must be given before a suspect's statement made during custodial interrogation could be admitted in evidence. In the wake of that decision, Congress enacted 18 U.S.C. §3501, which in essence laid down a rule that the admissibility of such statements should turn only on whether or not they were voluntarily made. We hold that *Miranda*, being a constitutional decision of this Court, may not be in effect overruled by an Act of Congress, and we decline to overrule *Miranda* ourselves. We therefore hold that *Miranda* and its progeny in this Court govern the admissibility of statements made during custodial interrogation in both state and federal courts.

Petitioner Dickerson was indicted for bank robbery, conspiracy to commit bank robbery, and using a firearm in the course of committing a crime of violence. . . . Before trial, Dickerson moved to suppress a statement he had made at a Federal Bureau of Investigation field office, on the grounds that he had not received "*Miranda* warnings" before being interrogated. The District Court granted his motion to suppress, and the Government took an interlocutory appeal to the United States Court of Appeals for the Fourth Circuit. That court, by a divided vote, reversed the District Court's suppression order. It agreed with the District Court's conclusion that petitioner had not received *Miranda* warnings before making his statement. But it went on to hold that §3501, which in effect makes the admissibility of statements such as Dickerson's turn solely on whether they were made voluntarily, was satisfied in this case. It then concluded that our decision in *Miranda* was not a constitutional holding, and that therefore Congress could by statute have the final say on the question of admissibility. . . .

Prior to *Miranda*, we evaluated the admissibility of a suspect's confession under a voluntariness test. The roots of this test developed in the common law, as the courts of England and then the United States recognized that coerced confessions are inherently untrustworthy. See, e.g., King v. Rudd, 168 Eng. Rep. 160 (K. B. 1783) (Lord Mansfield, C. J.) (stating that the English courts excluded confessions obtained by threats and promises); King v. Warickshall, 168 Eng. Rep. 234 (K. B.

1783) ("A free and voluntary confession [deserves] the highest credit, because it is presumed to flow from the strongest sense of guilt . . . but a confession forced from the mind by the flattery of hope, or by the torture of fear, comes in so questionable a shape . . . that no credit ought to be given to it; and therefore it is rejected"). Over time, our cases recognized two constitutional bases for the requirement that a confession be voluntary to be admitted into evidence: the Fifth Amendment right against self-incrimination and the Due Process Clause of the Fourteenth Amendment.

[F]or the middle third of the twentieth century our cases based the rule against admitting coerced confessions primarily, if not exclusively, on notions of due process. We applied the due process voluntariness test in some 30 different cases decided during the era that intervened between Brown v. Mississippi, 297 U. S. 278 (1936), and Escobedo v. Illinois, 378 U. S. 478 (1964). Those cases refined the test into an inquiry that examines "whether a defendant's will was overborne" by the circumstances surrounding the giving of a confession. The due process test takes into consideration "the totality of all the surrounding circumstances—both the characteristics of the accused and the details of the interrogation." The determination depends upon a weighing of the circumstances of pressure against the power of resistance of the person confessing.

We have never abandoned this due process jurisprudence, and thus continue to exclude confessions that were obtained involuntarily. But our decisions in Malloy v. Hogan, 378 U. S. 1 (1964), and *Miranda* changed the focus of much of the inquiry in determining the admissibility of suspects' incriminating statements. In *Malloy*, we held that the Fifth Amendment's Self-Incrimination Clause is incorporated in the Due Process Clause of the Fourteenth Amendment and thus applies to the States. We decided *Miranda* on the heels of *Malloy*.

In *Miranda*, we noted that the advent of modern custodial police interrogation brought with it an increased concern about confessions obtained by coercion. Because custodial police interrogation, by its very nature, isolates and pressures the individual, we stated that "[e]ven without employing brutality, the 'third degree' or [other] specific stratagems, . . . custodial interrogation exacts a heavy toll on individual liberty and trades on the weakness of individuals." We concluded that the coercion inherent in custodial interrogation blurs the line between voluntary and involuntary statements, and thus heightens the risk that an individual will not be "accorded his privilege under the Fifth Amendment . . . not to be compelled to incriminate himself." Accordingly, we laid down "concrete constitutional guidelines for law enforcement agencies and courts to follow." Those guidelines established that the admissibility in evidence of any statement given during custodial interrogation of a suspect would depend on whether the police provided the suspect with four warnings. . . .

Two years after *Miranda* was decided, Congress enacted §3501 [reprinted on page 671 of the casebook]. Given §3501's express designation of voluntariness as the touchstone of admissibility, its omission of any warning requirement, and the instruction for trial courts to consider a nonexclusive list of factors relevant to the circumstances of a confession, we agree with the Court of Appeals that Congress intended by its enactment to overrule *Miranda*. Because of the obvious conflict between our decision in *Miranda* and §3501, we must address whether Congress has constitutional authority to thus supersede *Miranda*. If Congress has such authority, §3501's totality-of-the-circumstances approach must prevail over *Miranda*'s requirement of warnings; if not, that section must yield to *Miranda*'s more specific requirements.

The law in this area is clear. This Court has supervisory authority over the federal courts, and we may use that authority to prescribe rules of evidence and procedure that are binding in those tribunals. However, the power to judicially create and enforce nonconstitutional rules of procedure and evidence for the federal courts exists only in the absence of a relevant Act of Congress. Congress retains the ultimate authority to modify or set aside any judicially created rules of evidence and procedure that are not required by the Constitution.

But Congress may not legislatively supersede our decisions interpreting and applying the Constitution. This case therefore turns on whether the *Miranda* Court announced a constitutional rule or merely exercised its supervisory authority to regulate evidence in the absence of congressional direction. Recognizing this point, the Court of Appeals surveyed *Miranda* and its progeny to determine the constitutional status of the *Miranda* decision. Relying on the fact that we have created several exceptions to *Miranda*'s warnings requirement and that we have repeatedly referred to the *Miranda* warnings as "prophylactic," New York v. Quarles, 467 U. S. 649 (1984), and "not themselves rights

161

protected by the Constitution," Michigan v. Tucker, 417 U. S. 433 (1974), the Court of Appeals concluded that the protections announced in *Miranda* are not constitutionally required.

We disagree with the Court of Appeals' conclusion, although we concede that there is language in some of our opinions that supports the view taken by that court. But first and foremost of the factors on the other side—that *Miranda* is a constitutional decision—is that both *Miranda* and two of its companion cases applied the rule to proceedings in state courts—to wit, Arizona, California, and New York. Since that time, we have consistently applied *Miranda*'s rule to prosecutions arising in state courts. It is beyond dispute that we do not hold a supervisory power over the courts of the several States. With respect to proceedings in state courts, our authority is limited to enforcing the commands of the United States Constitution.

The *Miranda* opinion itself begins by stating that the Court granted certiorari "to explore some facets of the problems . . . of applying the privilege against self-incrimination to in-custody interrogation, *and to give concrete constitutional guidelines for law enforcement agencies and courts to follow*" (emphasis added). In fact, the majority opinion is replete with statements indicating that the majority thought it was announcing a constitutional rule. . . .

Additional support for our conclusion that *Miranda* is constitutionally based is found in the *Miranda* Court's invitation for legislative action to protect the constitutional right against coerced self-incrimination. After discussing the "compelling pressures" inherent in custodial police interrogation, the *Miranda* Court concluded that, "in order to combat these pressures and to permit a full opportunity to exercise the privilege against self-incrimination, the accused must be adequately and effectively appraised of his rights and the exercise of those rights must be fully honored." However, the Court emphasized that it could not foresee "the potential alternatives for protecting the privilege which might be devised by Congress or the States," and it accordingly opined that the Constitution would not preclude legislative solutions that differed from the prescribed *Miranda* warnings but which were "at least as effective in apprising accused persons of their right of silence and in assuring a continuous opportunity to exercise it."

[Admittedly, we have], after our *Miranda* decision, made exceptions from its rule in cases such as New York v. Quarles and Harris

v. New York. But we have also broadened the application of the *Miranda* doctrine in cases such as Doyle v. Ohio, 426 U. S. 610 (1976), and Arizona v. Roberson, 486 U. S. 675 (1988). These decisions illustrate the principle—not that *Miranda* is not a constitutional rule— but that no constitutional rule is immutable. No court laying down a general rule can possibly foresee the various circumstances in which counsel will seek to apply it, and the sort of modifications represented by these cases are as much a normal part of constitutional law as the original decision.

[T]he court-invited *amicus curiae* contends that the section complies with the requirement that a legislative alternative to *Miranda* be equally as effective in preventing coerced confessions. We agree with the *amicus'* contention that there are more remedies available for abusive police conduct than there were at the time *Miranda* was decided, see, e.g., Wilkins v. May, 872 F. 2d 190 (7th Cir. 1989) (applying Bivens v. Six Unknown Fed. Narcotics Agents, 403 U. S. 388 (1971), to hold that a suspect may bring a federal cause of action under the Due Process Clause for police misconduct during custodial interrogation). But we do not agree that these additional measures supplement §3501's protections sufficiently to meet the constitutional minimum. *Miranda* requires procedures that will warn a suspect in custody of his right to remain silent and which will assure the suspect that the exercise of that right will be honored. . . . The additional remedies cited by *amicus* do not, in our view, render them, together with §3501 an adequate substitute for the warnings required by *Miranda*.

The dissent argues that it is judicial overreaching for this Court to hold §3501 unconstitutional unless we hold that the *Miranda* warnings are required by the Constitution, in the sense that nothing else will suffice to satisfy constitutional requirements. But we need not go farther than *Miranda* to decide this case. In *Miranda*, the Court noted that reliance on the traditional totality of the circumstances test raised a risk of overlooking an involuntary custodial confession, a risk that the Court found unacceptably great when the confession is offered in the case in chief to prove guilt. The Court therefore concluded that something more than the totality test was necessary. As discussed above, §3501 reinstates the totality test as sufficient. Section 3501 therefore cannot be sustained if *Miranda* is to remain the law.

Whether or not we would agree with *Miranda*'s reasoning and its resulting rule, were we addressing the issue in the first instance, the principles of stare decisis weigh heavily against overruling it now. While stare decisis is not an inexorable command, particularly when we are interpreting the Constitution, even in constitutional cases, the doctrine carries such persuasive force that we have always required a departure from precedent to be supported by some special justification.

We do not think there is such justification for overruling *Miranda*. *Miranda* has become embedded in routine police practice to the point where the warnings have become part of our national culture. While we have overruled our precedents when subsequent cases have undermined their doctrinal underpinnings, we do not believe that this has happened to the *Miranda* decision. If anything, our subsequent cases have reduced the impact of the *Miranda* rule on legitimate law enforcement while reaffirming the decision's core ruling that unwarned statements may not be used as evidence in the prosecution's case in chief.

The disadvantage of the *Miranda* rule is that statements which may be by no means involuntary, made by a defendant who is aware of his "rights," may nonetheless be excluded and a guilty defendant go free as a result. But experience suggests that the totality-of-the-circumstances test which §3501 seeks to revive is more difficult than *Miranda* for law enforcement officers to conform to, and for courts to apply in a consistent manner. . . .

In sum, we conclude that *Miranda* announced a constitutional rule that Congress may not supersede legislatively. Following the rule of stare decisis, we decline to overrule *Miranda* ourselves. . . .

SCALIA, J., dissenting.

Those to whom judicial decisions are an unconnected series of judgments that produce either favored or disfavored results will doubtless greet today's decision as a paragon of moderation, since it declines to overrule Miranda v. Arizona.  Those who understand the judicial process will appreciate that today's decision is not a reaffirmation of *Miranda*, but a radical revision of the most significant element of *Miranda* (as of all cases): the rationale that gives it a permanent place in our jurisprudence.

Marbury v. Madison, 1 Cranch 137 (1803), held that an Act of Congress will not be enforced by the courts if what it prescribes violates the Constitution of the United States. That was the basis on which

*Miranda* was decided. One will search today's opinion in vain, however, for a statement (surely simple enough to make) that what §3501 prescribes—the use at trial of a voluntary confession, even when a *Miranda* warning or its equivalent has failed to be given—violates the Constitution. The reason the statement does not appear is not only (and perhaps not so much) that it would be absurd, inasmuch as §3501 excludes from trial precisely what the Constitution excludes from trial, viz., compelled confessions; but also that Justices whose votes are needed to compose today's majority are on record as believing that a violation of *Miranda* is not a violation of the Constitution. And so, to justify today's agreed-upon result, the Court must adopt a significant new, if not entirely comprehensible, principle of constitutional law. As the Court chooses to describe that principle, statutes of Congress can be disregarded, not only when what they prescribe violates the Constitution, but when what they prescribe contradicts a decision of this Court that "announced a constitutional rule." [T]he only thing that can possibly mean in the context of this case is that this Court has the power, not merely to apply the Constitution but to expand it, imposing what it regards as useful "prophylactic" restrictions upon Congress and the States. That is an immense and frightening antidemocratic power, and it does not exist. . . .

The power we recognized in *Marbury* [requires] us to disregard §3501, a duly enacted statute governing the admissibility of evidence in the federal courts, only if it "be in opposition to the constitution"—here, assertedly, the dictates of the Fifth Amendment. It was once possible to characterize the so-called *Miranda* rule as resting (however implausibly) upon the proposition that . . . the admission at trial of un-Mirandized confessions . . . violates the Constitution. That is the fairest reading of the *Miranda* case itself. The Court began by announcing that the Fifth Amendment privilege against self-incrimination applied in the context of extrajudicial custodial interrogation—itself a doubtful proposition as a matter both of history and precedent. Having extended the privilege into the confines of the station house, the Court liberally sprinkled throughout its sprawling 60-page opinion suggestions that, because of the compulsion inherent in custodial interrogation, the privilege was violated by any statement thus obtained that did not conform to the rules set forth in *Miranda*, or some functional equivalent.

[T]he decision in *Miranda*, if read as an explication of what the

Constitution requires, is preposterous. There is, for example, simply no basis in reason for concluding that a response to the very first question asked, by a suspect who already knows all of the rights described in the *Miranda* warning, is anything other than a volitional act. And even if one assumes that the elimination of compulsion absolutely requires informing even the most knowledgeable suspect of his right to remain silent, it cannot conceivably require the right to have counsel present. There is a world of difference, which the Court recognized under the traditional voluntariness test but ignored in *Miranda*, between compelling a suspect to incriminate himself and preventing him from foolishly doing so of his own accord. Only the latter (which is not required by the Constitution) could explain the Court's inclusion of a right to counsel and the requirement that it, too, be knowingly and intelligently waived. Counsel's presence is not required to tell the suspect that he need not speak; the interrogators can do that. The only good reason for having counsel there is that he can be counted on to advise the suspect that he should not speak.

Preventing foolish (rather than compelled) confessions is likewise the only conceivable basis for the rules that courts must exclude any confession elicited by questioning conducted, without interruption, after the suspect has indicated a desire to stand on his right to remain silent, see Michigan v. Mosley, 423 U. S. 96 (1975), or initiated by police after the suspect has expressed a desire to have counsel present, see Edwards v. Arizona, 451 U. S. 477 (1981). Nonthreatening attempts to persuade the suspect to reconsider that initial decision are not, without more, enough to render a change of heart the product of anything other than the suspect's free will. Thus, what is most remarkable about the *Miranda* decision—and what made it unacceptable as a matter of straightforward constitutional interpretation in the *Marbury* tradition—is its palpable hostility toward the act of confession per se, rather than toward what the Constitution abhors, compelled confession. The Constitution is not, unlike the *Miranda* majority, offended by a criminal's commendable qualm of conscience or fortunate fit of stupidity.

[The Court tries to avoid the impact of its post-*Miranda* cases by disclaiming] responsibility for reasoned decisionmaking. It says [that the cases simply show that no constitutional rule is "immutable"]. The issue, however, is not whether court rules are "mutable"; they assuredly are. It is not whether, in the light of "various circumstances," they can be "modified"; they assuredly can. The issue is whether, as mutated and modified, they must make sense. The requirement that they do so is the only thing that prevents this Court from being some sort of nine-headed Caesar, giving thumbs-up or thumbs-down to whatever outcome, case by case, suits or offends its collective fancy. . . .

Finally, the Court asserts that *Miranda* must be a "constitutional decision" announcing a "constitutional rule," and thus immune to congressional modification, because we have since its inception applied it to the States. [If ] the argument is meant as an appeal to logic rather than stare decisis, it is a classic example of begging the question: Congress's attempt to set aside *Miranda*, since it represents an assertion that violation of *Miranda* is not a violation of the Constitution, also represents an assertion that the Court has no power to impose *Miranda* on the States. To answer this assertion—not by showing why violation of *Miranda* is a violation of the Constitution—but by asserting that *Miranda* does apply against the States, is to assume precisely the point at issue. . . .

Neither am I persuaded by the argument for retaining *Miranda* that touts its supposed workability as compared with the totality of the circumstances test it purported to replace. *Miranda*'s proponents cite ad nauseam the fact that the Court was called upon to make difficult and subtle distinctions in applying the "voluntariness" test in some 30-odd due process "coerced confessions" cases in the 30 years between Brown v. Mississippi, 297 U. S. 278 (1936), and *Miranda*. It is not immediately apparent, however, that the judicial burden has been eased by the "bright-line" rules adopted in *Miranda*. In fact, in the 34 years since *Miranda* was decided, this Court has been called upon to decide nearly 60 cases involving a host of *Miranda* issues, most of them predicted with remarkable prescience by Justice White in his *Miranda* dissent. . . .

Finally, I am not convinced by petitioner's argument that *Miranda* should be preserved because the decision occupies a special place in the "public's consciousness." As far as I am aware, the public is not under the illusion that we are infallible. I see little harm in admitting that we made a mistake in taking away from the people the ability to decide for themselves what protections (beyond those required by the Constitution) are reasonably affordable in the criminal investigatory process. And I see much to be gained by reaffirming for the people the wonderful reality that they govern themselves. . . .

Today's judgment converts *Miranda* from a milestone of judicial overreaching into the very Cheops' Pyramid (or perhaps the Sphinx would be a better analogue) of judicial arrogance. In imposing its Court-made code upon the States, the original opinion at least asserted that it was demanded by the Constitution. Today's decision does not pretend that it is—and yet still asserts the right to impose it against the will of the people's representatives in Congress. Far from believing that stare decisis compels this result, I believe we cannot allow to remain on the books even a celebrated decision—especially a celebrated decision—that has come to stand for the proposition that the Supreme Court has power to impose extraconstitutional constraints upon Congress and the States. This is not the system that was established by the Framers, or that would be established by any sane supporter of government by the people. I dissent from today's decision, and, until §3501 is repealed, will continue to apply it in all cases where there has been a sustainable finding that the defendant's confession was voluntary.

## *NOTES*

1.   *Constitutional foundations of* Miranda. Justice Scalia in his dissent asserts that the majority fails to articulate the constitutional foundations of *Miranda*. The majority acknowledges that intervening Supreme Court cases had clouded the constitutional basis for *Miranda*, and then reaffirms the holding in *Miranda* that the Fifth Amendment protection against compelled self-incrimination (applied to the states through the Fourteenth Amendment) provides the foundation for the *Miranda* warnings. Why does this not satisfy the dissenters? Do you have an answer to the claim that the majority is simply exercising a form of legislative power in reauthorizing its "Court-made code?"

2.   *Delayed constitutional reactions.* Section 3501 was enacted in 1968, two years after *Miranda*. *Dickerson* was decided in 2000, 32 years later. How could it possibly take 32 years to test this statute? For the statute to be tested in court, federal investigators and prosecutors had to try to enforce it, and that happened rarely. The most likely explanation is that §3501 was such a stark rejection of the Supreme Court's decision that most federal prosecutors felt they should not, and perhaps could not, rely upon it, since they, too, are sworn to uphold the constitution. In 1969, the Department of Justice under Attorney General John Mitchell

issued a memorandum to U.S. Attorneys suggesting that §3501 might be constitutional. Memorandum for the Department of Justice to the United States Attorneys (June 11, 1969), 5 Crim L. Rep. 2350 (1969). See Yale Kamisar, Can (Did) Congress "Overrule" Miranda, 85 Cornell L. Rev. 883, 925 (2000). For many years and through many administrations, however, federal prosecutors appear to have made only modest use of §3501. See Paul Cassell, The Statute That Time Forgot: 18 U.S.C. §3501 and the Overhauling of Miranda, 85 Iowa L. Rev. 175, 197-225 (1999).

3.   *Real* Miranda *reforms.* Again and again courts and commentators have noted that the *Miranda* court left open "potential alternatives for protecting the privilege which might be devised by Congress or the States," and allowed legislative solutions different from *Miranda* warnings, so long as the alternatives were "at least as effective in apprising accused persons of their right of silence and in assuring a continuous opportunity to exercise it." If *Miranda* warnings are problematic for law enforcement, why hasn't Congress enacted alternatives more substantial than §3501, which for 32 years was seen by most people not as an alternative to *Miranda*, but as a rejection of it? Should Congress require that all confessions be videotaped but eliminate the element of the warnings that notify defendants of a right to counsel? Should Congress require that counsel be provided before any interrogation is allowed? Would either of these proposals satisfy the U.S. Supreme Court? Under the language of *Miranda*, can't any state test alternatives as easily as Congress?

# Chapter 9

# Identifications

## A. Risks of Mistaken Identification

**Page 686.** **Add this material before the last sentence at the bottom of the page.**

The availability of DNA testing has uncovered a new supply of wrongful conviction cases. These cases point even more emphatically at faulty eyewitness testimony as the single most important source of wrongful convictions. The "Innocence Project," a nationwide effort based at the Cardozo School of Law in New York uses DNA testing to identify people who have been wrongfully convicted. A recent account of selected cases from the Innocence Project points to the role of cross-racial eyewitness testimony in many of the cases. Jim Dwyer, Peter Neufeld & Barry Scheck, Actual Innocence: Five Days to Execution and Other Dispatches From the Wrongly Convicted (2000).

## C. Remedies for Improper Identification Procedures

**Page 737.** **Add the following material before the notes.**

The following case considers the need for a jury instruction that highlights the difficulties of cross-racial identifications. Do you believe that the arguments in favor of such an instruction are basically the same as those supporting instructions about identifications more generally, or is there something distinctively difficult about cross-racial identifications? What is the role of social science in answering this question for a particular case or for a particular state system? Will jury instructions of the sort described in this opinion actually change juror conduct?

## State v. McKinley Cromedy
### 727 A.2d 457 (N.J. 1999)

COLEMAN, J.

This appeal involves a rape and robbery in which a cross-racial identification was made of defendant as the perpetrator seven months after the offenses occurred. The identification of the perpetrator was the critical issue throughout the trial. The trial court denied defendant's request to have the jury instructed concerning the cross-racial nature of the identification. . . . The novel issue presented is whether a cross-racial identification jury instruction should be required in certain cases before it is established that there is substantial agreement in the scientific community that cross-racial recognition impairment of eyewitnesses is significant enough to warrant a special jury instruction. Our study of the recommendations of a Court-appointed Task Force, judicial literature, and decisional law from other jurisdictions persuades us that there exists a reliable basis for a cross-racial identification charge. We hold that the trial court's failure to submit to the jury an instruction similar to the one requested by defendant requires a reversal of defendant's convictions.

On the night of August 28, 1992, D.S., a white female student then enrolled at Rutgers University in New Brunswick, was watching television in her basement apartment. While she was relaxing on the couch, an African-American male entered the brightly lit apartment and demanded money from D.S., claiming that he was wanted for murder and that he needed funds to get to New York. After D.S. told the intruder that she had no money, he spotted her purse, rifled through it, and removed money and credit cards.

The intruder then [demanded that she remain quiet and led her by the arm into the brightly lit kitchen. He sexually assaulted her.] Throughout the sexual assault, D.S. was facing the kitchen door with her eyes closed and hand over her mouth to avoid crying loudly. Once the assault was over, D.S. faced her attacker who, after threatening her again, turned around and left the apartment. At the time of the second threat, D.S. was standing approximately two feet away from her assailant. The attacker made no attempt to conceal his face at any time. D.S. immediately called the New Brunswick Police Department after the intruder left the apartment. . . .

D.S. described her assailant as an African-American male in his late 20s to early 30s, full-faced, about five feet five inches tall, with a medium build, mustache, and unkempt hair. She stated that the intruder was wearing a dirty gray button-down short-sleeved shirt, blue warm-up pants with white and red stripes, and a Giants logo on the left leg. D.S. was then taken to Roosevelt Hospital where rape samples were taken. The next day, D.S. made a formal statement to the police in which she again described the intruder. Three days later, a composite sketch was drawn by an artist with her assistance. The following day at police headquarters, D.S. was shown many slides and photographs, including a photograph of defendant, in an unsuccessful attempt to identify her assailant.

On April 7, 1993, almost eight months after the crimes were committed, D.S. saw an African-American male across the street from her who she thought was her attacker. She spotted the man while she was standing on the corner of a street in New Brunswick waiting for the light to change. As the two passed on the street, D.S. studied the individual's face and gait. Believing that the man was her attacker, D.S. ran home and telephoned the police, giving them a description of the man she had just seen. Defendant was picked up by the New Brunswick police and taken to headquarters almost immediately. Within fifteen minutes after seeing defendant on the street, D.S. viewed defendant in a "show-up" from behind a one-way mirror and immediately identified him as the man she had just seen on the street and as her attacker. Defendant was then arrested and, with his consent, saliva and blood samples were taken for scientific analysis. [The State Police Laboratory was unable to determine whether those samples matched the samples obtained from D.S.'s Rape Crisis Intervention Kit.]

Because of the nature of the crimes, the races of the victim and defendant, and the inability of the victim to identify defendant from his photograph, and because defendant was not positively identified until almost eight months after the date of the offenses, defense counsel sought a cross-racial identification jury charge. The following language was proposed:

> [Y]ou know that the identifying witness is of a different race than the defendant. When a witness who is a member of one race identifies a member who is of another race we say there has been a cross-racial identification. You may consider, if you think it is appropriate to do so, whether the cross-racial nature of the identification has affected the accuracy of the witness's original perception and/or accuracy of a subsequent identification.

In support of that request, defendant cited the June 1992 New Jersey Supreme Court Task Force on Minority Concerns Final Report, 131 N.J.L.J. 1145 (1992) (Task Force Report).

The trial court denied the request because this Court had not yet adopted the Task Force Report and because there had been no expert testimony with respect to the issue of cross-racial identification. The trial court instead provided the jury with the Model Jury Charge on Identification. The jury convicted defendant of first-degree aggravated sexual assault. . . .

For more than forty years, empirical studies concerning the psychological factors affecting eyewitness cross-racial or cross-ethnic identifications have appeared with increasing frequency in professional literature of the behavioral and social sciences. People v. McDonald, 690 P.2d 709, 717-18 (Cal. 1984). [Studies] have concluded that eyewitnesses are superior at identifying persons of their own race and have difficulty identifying members of another race. See generally Gary Wells & Elizabeth Loftus, Eyewitness Testimony: Psychological Perspectives 1 (1984); Elizabeth Loftus, Eyewitness Testimony (1979). This phenomenon has been dubbed the "own-race" effect or "own-race" bias. Its corollary is that eyewitnesses experience a "cross-racial impairment" when identifying members of another race. Studies have consistently shown that the "own-race effect" is strongest when white witnesses attempt to recognize black subjects.

Although researchers generally agree that some eyewitnesses exhibit an own-race bias, they disagree about the degree to which own-race bias affects identification. In one study, African-American and white "customers" browsed in a convenience store for a few minutes and then went to the register to pay. Researchers asked the convenience store clerks to identify the "customers" from a photo array. The white clerks were able to identify 53.2% of the white customers but only 40.4% of the African-American subjects. Stephanie Platz & Harmon Hosch, Cross-Racial/Ethnic Eyewitness Identification: A Field Study, 18 J. Applied Soc. Psychol. 972, 977-78 (1988). . . .

Many studies on cross-racial impairment involve subjects observing photographs for a few seconds. Because the subjects remembered the white faces more often than they recalled the African-American faces, researchers concluded that they were biased towards their own race. See Paul Barkowitz & John C. Brigham, Recognition of Faces: Own-Race Bias, Incentive, and Time Delay, 12 J. Applied Soc. Psychol. 255 (1982). Yet, there is disagreement over whether the results of some of the tests can be generalized to real-world situations in which a victim or witness confronts an assailant face-to-face and experiences the full range of emotions that accompany such a traumatic event.

The debate among researchers did not prevent the Supreme Court of the United States, in the famous school desegregation case of Brown v. Board of Education of Topeka, 347 U.S. 483, 494 n. 11 (1954), from using behavioral and social sciences to support legal conclusions without requiring that the methodology employed by those scientists have general acceptance in the scientific community. . . . Thus, Brown v. Board of Education is the prototypical example of an appellate court using modern social and behavioral sciences as legislative evidence to support its choice of a rule of law.

In United States v. Telfaire, 469 F.2d 552 (D.C. Cir. 1972), Chief Judge Bazelon urged in his concurring opinion that juries be charged on the pitfalls of cross-racial identification. He believed that the cross-racial nature of an identification could affect accuracy in the same way as proximity to the perpetrator and poor lighting conditions. He felt that a meaningful jury instruction would have to apprise jurors of that fact. . . . Judge Bazelon rejected the notion that instructions on interracial identifications "appeal to racial prejudice." Rather, he believed that an explicit jury instruction would safeguard against improper uses of race by the jury and would delineate the narrow context in which it is appropriate to consider racial differences. . . .

The Supreme Court of the United States has acknowledged that problems exist with eyewitness identifications in general and cross-racial identifications in particular. Manson v. Brathwaite, 432 U.S. 98 (1977).

Although there have been no reported decisions in our own State addressing the propriety of requiring a cross-racial identification jury instruction, decisions have been rendered by courts in other jurisdictions. The majority of courts allowing cross-racial identification charges hold that the decision to provide the instruction is a matter within the trial judge's discretion. Omission of such a cautionary instruction has been held to be prejudicial error where identification is the critical or central issue in the case, there is no corroborating evidence, and the circumstances of the case raise doubts concerning the reliability of the identification. See United States v. Thompson, 31 M.J. 125 (C.M.A. 1990) (calling for cross-racial identification instruction when requested by counsel and when cross-racial identification is a "primary issue"); People v. Wright, 755 P.2d 1049 (Cal. 1988); State v. Long, 721 P.2d 483 (Utah 1986). . . .

Courts typically have refused the instruction where the eyewitness or victim had an adequate opportunity to observe the defendant, there was corroborating evidence bolstering the identification, and/or there was no evidence that race affected the identification. See Commonwealth v. Hyatt, 647 N.E.2d 1168 (Mass. 1995) (declining instruction in rape and robbery case where victim was terrorized for fifteen to twenty minutes in broad daylight and could see the attacker's face).

A number of courts have concluded that cross-racial identification simply is not an appropriate topic for jury instruction. See State v. Willis, 731 P.2d 287, 292-93 (Kan. 1987); People v. McDaniel, 630 N.Y.S.2d 112, 113 (N.Y. App. Div. 1995). Those courts have determined that the cross-racial instruction requires expert guidance, and that cross-examination and summation are adequate safeguards to highlight unreliable identifications. Other jurisdictions have denied the instruction, finding that the results of empirical studies on cross-racial identification are questionable. People v. Bias, 475 N.E.2d 253, 257 (Ill. App. Ct. 1985) (rejecting instruction in robbery case where eyewitness failed to describe key distinguishing facial features and gave inconsistent descriptions because empirical studies are not unanimous). One jurisdiction has even rejected cross-racial identification instructions as improper commentary on "the nature and quality" of the evidence. See State v. Hadrick, 523 A.2d 441, 444 (R.I. 1987) (rejecting such instruction in robbery case where victim viewed perpetrator for two to three minutes at close range during robbery and identified him from a line-up). . . .

It is well-established in this State that when identification is a critical issue in the case, the trial court is obligated to give the jury a discrete and specific instruction that provides appropriate guidelines to focus the jury's attention on how to analyze and consider the trustworthiness of eyewitness identification. State v. Green, 430 A.2d 914 (N.J. 1981). *Green* requires that as a part of an identification charge a trial court inform the jury that [it] should consider, among other things, "the capacity or the ability of the witness to make observations or perceptions . . . at the time and under all of the attendant circumstances for seeing that which he says he saw or that which he says he perceived with regard to his identification." What defendant sought through the requested charge in the present case was an instruction that informed the jury that it could consider the fact that the victim made a cross-racial identification as part of the "attendant circumstances" when evaluating the reliability of the eyewitness identification.

The Court-appointed Task Force discussed and debated the issue of the need for a cross-racial and cross-ethnic identification jury instruction for more than five years. That Task Force was comprised of an appellate judge, trial judges, lawyers representing both the prosecution and defense, social scientists, and ordinary citizens. . . . Task Force sessions were conducted in much the same way as legislative committees conduct hearings on proposed legislation. . . . Ultimately, in 1992 the Task Force submitted its final report to the Court in which it recommended, among other things, that the Court develop a special jury charge regarding the unreliability of cross-racial identifications.

The Court referred that recommendation to the Criminal Practice Committee. . . . The Criminal Practice Committee has submitted that proposed charge to the Model Jury Charge Committee for its review. That Committee is withholding further consideration of the proposed charge pending the Court's decision in the present case.

We reject the State's contention that we should not require a cross-racial identification charge before it has been demonstrated that there is substantial agreement in the relevant scientific community that cross-racial recognition impairment is significant enough to support the need for such a charge. This case does not concern the introduction of scientific evidence to attack the reliability of the eyewitness's identification. Defendant's requested jury instruction was not based upon any "scientific, technical, or other specialized knowledge" to assist the jury. N.J.R.E. 702. He relied instead on ordinary human experience and the legislative-type findings of the Task Force because the basis for his request did not involve a matter that was beyond the ken of the average juror.

[I]n a prosecution in which race by definition is a patent factor, race must be taken into account to assure a fair trial. At the same time, we recognize that unrestricted use of cross-racial identification instructions could be counter-productive. Consequently, care must be taken to insulate criminal trials from base appeals to racial prejudice. An appropriate jury instruction should carefully delineate the context in which the jury is permitted to consider racial differences. The simple fact pattern of a white victim of a violent crime at the hands of a black assailant would not automatically give rise to the need for a cross-racial identification charge. More is required.

A cross-racial instruction should be given only when, as in the present case, identification is a critical issue in the case, and an eyewitness's cross-racial identification is not corroborated by other evidence giving it independent reliability. Here, the eyewitness identification was critical; yet it was not corroborated by any forensic evidence or other eyewitness account. The circumstances of the case raise some doubt concerning the reliability of the victim's identification in that no positive identification was made for nearly eight months despite attempts within the first five days following the commission of the offenses. Under those circumstances, turning over to the jury the vital question of the reliability of that identification without acquainting the jury with the potential risks associated with such identifications could have affected the jurors' ability to evaluate the reliability of the identification. We conclude, therefore, that it was reversible error not to have given an instruction that informed the jury about the possible significance of the cross-racial identification factor, a factor the jury can observe in many cases with its own eyes, in determining the critical issue — the accuracy of the identification. . . . We request the Criminal Practice Committee and the Model Jury Charge Committee to revise the current charge on identification to include an appropriate statement on cross-racial eyewitness identification that is consistent with this opinion. . . .

# Chapter 10

# Complex Investigations

## A.  Selection and Pursuit of Targets

### 2.  Entrapment Defenses

**Page 770.  Add this material to the end of note 4.**

Although the amounts of money paid to informants are often small, some cases involve huge sums. See David Rosenzweig, Undercover Informant Got $2 Million for Aiding Drug Probe, Los Angeles Times, Jan. 30, 1999, at B1. In some money laundering or fraud cases, the compensation for the witness comes from commissions paid by banks or other participants in the criminal scheme. Should the amount of compensation be based on the amount of physical danger an informant faces, the amount of loss to crime victims, the amount of gain to criminals, or simply the amount that the suspects are willing to pay the informant?

# B.  The Investigative Grand Jury

## 1.  Document Subpoenas

**Page 780.   Add this material to the end of note 2.**

Should the level of justification to support a grand jury subpoena turn on the type of document involved? See State v. Nelson, 941 P.2d 441 (Mont. 1997) (state constitution requires state to show probable cause to support investigative subpoena for discovery of medical records).

**Page 782.   Add this material to the end of note 6.**

In United States v. Hubbell, 530 U.S. 27 (2000), the Supreme Court expanded the effects of the self-incrimination privilege for parties responding to grand jury document subpoenas. Independent Counsel Kenneth Starr served Webster Hubbell with a grand jury subpoena calling for the production of documents. Hubbell invoked his Fifth Amendment privilege and refused to state whether he had the documents. The IC then obtained an immunity order from the court, compelling him to respond to the subpoena. Later, the IC brought tax and fraud charges against Hubbell and used the contents of the documents as evidence in the case. The Supreme Court held that the use of the subpoenaed documents violated the immunity statute because they constituted a "derivative use" of compelled "testimony."

The Court reaffirmed its earlier cases holding that the "act of production" could communicate information about the documents' existence, custody, and authenticity. The prosecutor needed Hubbell's help both to identify potential sources of information and to produce those sources. When Hubbell provided a catalog of existing documents fitting within the 11 broadly worded subpoena categories, he gave prosecutors "a link in the chain of evidence needed to prosecute." The IC in this case showed no prior knowledge of either the existence or the whereabouts of the documents ultimately produced.

**Page 786.  Add this material at the end of note 4.**

5. *Search warrants for attorneys' offices.* Section 9-2.161(b) of the U.S. Attorney's Manual, issued in November 1995, creates special rules for the use of search warrants to search the offices of attorneys who are suspects, subjects, or targets of a criminal investigation. The U.S. Attorney or an Assistant Attorney General must authorize any application for such a warrant. The application may go forward only if there is a "strong need" for material and if alternatives (such as a subpoena) will not work because of a risk of destroyed documents. The rules call for the creation of a "privilege team" consisting of agents and lawyers not involved in the investigation, who must review seized documents to identify those containing possibly privileged information. The privilege team cannot reveal the contents of privileged documents to the investigating agents and attorneys. The rule encourages agents to provide copies of all seized documents to the attorney to prevent disruption of his or her legal practice.

Perhaps more than with other suspects, the government can influence whether an attorney will be present at a location when the search warrant is executed. See Connecticut v. Gabbert, 526 U.S. 286 (1999) (Court rejected due process challenges raised in civil rights suit by attorney against prosecutors who executed a search for attorney's papers at same time they were calling attorney's client to testify before grand jury).

## 2. Witnesses

### a.  *Witnesses and Grand Jury Secrecy*

**Page 789.  Add this material at the end of note 1.**

Professor Daniel Richman points out that there are reasons to prevent law enforcement personnel from disclosing *any* investigative data, and not just grand jury information. The statutory protections for grand jury secrecy give white-collar crime defendants a tactical benefit that other defendants do not hold. See Richman, Grand Jury Secrecy: Plugging the Leaks in an Empty Bucket, 36 Am. Crim. L. Rev. 339 (1999).

**Page 791.    Add this material at the end of note 6.**

The dispute between the U.S. Department of Justice and the ethics enforcers for the state bars has continued. The state courts, for their part, have insisted that the Justice Department cannot exempt its attorney employees from state ethical rules. See In re Howes, 940 P.2d 159 (N.M. 1997) (court censures former federal prosecutor for contacts with represented defendant). In 1998, Congress repealed the Thornburgh rule and required federal prosecutors to follow all ethical obligations of the states where they are licensed. The statute, known as the "McDade amendment," was part of a large budget bill. Despite a powerful lobbying effort by the Department of Justice, the law took effect without changes in April 1999. What incentive does the U.S. Congress have to ignore the request of the Department of Justice and to impose state ethical rules on federal attorneys?

### b.    Immunity

**Page 803.    Add this material to the end of note 6.**

In United States v. Balsys, 524 U.S. 666 (1998), the government issued an administrative subpoena to determine whether Balsys lied in his immigration application about his activities during World War II. He claimed that any answer to the questions might expose him to prosecution in foreign countries. The Court held that concern with foreign prosecution was not an adequate basis for invoking the Fifth Amendment privilege against self-incrimination.

# Chapter 11 / 1

# Defense Counsel

## A. When Will Counsel Be Provided?

### 1. Types of Charges

**Page 821 (page 819 in Police paperback; page 17 in Prosecution paperback).  Add this material to note 5.**

By the time *Gideon* was decided in 1963, most states appointed counsel for all indigent felons. Although the source of the legal obligation was not always clear, some states did so based on a reading of the state constitutional right to counsel. See Carpenter v. County of Dane, 9 Wis. 274, 278 (1859) (Wisconsin Constitution interpreted to require counties to appoint counsel for indigent felons at county expense).

**Page 822 (page 820 in Police paperback; page 18 in Prosecution paperback).  Add this material to note 7.**

The *Nichols* case has received mixed reviews from state courts interpreting the state constitutional right to counsel. Compare Brisson v. State, 955 P.2d 888 (Wyo. 1998) (rejects *Nichols*, holds that use of prior uncounseled misdemeanor conviction to enhance later sentence is violation of right to counsel); State v. Woodruff, 951 P.2d 605 (N.M. 1997) (adopts *Nichols* under state constitution).

The U.S. Supreme Court settled a longstanding question about suspended sentences in Alabama v. Shelton, 122 S. Ct. 1764 (2002). The Court held that a suspended sentence "that may end up in the actual deprivation of a person's liberty" may not be imposed unless the defendant was provided with "the guiding hand of counsel in the prosecution for the crime charged."

## 2. Point in the Proceedings

**Page 835 (page 833 in Police paperback; page 31 in Prosecution paperback).   Add this material at the end of note 1.**

According to a survey by Douglas Colbert, defense attorneys are usually not available when the judge makes the first determination of bail or pretrial detention at the initial appearance. Eight states provide counsel when a judge decides whether to order pretrial release or bail. Nineteen states provide no counsel at the time of bail, while the remaining twenty-three provide counsel only in urban centers. See Douglas Colbert, Thirty Five Years After *Gideon*: The Illusory Right to Counsel, 1998 Ill. L. Rev. 1 (1998).

**Page 836 (page 834 in Police paperback; page 32 in Prosecution paperback).  Insert the following material after note 6.**

## 3. Counsel for Other Charges

When counsel is hired or appointed to represent a defendant on specific charges, and a new criminal charge is filed against the defendant, what is the scope of representation? There are at least two significant aspects of this question: first, what is the scope of the lawyer's duties, and second, what is the effect of the representation on further government investigation of the defendant?

Are lawyers hired to represent the defendant, or only to represent the defendant on specific charges? Perhaps this is simply a matter of contract, and a private lawyer could agree only to represent the defendant on specific charges, but not on other charges. But would such an agreement satisfy the ethical obligation to zealously represent the client? Can an appointed lawyer similarly limit her representation, or is her representation limited by the terms of the initial appointment? What if the judge simply appoints a lawyer "to represent the defendant"?

On the question of the investigative effects of obtaining counsel (whether through private agreement or appointment), the impact in related cases could be very broad indeed. Initial charges will often be filed with little investigation. With respect to the filed charges, there are sharp limits on further police interrogations without providing counsel with notice. Michigan v. Jackson, 425 U.S. 625 (1986). These limits include not only deliberate efforts to elicit information, but also such indirect efforts as placing another person in a jail cell to encourage conversation. See Massiah v. United States, 377 U.S. 201 (1964); United States v. Henry, 447 U.S. 264 (1980); Maine v. Moulton, 474 U.S. 159 (1985); Kuhlmann v. Wilson, 477 U.S. 436 (1986). For further discussion, see Chapters 7 and 8.

But what if police and prosecutors become convinced that the defendant committed other, related crimes? Can they interrogate a defendant without notice to counsel on the different charges (assuming that other limits on interrogation, such as *Miranda* warnings, are followed)? Consider the following problem.

### Problem 11-2A.   Counsel for Which Offense?

Raymond Levi Cobb was indicted for the burglary of a home in August 1994. Hal Ridley was appointed to represent him. Cobb said he knew nothing about the murder of the woman and child who lived in the home, and he was not initially indicted for the killings. Shortly after Ridley's appointment, investigators asked and received his permission to question Cobb about the killings. Cobb continued to deny involvement. Investigators spoke with Cobb again in September 1995 (with Ridley's permission) and again obtained no confession.

In November 1995, while free on bond on the burglary charge, Cobb confessed to his father that he had killed the woman and child. Cobb's father gave a statement to the authorities, and they arrested Cobb. Police questioned Cobb again—this time without contacting Ridley for permission. Cobb waived his rights after a full *Miranda* warning and confessed to the police. He was then charged with capital murder, tried, and sentenced to death.

On appeal, Cobb challenged the use of the confession, arguing that police violated his Sixth Amendment right to counsel when they interrogated him after counsel had been appointed in the burglary case. The government argued that the murders were a different case for which the right to counsel had not attached. How would you rule?

## NOTES

1. *Other charges, Sixth Amendment limits on further uncounseled interrogation: majority position.* In Texas v. Cobb, 532 U.S. 162 (2001), a sharply divided Supreme Court held that the Sixth Amendment right to counsel is "offense specific" and does not extend to offenses that are "factually related" to those that have actually been charged unless the relationship is so close that conviction on the new charges would violate federal double jeopardy standards against prosecution for the "same offense" (the so-called "*Blockburger*" test). See Chapter 14. Before *Cobb*, most federal and state courts had held that the protection against uncounseled interrogations extended at least to new charges that were factually related. See, e.g., Whittlesey v. State, 665 A.2d 223 (Md. 1995). In *Cobb* itself, the Texas Court of Criminal Appeals read federal law such that "once the right to counsel attaches to the offense charged, it also attaches to any other offense that is very closely related factually to the offense charged." Lower federal courts and state courts applying federal law will now be bound by *Cobb*. Many state court decisions on this question have lacked clarity on whether they were applying federal law, state law, or both. Now state courts will be asked to clarify their position. Are state courts applying state law likely to follow the federal lead?

2. *Other charges, lawyers' duties: majority position.* What would a judge say if a lawyer refused to handle related charges after an initial appointment? If the court would find that the attorney's ethical duty to zealously represent her client would extend to new, related charges, then how can the Sixth Amendment's "shield" be limited to the offense rather than apply to the offender, or at least to the behavior for which the offender is being prosecuted? There is a substantial literature on the range of important questions related to the defense attorney's ethical obligation to her client. See, e.g., Fred Zacharias, "The Civil-Criminal

Distinction in Professional Responsibility," 7 J. Contemp. Legal Issues 165 (1996); Monroe Freedman, Lawyers' Ethics in an Adversary System (1975); David Luban, "Are Criminal Defenders Different?," 91 Mich. L. Rev. 1729 (1993). See also ABA Model Rule of Professional Conduct 4.2 (2001) (lawyer is generally prohibited from communicating with a person known to be represented by counsel "about the subject of the representation" without counsel's consent).

## B. Selection and Rejection of Counsel

**Page 846 (page 844 in Police paperback; page 42 in Prosecution paperback).** Add this material after note 8.

9. *Self-representation on appeal.* In Martinez v. Court of Appeal of California, 528 U.S. 152 (2000), the Supreme Court refused to extend the *Faretta* right of self-representation to a direct appeal. The appellate courts may properly appoint counsel for the appellant, even if the appellant objects. Are trial judges better able than appellate judges to manage the difficulties presented by defendants who represent themselves? Are a defendant's interests in self-representation stronger at trial than during an appeal?

## C. Adequacy of Counsel

**Page 860 (page 858 in Police paperback; page 56 in Prosecution paperback).** Replace the *Durpree* case with the following material.

### People v. Nicholas Benevento
697 N.E.2d 584 (N.Y. 1998)

SMITH, J.

. . . Shortly after 2:00 A.M. on June 17, 1993, the complainant was walking down Bleecker Street in Manhattan when she noticed a man following closely behind her. After a brief verbal exchange with defendant, she crossed the street and turned away. At this point, defendant ran up behind her and knocked her to the ground. Defendant began slapping and punching the woman in the face while screaming obscenities at her. . . . When some bystanders approached to assist the woman, defendant stole $15 from her pocket and ran off. Chased by the group, defendant discarded the stolen money but ultimately surrendered to one of his pursuers.

As he was escorted to the crime scene, defendant admitted to stealing the complainant's money. Defendant made a similar confession to the police officers upon his arrest and confessed a third time to an Assistant District Attorney during later questioning. Defendant tried to explain that, prior to the incident, he had been drinking "a lot of Jack Daniels," and, upon observing the complainant, he "said something stupid to her and then went crazy on her." Defendant was indicted and charged with robbery in the second degree.

From his opening statement to the jury, defense counsel indicated that his strategy was to convince the jury that defendant lacked the requisite intent to deprive the complainant of her property. While counsel conceded that defendant assaulted the complainant, counsel argued "that there [was] abundant doubt, not just reasonable doubt that [defendant] intended to deprive the complaining witness of any property whatsoever," an essential element to convict defendant of the sole crime charged in the indictment. In light of that strategy, counsel noted that defendant already had $200 on his person at the time of the alleged robbery. Counsel also adduced evidence that defendant was too intoxicated to form the requisite intent. Although counsel did not highlight the evidence of intoxication during his summation to the jury, he requested and received a jury instruction in that regard.

Defendant points to counsel's other efforts that he now claims were deficient. For example, counsel indicated during his opening statement that defendant would testify as to a lack of intent, but defendant ultimately did not take the stand. Counsel also . . . delivered a summation and used hypotheticals that the Trial Judge ruled, on objection by the People, irrelevant to the case. Nevertheless, counsel's summation reiterated the primary strategy of the defense, that defendant lacked the requisite intent to deprive the complainant of her property.

The jury convicted defendant of second degree robbery. . . . A majority at the Appellate Division found that the trial record

188

demonstrated that defendant had not received "meaningful assistance" because counsel's conduct indicated "no discernible defense strategy."

. . . An essential ingredient in our system of criminal jurisprudence, rooted deeply in our concept of a fair trial within the adversarial context, is the right to the assistance of counsel guaranteed under both the Federal and State Constitutions. The constitutional mandate extends to the giving of "effective" aid which generally means the reasonably competent services of an attorney devoted to the client's best interests. The fundamental right to the effective assistance of counsel is recognized not for its own sake, but because of the effect it has on the ability of the accused to receive a fair trial in an adversarial system of justice.

The phrase "effective assistance" is not, however, amenable to precise demarcation applicable in all cases. See People v. Baldi, 429 N.E.2d 400 (N.Y. 1981) ("what constitutes effective assistance . . . varies according to the unique circumstances of each representation"). Thus, this Court has long applied a flexible standard to analyze claims based upon a deprivation of rights guaranteed under the New York State Constitution due to counsel's alleged ineffectiveness. As we have held, "so long as the evidence, the law, and the circumstances of a particular case, viewed in totality and as of the time of the representation, reveal that the attorney provided meaningful representation, the constitutional requirement will have been met." People v. Baldi. The core of the inquiry is whether defendant received "meaningful representation."

In applying this standard, counsel's efforts should not be second-guessed with the clarity of hindsight to determine how the defense might have been more effective. The Constitution guarantees the accused a fair trial, not necessarily a perfect one. That a defendant was convicted may have little to do with counsel's performance, and courts are properly skeptical when "disappointed prisoners try their former lawyers on charges of incompetent representation." People v. Brown, 165 N.E.2d 557 (N.Y. 1960).

Accordingly, a reviewing court must avoid confusing true ineffectiveness with mere losing tactics and according undue significance to retrospective analysis. Rather, it is incumbent on defendant to demonstrate the absence of strategic or other legitimate explanations for counsel's alleged shortcomings. Counsel's performance should be objectively evaluated to determine whether it was consistent with strategic decisions of a reasonably competent attorney. As long as the defense reflects a reasonable and legitimate strategy under the circumstances and evidence presented, even if unsuccessful, it will not fall to the level of ineffective assistance. . . .

The Federal standard for claims of ineffective assistance based upon a counsel's performance was set forth by the Supreme Court in Strickland v. Washington. The two-part *Strickland* test requires a showing that counsel's performance was deficient and that the deficiency in performance prejudiced defendant. [P]rior to Strickland, we had developed a somewhat different test for ineffective assistance of counsel under article I, §6 of the New York Constitution from that employed by the Supreme Court in applying the Sixth Amendment. Under the State Constitution, "prejudice" is examined more generally in the context of whether defendant received meaningful representation.

The question is whether the attorney's conduct constituted "egregious and prejudicial" error such that defendant did not receive a fair trial. Stated another way, a court must examine whether counsel's acts or omissions prejudiced the defense or defendant's right to a fair trial. While the inquiry focuses on the quality of the representation provided to the accused, the claim of ineffectiveness is ultimately concerned with the fairness of the process as a whole rather than its particular impact on the outcome of the case. [W]hether defendant would have been acquitted of the charges but for counsel's errors is relevant, but not dispositive under the State constitutional guarantee of effective assistance of counsel. The safeguards provided under the Constitution must be applied in all cases to be effective and, for that reason, our legal system is concerned as much with the integrity of the judicial process as with the issue of guilt or innocence.

Applying the well-settled *Baldi* test to the facts before us, we conclude that this defendant received effective assistance of counsel. Far from being inconsistent with reasonable representation, counsel logically attempted to disprove an element of the charged crime — a standard defense tactic. The claimed deficiencies in counsel's performance do not undercut the conclusion that defendant, who had previously confessed to the crime, received meaningful representation. The defense strategy remained clear from counsel's opening remarks through his summation. Counsel supported the strategy by introducing evidence of intoxication and requesting relevant jury instructions. Moreover, counsel's ultimate decision not to call defendant to the stand — albeit following representations to the contrary made in opening remarks — does not constitute an objectively incompetent performance. Thus, defendant was provided with meaningful representation.

In light of our conclusion, we have no occasion to consider whether we should adopt *Strickland* or otherwise abandon our discrete approach which predates the Supreme Court's formulation of the Federal standard.

**Page 861 (page 859 in Police paperback; page 57 in Prosecution paperback).   Add the following material to note 1.**

New York takes a minority position when it rejects the *Strickland* framework, but New York is not alone. See State v. Smith, 712 P.2d 496 (Haw. 1986); Briones v. State, 848 P.2d 966 (Haw. 1993). Is there any functional difference between the New York test and the federal standard? While *Benevento* has been raised and cited in more than 50 appellate decisions in two years, not one of these decisions finds ineffective assistance. In People v. Wright, 681 N.Y.S.2d 803 (N.Y. App. Div. 1999), the court found effective assistance of counsel where the lawyer had failed to meet with the client before filing a motion that required factual details. Similarly in Hawaii, no published case applying the more liberal effectiveness standards of *Briones* has found ineffective assistance.

**Page 862 (page 860 in Police paperback; page 58 in Prosecution paperback).   Add the following material to note 2.**

The U.S. Supreme Court has issued a series of recent rulings on this cluster of questions. See Roe v. Flores-Ortega, 528 U.S. 470 (2000) (ineffectiveness often present but not presumed when counsel fails to consult client about appeal and misses deadline for filing notice of appeal); Glover v. United States, 531 U.S. 198 (2001) (increase in prison sentence due to inadequate performance by attorney does not have to meet any particular "significance" threshhold to qualify as potential prejudice); Mickens v. Taylor, 122 S. Ct. 1227 (2002) (defendant must show prejudice where defense lawyer had potential conflict of interest based on former representation of murder victim in juvenile proceedings; conflict of interest must be actual before prejudice is presumed).

**Page 868 (page 866 in Police paperback; page 64 in Prosecution paperback).   Add the following material to note 3.**

For one effort to obtain more monitoring benefits from ineffective assistance claims, see Rule 13 of the Rules of the Supreme Court of the State of Hawaii. Under Rule 13, after a conviction has been overturned because of ineffective assistance of counsel, the Supreme Court appoints a special master to "determine whether action against the counsel alleged to have been incompetent is warranted." The special master can recommend "corrective action" against the attorney such as remedial education, suspension of the attorney's license to practice law, and referral to the state legal ethics authorities.

## D.  Systems for Providing Counsel

**Page 894 (page 892 in Police paperback; page 90 in Prosecution paperback).   Add the following material to note 7.**

For an effort to contrast the "ex post" evaluation of a lawyer's performance under *Strickland* with an "ex ante" evaluation of the resources available to prosecution and defense, see Donald Dripps, Ineffective Assistance of Counsel: The Case for an Ex Ante Parity Standard, 88 J. Crim. L. & Criminology 242-308 (1997); cf. Albert Alschuler, Personal Failure, Institutional Failure, and the Sixth Amendment, 14 N.Y.U. Rev. L. & Soc. Change 149 (1986).

## E.  The Ethics of Defending Criminals

**Page 906 (page 904 in Police paperback; page 102 in Prosecution paperback).   Add the following material after note 2.**

3.  *Asking the question.*  Some of the justifications for representing potentially guilty defendants depend on the possibility (however slim) that a client could be innocent of the charges. If a defense lawyer learns that a particular client did indeed commit the crime as charged, what

justifications remain for going forward with the case? Should a defense lawyer ever ask a client, "Are you guilty?" Experienced lawyers give different answers to this question. Some insist on asking their clients, because they believe they cannot prepare a good defense unless they know "the whole truth." Others do not ask, because they believe the answer would be irrelevant to the defense.

During the 1997 trial of Timothy McVeigh, who was ultimately convicted of bombing a federal courthouse in Oklahoma City and killing hundreds of people, reports circulated that McVeigh had confessed to his lawyers. The lead defense attorney, Stephen Jones, appeared on a nationally televised talk show to discuss the case with the viewers:

*Host*:    Tulsa, Oklahoma. Hello.
*Oklahoma Caller*:    Yes, Mr. Jones, assuming McVeigh told you he was guilty, and assuming you got him off, how can you live with yourself morally the rest of your life?
*Jones*:    Well, I think that's a fair question.
*Host*:    It is.
*Jones*:    I'm not a judge. I'm a defense lawyer. I don't ask a client whether they're guilty. I ask them to tell me what happened. And then I compare what they tell me with what the evidence is. It's the prosecution's job to prosecute him, the jury's job to judge the facts, my job to represent him. That's the system, has been the system for over 250 years. I don't have trouble sleeping at night. I have confidence in the system.

CNN Larry King Live, March 17, 1997 (Transcript #97031700V22). How might the Oklahoma caller respond to Jones's answer?

# Chapter 12 / 2

# Pretrial Release
# and Detention

## A.  Pretrial Release

**Page 921 (Prosecution paperback page 117).    Add this material to note 2.**

The average rate of failure to appear based on nationwide data in 1992 was about 25 percent, with jurisdictions varying between 2 percent and 56 percent. See John Clark and D. Alan Henry, The Pretrial Release Decision, 81 Judicature 76, 77 (Sept.-Oct. 1997).

**Page 922 (Prosecution paperback page 118).    Add this material to note 3.**

Based on 1992 data gathered in 40 large urban jurisdictions in the United States, bonding agents were available as a method of pretrial release in at least 37 percent of all felony cases. See John Clark and D. Alan Henry, The Pretrial Release Decision, 81 Judicature 76, 77 (Sept.-Oct. 1997).

**Page 940 (Prosecution paperback page 136).    Add this material to note 5.**

All 50 states have passed statutes offering protections to victims during the criminal justice process, and about 30 have given some of these protections constitutional status. But the implementation and effects of these laws have been uneven. According to a 1995 survey, over 60 percent of crime victims living in states with "strong" legal protections for victims were notified about the dates for bond hearings for the defendants, while about 40 percent of crime victims living in states with weaker legal provisions received this information. Almost 40 percent of victims in "strong protection" states received notice about the pretrial release of a defendant, compared to 25 percent of the victims in "weak protection" states. About 40 percent of victims in the strong states made a recommendation to the court at the bond hearing; about 25 percent in the weak states did. See Dean Kilpatrick, et al., The Rights of Crime Victims — Does Legal Protection Make a Difference? (Research in Brief) (NCJ 173839, Dec. 1998).

# B.  Pretrial Detention

**Page 941 (Prosecution paperback page 137).    Replace the provision from the Ohio Constitution with the following material.**

## TENNESSEE CONSTITUTION ART. I, §§15, 16

15. That all prisoners shall be bailable by sufficient sureties, unless for capital offences, when the proof is evident or the presumption great. And the privilege of the writ of habeas corpus shall not be suspended, unless when in case of rebellion or invasion the public safety may require it.

16. That excessive bail shall not be required, nor excessive fines imposed, nor cruel and unusual punishments inflicted.

# 18 U.S.C. §3142(e), (f)

(e) If, after a hearing pursuant to the provisions of subsection (f) of this section, the judicial officer finds that no condition or combination of conditions will reasonably assure the appearance of the person as required and the safety of any other person and the community, such judicial officer shall order the detention of the person before trial. In a case described in subsection (f)(1) of this section, a rebuttable presumption arises that no condition or combination of conditions will reasonably assure the safety of any other person and the community if such judicial officer finds that —

(1) the person has been convicted of a Federal offense that is described in subsection (f)(1) of this section, or [a similar] State or local offense . . . ;

(2) the offense described in paragraph (1) of this subsection was committed while the person was on release pending trial for a Federal, State, or local offense; and

(3) a period of not more than five years has elapsed since the date of conviction, or the release of the person from imprisonment, for the offense described in paragraph (1) of this subsection, whichever is later.

Subject to rebuttal by the person, it shall be presumed that no condition or combination of conditions will reasonably assure the appearance of the person as required and the safety of the community if the judicial officer finds that there is probable cause to believe that the person committed an offense for which a maximum term of imprisonment of ten years or more is prescribed in the [federal laws proscribing drug trafficking and crimes of violence].

(f) The judicial officer shall hold a hearing to determine whether any condition or combination of conditions . . . will reasonably assure the appearance of the person as required and the safety of any other person and the community —

(1) upon motion of the attorney for the Government, in a case that involves — (A) a crime of violence; (B) an offense for which the maximum sentence is life imprisonment or death; (C) an offense for which a maximum term of imprisonment of ten years or more is prescribed in the [federal drug trafficking laws]; (D) any felony if the person has been convicted of two or more offenses described in

subparagraphs (A) through (C) of this paragraph, or two or more [similar] State or local offenses . . . , or a combination of such offenses; or

(2) Upon motion of the attorney for the Government or upon the judicial officer's own motion, in a case that involves — (A) a serious risk that the person will flee; or (B) a serious risk that the person will obstruct or attempt to obstruct justice, or threaten, injure, or intimidate, or attempt to threaten, injure, or intimidate, a prospective witness or juror. . . .

The facts the judicial officer uses to support a finding pursuant to subsection (e) that no condition or combination of conditions will reasonably assure the safety of any other person and the community shall be supported by clear and convincing evidence. . . .

**Page 951 (Prosecution paperback page 147).    Replace note 1 with the following material.**

1. *Preventive detention: majority position.* Like the federal system, about half the states authorize courts to detain defendants before trial for the purpose of preventing the commission of new crimes ("preventive detention"). On the other hand, about 25 states have constitutional provisions that, like Tennessee, guarantee the right to bail except in capital cases. Detention based on risk of future crime is often distinguished from detention based on fear of flight or threat to witnesses. Do the categories of fear of flight or threat to witnesses overlap with risk of future crime? Most of the roughly 25 states addressing the subject of preventive detention since the federal Bail Reform Act of 1984 was passed have authorized detention. See, e.g., Md. Code art. 27, §616½; Mass. Gen. L. ch. 276, §58A. The details vary substantially among the states, with a handful creating a presumption against bail and most allowing detention in the discretion of the court. Some states limit preventive detention to "serious crimes"; others require special hearings on future dangerousness or limit detention to offenders with specific combinations of prior record and sufficiently serious current charges. A handful of states have enacted limits on the maximum time a defendant may be detained to prevent crimes. See, e.g., Mass. Gen. L. ch. 276, §58A (90 days); Wis. Stat. §969-035 (60 days). Why have so many states continued to reject preventive detention laws

over the more than 10 years since passage of the federal Bail Reform Act and the decision of the Supreme Court in *Salerno*? Are other states likely, over time, to make the statutory and constitutional changes necessary to allow preventive detention? Some state constitutional provisions that seemed to bar the use of preventive detention have either been amended by the voters (e.g., Ohio Const. art. I, §9 was amended in 1997) or read restrictively to avoid any inconsistency with a new preventive detention statute. See State v. Ayala, 610 A.2d 1162 (Conn. 1992). See also Mo. Rev. Stat. §544.457 (allowing preventive detention "notwithstanding" constitutional guarantee of bail).

**Page 954 (Prosecution paperback page 150).    Add this material to note 6.**

The number of defendants detained in the federal system is creeping upward. While 29.1 percent of the federal defendants in 1992 were detained without bail, the number had reached 34 percent by 1996. Bureau of Justice Statistics, Federal Pretrial Release and Detention, 1996 (NCJ 168635 Feb. 1999). Of those federal defendants released pending trial, almost two-thirds were released on their own recognizance or on an unsecured bond.

**Page 954 (Prosecution paperback page 150). Add this material after note 8.**

9. *Detention after completion of sentence.* States are now using post-sentence detention to control some persons convicted of sex offenses. Statutes passed since the mid-1990s authorize the government to request continued detention of convicted sex offenders after they have completed their sentences. These statutes typically require the government to demonstrate, on a year-to-year basis, that the offender remains "dangerous." The Supreme Court has upheld such a statute against challenges based on the due process, ex post facto, and double jeopardy clause of the federal constitution. Kansas v. Hendricks, 521 U.S. 346 (1997). Employing the same distinction that it used in *Salerno*, the court said that this detention was "regulatory" rather than "punitive." See also Kansas v. Crane, 534 U.S. 407 (2002) (constitution does not require judicial finding of total or complete lack of control to support regulatory detention of sexual offender, but Constitution does require a showing that person does lack some control over his or her behavior).

# Chapter 13 / 3

# Charging

## A. Police Screening

**Page 961 (Prosecution paperback page 157).** **Add this material at the end of note 2.**

A practice resembling the use of police courts has developed in England. Because the police in England make the initial decision whether to prosecute a criminal case, a practice has grown up (without a statutory basis) known as a "police caution." The caution is a warning to an arrested person, delivered by a senior police officer. If the person accepts the caution, the police agree not to refer the case to the Crown Prosecution Service. The caution becomes part of the offender's prior record. The Home Secretary has issued "National Standards for Cautioning" to guide police decisions in this area. See Home Office Circular 18/1994, The Cautioning of Offenders; Andrew Ashworth, The Criminal Process (2d ed. 1998). Does the consent of the suspect (when he accepts a caution) make the caution fundamentally different from a conviction in police court?

# B. *Prosecutorial Screening*

## 2.   Encouraging or Mandating Criminal Charges

**Page 993 (Prosecution paperback page 189).    Add this material at the end of note 3.**

The relationship between no-drop policies and shall-arrest policies is not yet well understood. According to one analysis of arrest and prosecution records in domestic violence cases in Ann Arbor and Ypsilanti, Michigan, a shall-arrest policy leads to more frequent dismissal of charges and to more frequent acquittals after trial. Andrea Lyon, Be Careful What You Wish For: An Examination of Arrest and Prosecution Patterns of Domestic Violence Cases in Two Cities in Michigan, 5 Mich. J. Gender & L. 253-298 (1999). The same study found that the police arrested women in 12 percent of the cases. If the police found out about a prior history of abuse, they were more likely to arrest a man. On the other hand, if they had been called to that residence before, they were more likely to arrest a woman — possibly a form of retaliation against women for staying in an abusive situation.

**Page 994 (Prosecution paperback page 190).    Add this material after note 5.**

6. *Prosecutorial office structure.* Although the criminal code might give prosecutors huge amounts of discretion over whether to file criminal charges, the legislature or the chief prosecutor might structure the prosecutor's office in ways that will encourage the filing of some criminal charges and discourage the filing of others. For instance, the office might have specialized units, whose work is easy to monitor. Line items in budgets give strong incentives to pursue certain charges. Some investigative techniques or charging decisions require special authorization from those high in the prosecutorial hierarchy. As Professor Daniel Richman points out, these office structures operate as predictable limits on the reach of substantive criminal law, even when those criminal laws are drafted very broadly and delegate nominally large powers to the prosecutor. Richman, Federal Criminal Law,

Congressional Delegation, and Enforcement Discretion, 46 UCLA L. Rev. 757 (1999).

## 3.   Selection of Charges and System

### b. Selection of System

**Page 1018 (Prosecution paperback page 214).   Add this material at the end of note 1.**

Franklin Zimring's recent study indicates that, despite major changes in the laws dealing with the assignment of juveniles to the adult criminal justice system, the legal changes have made little or no difference in the numbers of juvenile cases actually resolved in the adult system. See Zimring, American Youth Violence (1998). In 1994, about 1 percent of all felony defendants in the nation's 75 largest counties were juveniles. Two-thirds of the juveniles transferred to criminal court were charged with a violent offense; 59 percent of the juveniles transferred were convicted of a felony. In the 75 largest counties in 1994, almost 2 percent of juveniles older than age 14 were transferred to adult criminal courts by judicial waiver. See Bureau of Justice Statistics, Juvenile Felony Defendants in Criminal Courts (Sept. 1998, NCJ 165815).

**Page 1019 (Prosecution paperback page 215).   Add this material after note 6.**

7. *Disparate racial impact in juvenile justice.* A report funded by the U.S. Department of Justice and several private foundations, released in April 2000, documented some major disparities in the treatment of white and black defendants in the juvenile justice system. Some of the findings of the report are as follows:

> It is clear that minority youth are more likely than others to come into contact with the juvenile justice system. Research suggests that this disparity is most pronounced at the beginning stages of involvement with the juvenile justice system.  When racial / ethnic differences are found, they tend to accumulate as youth are processed through the system. . . .

• In 1998, African American youth were overrepresented as a proportion of arrests in 26 of 29 offense categories documented by the FBI.
• In 1997, the majority of cases referred to juvenile court involved White youth. Minority youth were overrepresented in the referral cohort.
• While White youth comprised 66 percent of the juvenile court referral population they comprised 53 percent of the detained population. In contrast, African American youths made up 31 percent of the referral population and 44 percent of the detained population. . . .
• African American youth are more likely than White youth to be formally charged in juvenile court, even when referred for the same type of offense.
• Although just over half of drug cases involving White youth and youth of other races result in formal processing, three-quarters of drug cases involving African American youth result in formal processing.
• Minority youth were much more likely to be waived to adult criminal court named White youth. This was true in whole offense categories.
• For offenses against persons, White youth were 57 percent of cases petitioned but only 45 percent of cases waived to adult court. African American youth charged with similar offenses were 40 percent of the cases petitioned but rose to 50 percent of cases waived to adult court. Similarly, in drug cases, White youth were 59 percent of cases petitioned but only 35 percent of cases waived to adult court. African American youth charged with drug offenses were 39 percent of cases petitioned but rose 263 percent of the cases waived to adult court. With us, among drug offense cases referred to juvenile court, White youth enjoy a 24 percent "waiver advantage," while African American youth carry a 24 percent "waiver disadvantage."
• African American youth were overrepresented among cases receiving a disposition of out-of-home placement (e.g., commitment to a locked institution). This was true in offense categories and was most pronounced among drug offense cases. . . .
• In 1993, when controlling for current offense and prior admissions, incarceration rates to state public facilities were higher for African American and Latino youth than White youth.
• When White youth and minority youth were charged with the same offenses, African American youth with no prior admissions were six times more likely to be incarcerated in public facilities in White youth with the same background. Latino youth were three times more likely than White youth to be incarcerated.
• In 1993, African American youth were confined on average for 61 days more than White youth, and Latino youth were confined 112 days more than white youth.

Eileen Poe-Yamagata & Michael Jones, "And Justice for Some" (Building Blocks for Youth, 2000). The racial disparities described in the report are larger than disparities found in some studies of the adult criminal justice system. As a legislator, how would you respond to this study? Would you argue to transfer fewer juveniles into the adult system (even though the racial disparities in the adult system might be smaller overall)? To make the juvenile system less discretionary?


**Page 1020 (page 216 in Prosecution paperback).   Add this material after Problem 13-2 (Problem 3-2 in Prosecution paperback).**

## NOTE

*The federalization trend.* The federal government has been exerting more authority and money on criminal matters during the last few decades than at any previous point in the nation's history. The 1999 report of the American Bar Association's Task Force on Federalization of Criminal Law documents various aspects of this growth. Federal crime legislation has become more common: "more than forty percent of the federal criminal provisions enacted since the Civil War have been enacted since 1970." The number of federal investigators and prosecutors has expanded along with the number of available federal crimes. The types of cases making up the federal criminal docket have also shifted in recent decades. Federal theft and forgery cases have become less common; the number of federal fraud cases have increased. Narcotics offenses have increased more than any other category (18 percent of the caseload in 1977 and 36 percent in 1997). The report lists some negative consequences of federalization: "diminution of the stature of the state courts in the perception of citizens" and "disparate results for the same conduct." What would be a legitimate basis for extending federal law to criminalize additional conduct? Would the same arguments support a new emphasis in enforcing existing federal laws?


## 4.   Selective Prosecution

**Page 1029 (Prosecution paperback page 225).   Add this material after note 4.**

5. *Racial discrimination and written charging policies.* Do charging policies reduce the likelihood that individual prosecutors will consider race as a factor in charging decisions? As we saw earlier in this

chapter, the state of Washington has passed a statute instructing prosecutors on the general factors to consider when making a charging decision. See pages 968–969 (Prosecution paperback pages 164–165). A 1994 study of King County, Washington (where written office policies supplement the state statutes) attempted to determine whether race influenced the charging decisions of prosecutors. See Larry Michael Fehr, Racial and Ethnic Disparities in Prosecution and Sentencing: Empirical Research of the Washington State Minority and Justice Commission, 32 Gonz. L. Rev. 577 (1996/97). The study found that white defendants were charged in 60 percent of the cases referred to prosecutors, while black defendants were charged in 65 percent. The researchers could explain only part of this difference based on legally relevant factors, such as the type of crime involved.

6. *Prosecution in the sunshine.* Would prosecutors benefit or lose more from the collection and publication of data on the race of every defendant and victim for every criminal matter the office encounters? If a chief prosecutor were to carry out this policy (either voluntarily or pursuant to a statute), would she want to show the data broken down by type of crime and by the action the office chose to pursue? If you believe prosecutors would resist the collection and publication of such data, what arguments might they raise against this proposal? What if the legislature were willing to provide funds for any extra personnel needed to collect and analyze the data? See Angela J. Davis, Prosecution and Race: The Power and Privilege of Discretion, 67 Fordham L. Rev. 13 (1998) (proposing a requirement that prosecutors publish "racial impact studies").

# Chapter 14 / 4

# Jeopardy and Joinder

## A. Double Jeopardy

### 2. "Same Offence"

#### a. Defining "Offences"

**Page 1077 (Prosecution paperback page 273).** **Replace the paragraph before the *Lessary* opinion with the following material.**

509 U.S. at 704, 709-711. The first of the following two cases shows the *Blockburger* test at work. The second case discusses the choices among different tests for the "same offense" and illustrates the response of state courts to the leadership of the U.S. Supreme Court in this difficult area.

## Robert Taylor v. Commonwealth
### 995 S.W.2d 355 (Ky. 1999)

COOPER, J.

. . . On the afternoon of October 9, 1996, Appellant, then seventeen years of age, his girlfriend, Lucy Cotton, and Cotton's infant son had attended the Daniel Boone Festival and were traveling through rural Knox County in a 1985 Buick owned by Cotton's mother. They had with them a .22 rifle, a .38 Derringer handgun, and two shotguns. When the vehicle stalled, Appellant sought assistance from Herman McCreary, who lived nearby. McCreary agreed to help and drove his 1984 Ford pickup truck to the location of the stalled vehicle. Upon arrival, he observed Cotton sitting in the passenger seat of the Buick holding a child in her lap. Several attempts to jump-start the Buick failed. According to Cotton, Appellant told her, "If it don't start this time, I'm gonna take his truck," and armed himself with the .22 rifle and the .38 handgun. According to Appellant, Cotton pointed the .38 handgun at him and threatened to shoot him if he did not steal McCreary's truck.

When a final attempt to jump-start the Buick was unsuccessful, Appellant got out of the vehicle, pointed the .22 rifle at McCreary, and ordered him to lie on the ground. When McCreary complied, Appellant fired a round from the rifle into the ground near McCreary's head. According to Cotton, Appellant then struck McCreary in the head with the stock of the rifle. McCreary temporarily lost consciousness. Upon regaining consciousness, McCreary experienced dizziness and noticed blood coming from the left side of his head. Appellant then told McCreary to get into the ditch beside the road or he would "blow his head off." McCreary again complied, whereupon Appellant, Cotton and the child departed the scene in McCreary's truck. McCreary walked to a neighbor's house and called the police. [Taylor and Cotton were later apprehended and Taylor was convicted of assault in second degree, robbery in first degree, and possession of handgun by a minor. Taylor] asserts that his convictions violated the constitutional proscription against double jeopardy. U.S. Const. amend. V; Ky. Const. §13.

In Commonwealth v. Burge, 947 S.W.2d 805, 809-11 (1997), we reinstated the "*Blockburger* rule," Blockburger v. United States, 284 U.S. 299 (1932), as incorporated in KRS §505.020, as the sole basis for determining whether multiple convictions arising out of a single course of conduct constitutes double jeopardy. The test in this case is not whether all three convictions were premised upon the use or possession of a firearm, or whether both the assault and the robbery occurred in the course of a single transaction. "The applicable rule is that, where the same act or transaction constitutes a violation of two distinct statutory provisions, the test to be applied to determine whether there are two offenses or only one is whether each provision requires proof of an additional fact which the other does not." Blockburger v. United States, 284 U.S. 299, 304 (1932).

KRS §515.020(1) defines robbery in the first degree as follows:

A person is guilty of robbery in the first degree when, in the course of committing a theft, he uses or threatens the immediate use of physical force upon another person with intent to accomplish the theft and when he:
>   (a) Causes physical injury to any person who is not a participant in the crime; or
>   (b) Is armed with a deadly weapon; or
>   (c) Uses or threatens the use of a dangerous instrument upon any person who is not a participant in the crime.

The first paragraph of the statute sets forth three elements which must be proven in any robbery case, viz: (1) In the course of committing a theft, (2) the defendant used or threatened the immediate use of physical force upon another person (3) with the intent to accomplish the theft. Subsections (a), (b), and (c) of the statute then describe three separate and distinct factual situations, any one of which could constitute the fourth element of the offense. The indictment of Appellant for robbery in the first degree in this case charged that he committed the offense "by being armed with a deadly weapon." The jury was instructed that it could convict Appellant of robbery in the first degree only if it believed beyond a reasonable doubt that "when he did so, he was armed with a .22 rifle." Thus, both the indictment and the instruction were predicated upon a violation of KRS 515.020(1)(b). Neither the indictment nor the instruction required Appellant to have caused a physical injury to McCreary or to have used or threatened the use of a dangerous instrument upon McCreary.

KRS 508.020(1) defines assault in the second degree as follows:

A person is guilty of assault in the second degree when:
>   (a) He intentionally causes serious physical injury to another person; or
>   (b) He intentionally causes physical injury to another person by means of a deadly weapon or a dangerous instrument; or
>   (c) He wantonly causes serious physical injury to another person by means of a deadly weapon or a dangerous instrument.

The statute sets forth three alternative factual situations by which the offense can be committed. Although the indictment charged Appellant with having committed the offense "by striking Herman McCreary with a pistol," the jury instruction conformed to the testimony of Lucy Cotton, who provided the only evidence with respect to this offense:

You will find the defendant guilty under this instruction if, and only if, you believe from the evidence beyond a reasonable doubt all of the following: (a) that in this county on or about October 9, 1996 and before the finding of the indictment herein, he inflicted an injury upon Herman McCreary by striking him with a .22 rifle, a deadly weapon; AND (b) that in so doing, the defendant intentionally caused physical injury to Herman McCreary.[1]

Thus, conviction of either the assault or the robbery of McCreary required proof of an element not required to prove the other. The conviction of robbery required proof of a theft, which was not required to convict of assault. The conviction of assault required proof of a physical injury to McCreary, whereas the conviction of robbery required proof only that Appellant used or threatened the use of physical force upon McCreary while armed with a .22 rifle. . . .

STUMBO, J., dissenting.

Respectfully, I must dissent. I believe Appellant's convictions for both assault and robbery violated the prohibition against double jeopardy. I would first note that, under the *Burge* test, the trial court correctly refused to dismiss the assault charge in the indictment. As written, the indictment did not violate the double jeopardy prohibition. The indictment charged Appellant with "Assault in the Second Degree by striking Herman McCreary with a pistol" and "Robbery in the First Degree by being armed with a deadly weapon while in the course of committing a theft of Herman McCreary." Clearly, these offenses arise from two distinct statutes. As charged, each would have required proof of a fact which the other did not. For the assault, the prosecution would have had to prove that Appellant struck McCreary with the .38 pistol causing a physical injury. For the robbery, the prosecution would have

---

1.  Appellant did not object to the variance of this instruction from the language of the indictment. The indictment described the weapon used to inflict the injury as a pistol, whereas the instruction described the weapon as a .22 rifle. Generally, instructions should be based on the evidence introduced at trial, and any variance between the language of the indictment and the language of the instruction is not deemed prejudicial unless the defendant was misled.

had to prove Appellant used or threatened to use physical force on McCreary while armed with a deadly weapon (presumably the .22 rifle) during the course of the theft of his truck.

In the end, however, the prosecution was unable to maintain this logically sound but practically impossible distinction. By the time the jury was instructed, the assault had merged into the robbery so that one was clearly included within the other. This is so because the jury instruction on second-degree assault required the jury to find the offense was accomplished "by striking him with a .22 rifle, a deadly weapon." The jury instruction on first-degree robbery required the jury to find Appellant "used or threatened the immediate use of physical force upon Herman McCreary; AND (c) that when he did so, he was armed with a .22 rifle." This melding of the charges allowed the jury to consider any assault with the .22 rifle during the incident as an element of the robbery and thus made the assault charge a lesser included offense of the robbery charge. Appellant may be convicted of only one of these offenses without violating the prohibition against double jeopardy. Burge v. Commonwealth, 947 S.W.2d at 805, 811 (1997). Therefore, I would vacate the conviction on the lesser charge of assault in the second degree.

**Page 1084 (Prosecution paperback page 280).   Replace notes 1 through 3 with the following material.**

1.   *Determining whether two charges are the "same offence": majority position.* The Supreme Court's decision in United States v. Dixon, 509 U.S. 688 (1993), reestablished the "same elements" test of Blockburger v. United States, 284 U.S. 299 (1932). Under this test, if the two offenses *each* have at least one distinct "element," they are not treated as the same offense. Hence, multiple trials or multiple punishments based on these offenses do not violate the protection against double jeopardy.

About 30 state courts follow *Dixon* and have adopted (or readopted) the *Blockburger* "same elements" test under state law. See, e.g., City of Fargo v. Hector, 534 N.W.2d 821 (N.D. 1995); State v. Kurzawa, 509 N.W.2d 712 (Wis. 1994). About 10 jurisdictions, like the Hawaii Supreme Court in *Lessary,* have interpreted their state constitutions to employ the *Grady* "same conduct" test (or the closely related "same evidence" test) in addition to the *Blockburger* analysis as a limit on multiple prosecutions. A smaller group of states (about a half dozen) apply a test that places even stronger limits on government attempts to bring multiple prosecutions: the "same transaction" test (also called the "same episode" or "same incident" test) suggested by Justice Brennan in his concurring opinion in Ashe v. Swenson, 397 U.S. 436 (1970). See, e.g., People v. Harding, 506 N.W.2d 482 (Mich. 1993); State v. Farley, 725 P.2d 359 (Or. 1986).

Around 15 states have adopted statutory tests for whether a second charge is for the "same offense"; some statutes mirror the *Blockburger* test, Fla. Stat. §775.021(4)(a), while others add a "same facts" or "same conduct" test. Some states apply different tests at different times or refer to both the "same offense" and "same transaction" tests. See, e.g., La. Code Crim. Proc. art. 596.

There is no shortage of suggestions in the academic literature for reworking this doctrine from the ground up. See Akhil Amar, Double Jeopardy Law Made Simple, 106 Yale L.J. 1807 (1997) (suggests due process rather than double jeopardy as remedy for vexatious litigation); George Thomas, A Blameworthy Act Approach to the Double Jeopardy Same Offense Problem, 83 Cal. L. Rev. 1027, 1041-1049 (1995) (looks to blameworthiness rather than *Blockburger* as best indicator of legislative intent as to multiple punishment and trials).

2. *Punishment for greater and lesser included offenses.* A lesser included offense is one that is necessarily included within the statutory elements of another offense. Thus, if Crime 1 has elements A and B, it is a lesser included offense for Crime 2, with elements A, B, and C. In a straightforward application of the *Blockburger* test, a prosecution for either Crime 1 or Crime 2 would prevent a later prosecution or punishment for the second crime. An exception to this bar would allow a prosecution for Crime 2 after a prosecution for Crime 1, if the additional element C had not yet occurred at the time of the Crime 1 prosecution (for instance, if an assault victim dies after the trial for assault goes forward). See Brown v. Ohio, 432 U.S. 161, 169 n.7 (1977).

But the courts have gone beyond this literal understanding of lesser included offenses. Both federal and state courts declare that double jeopardy limits for the "same offense" also apply to "a species of lesser included offense." In Harris v. Oklahoma, 433 U.S. 682 (1977), the court held that a conviction for felony murder barred a later trial of the defendant for the underlying robbery. Strictly speaking, the robbery and felony murder statutes pass the *Blockburger* test: felony murder requires proof of a killing (robbery does not), and robbery requires proof of forcible taking of property (which felony murder does not necessarily require). But the court was willing to treat robbery and felony murder as the "same offense" because in the *case at hand*, the prosecution was relying on forcible taking of property to establish the predicate felony for felony murder. See also United States v. Dixon, 509 U.S. 688, 697-700 (1993) (criminal contempt of court for violation of judicial order not to commit "any criminal offense" and possession of cocaine with intent to distribute are the same offense). On the other hand, the same logic does not seem to apply to conspiracy or "continuing criminal enterprise" crimes. See United States v. Felix, 503 U.S. 378, 387-392 (1992) (conspiracy to manufacture narcotics is not same offense as manufacturing narcotics); Garrett v. United States, 471 U.S. 773, 777-786 (1985) (distribution of marijuana is not same offense as conducting a continuing criminal enterprise to distribute marijuana).

3.  *The "multiple punishment" prong of double jeopardy.* Unlike the relatively clear rule against multiple *prosecutions* for the same offense, there are looser limits when the prosecutor files multiple charges in a *single proceeding*, and the defendant claims that the charges are actually an attempt to impose multiple punishments for what is really a single offense. In this setting, the legislature sets the constraints on the prosecutor. In Missouri v. Hunter, 459 U.S. 359 (1983), the Supreme Court held that "the Double Jeopardy Clause does no more than prevent the sentencing court from prescribing greater punishment than the legislature intended."

Most states follow Missouri v. Hunter and hold that in the context of a single prosecution, the *Blockburger* test (or an alternative test) only helps determine whether the legislature intended to allow separate convictions and punishments for a single criminal episode or event. See, e.g., State v. Smith, 547 So. 2d 613 (Fla. 1989). The courts reason that the legislature can select from a wide range of punishments for any particular offense. Other states have rejected the majority rule and have applied state law to limit cumulative punishments regardless of the legislature's intent. See, e.g., Ingram v. Commonwealth, 801 S.W.2d 321 (Ky. 1990). In one especially difficult area, states are split on whether punishment is acceptable for both felony murder and the underlying felony when they are tried together. See, e.g., Todd v. State, 917 P.2d 674 (Alaska 1996) (allowing multiple punishment); cf. Boulies v. People, 770 P.2d 1274 (Colo. 1989) (state merger rule barring multiple punishment).

What reasons might justify the different treatment of "multiple proceedings" on the one hand, and "multiple punishment" for the same conduct in a single proceeding on the other hand? Does this distinction make sense? See Nancy King, Portioning Punishment: Constitutional Limits on Successive and Excessive Penalties, 144 U. Pa. L. Rev. 101 (1995) (points to illogic of cases allowing multiple punishments in a single trial but not in successive trials; argues for limiting Eighth Amendment to a remedy for excessive punishments imposed in multiple proceedings).

Note that the legal doctrines discussed so far all involve criminal charges and criminal proceedings. Another body of law deals with efforts by the government to impose both civil and criminal penalties for wrongdoing. In a few settings, the civil sanctions qualify as "punishment" and trigger the double jeopardy protections. Chapter 15 considers the double jeopardy aspects of forfeitures and other civil sanctions.

# Chapter 15 / 5

# Forfeiture of Assets

## A. Property Subject to Forfeiture

### 1. Instrumentalities and Proceeds

**Page 1148 (Prosecution paperback page 344).** **Add this material at the end of note 3.**

For a discussion of the "widening net" of property subject to forfeiture under federal forfeiture laws, see Jimmy Gurulé and Sandra Guerra, The Law of Asset Forfeiture, Chapter 5 (1999).

### 2. Property Exempted

**Page 1156 (Prosecution paperback page 352).** **Add this material to the end of note 1.**

The Supreme Court returned to the question of what standard to use in measuring the excessiveness of a forfeiture in United States v. Bajakajian, 524 U.S. 321 (1998). Bajakajian was waiting in the Los Angeles airport to board an international flight when a customs inspector approached him and told him that he was required to report all cash in excess of $10,000 in his possession or baggage. Bajakajian lied about the amount of cash he was holding; cash-sniffing dogs indicated the presence of currency in his luggage. Customs inspectors found $357,144.

Bajakajian pleaded guilty to the currency reporting offense, and elected to have a bench trial on the forfeiture. The trial judge found that the funds were not connected to any other crime and that Bajakajian was transporting the money to repay a lawful debt; he held that forfeiture of the entire amount was constitutionally "excessive" and reduced the forfeiture to $15,000.

The Supreme Court held that the forfeiture was a "punishment" for purposes of the Excessive Fines Clause because the statute was an *in personem* forfeiture that applied only to the property of a person who willfully fails to report the cash. The Court then described the proper method for a court to use in determining whether a forfeiture is excessive:

> The text and history of the Excessive Fines Clause demonstrate the centrality of proportionality to the excessiveness inquiry; nonetheless, they provide little guidance as to how disproportional a punitive forfeiture must be to the gravity of an offense in order to be "excessive." . . . We must therefore rely on other considerations in deriving a constitutional excessiveness standard, and there are two that we find particularly relevant. The first, which we have emphasized in our cases interpreting the Cruel and Unusual Punishments Clause, is that judgments about the appropriate punishment for an offense belong in the first instance to the legislature. See, e.g., Solem v. Helm, 463 U.S. 277, 290 (1983) ("Reviewing courts . . . should grant substantial deference to the broad authority that legislatures necessarily possess in determining the types and limits of punishments for crimes"). The second is that any judicial determination regarding the gravity of a particular criminal offense will be inherently imprecise. Both of these principles counsel against requiring strict proportionality between the amount of a punitive forfeiture and the gravity of a criminal offense, and we therefore adopt the standard of gross disproportionality articulated in our Cruel and Unusual Punishments Clause precedents. See Solem v. Helm; Rummel v. Estelle, 445 U.S. 263 (1980).
>
> In applying this standard, the district courts in the first instance, and the courts of appeals, reviewing the proportionality determination de novo, must compare the amount of the forfeiture to the gravity of the defendant's offense. If the amount of the forfeiture is grossly disproportional to the gravity of the defendant's offense, it is unconstitutional.
>
> Under this standard, the forfeiture of respondent's entire $357,144 would violate the Excessive Fines Clause. Respondent's crime was solely a reporting offense. It was permissible to transport the currency out of the country so long as he reported it. . . . Furthermore, as the District Court found, respondent's violation was unrelated to any other illegal activities. The money was the proceeds of legal activity and was to be used to repay a lawful debt. Whatever his other vices, respondent does not fit into the class of persons for whom the statute was principally designed: He is not a money launderer, a drug trafficker, or a tax evader. And under the Sentencing Guidelines, the maximum sentence that could

have been imposed on respondent was six months, while the maximum fine was $5,000. . . .

The harm that respondent caused was also minimal. Failure to report his currency affected only one party, the Government, and in a relatively minor way. There was no fraud on the United States, and respondent caused no loss to the public fisc. Had his crime gone undetected, the Government would have been deprived only of the information that $357,144 had left the country. . . . Comparing the gravity of respondent's crime with the $357,144 forfeiture the Government seeks, we conclude that such a forfeiture would be grossly disproportional to the gravity of his offense.


**Page 1158 (Prosecution paperback page 354).    Add this material after note 6.**


7. *Incentives to reduce coverage.* The fact that most of the proceeds of forfeiture proceedings directly benefit law enforcement budgets surely creates some pressure to expand forfeiture programs. See Eric Blumenson and Eva Nilsen, Policing for Profit: The Drug War's Hidden Economic Agenda, 65 U. Chi. L. Rev. 35 (1998). On the other hand, large amounts of property can be seized in clear-cut narcotics cases, and public relations nightmares can happen when the law is used in less attractive cases (for instance, when federal agents confiscated a research ship owned by the Woods Hole Oceanographic Institution after finding a tiny amount of marijuana in a crew member's shaving kit). In such a setting, will political pressures create a willingness to make exceptions in the application of forfeiture laws? See David Johnston, Reprising Zero Tolerance; History Shows That Tough Talk Is Cheap, New York Times, Jan. 31, 1999, §4 at 1 ("after the klieg-light hype, the programs are usually quietly dumped or throttled back"). The federal Customs Service now apparently administers its forfeiture program in a way that allows exceptions for many of the least culpable claimants.

# B.  Procedures for Initiating Forfeitures

**Page 1164 (Prosecution paperback page 360).    Add this material at the end of the carryover paragraph at the top of the page.**

See also Florida v. White, 526 U.S. 559 (1999) (Fourth Amendment does not require the police to obtain a warrant before seizing an automobile from a public place when they have probable cause to believe that it is forfeitable contraband).

**Page 1169 (Prosecution paperback page 365).    Add this material at the end of note 4.**

The Civil Asset Forfeiture Reform Act of 2000, P.L. No. 106-185, expands access to attorneys for parties who have some claim to property that is the subject of civil asset forfeiture proceedings in federal court. The federal government now provides legal counsel for indigent claimants of property that the government is attempting to seize, along with attorneys' fees for winning claimants. Would this expanded access to attorneys in the civil proceedings have any impact on the willingness of private defense counsel to accept a criminal case?

**Page 1170 (Prosecution paperback page 366).    Add this material after note 7.**

8. *Notice of procedures for return of property.* In City of West Covina v. Perkins, 525 U.S. 234 (1999), police officers lawfully seized personal property from the Perkins' home and left behind a notice form specifying the fact of the search and some details about the search warrant. After the Perkins failed to recover their property through administrative channels, they filed a civil suit, claiming that due process required the police officers to give them notice of the state procedures for return of seized property and the information necessary to invoke those procedures. The Supreme Court held that the due process clause does not require the police to give such notice when they seize property for a criminal investigation. It only requires individualized notice that officers have taken property. The property owner can determine state

law remedies for recovery by consulting generally available state statutes and case law.

## C. Procedures for Resolving Forfeitures

**Page 1171 (Prosecution paperback page 367).    Replace the first sentence on the page with this material.**

In most states, civil forfeiture is far more common than criminal forfeiture. Until recently, this has also been true in the federal system. However, the Civil Asset Forfeiture Reform Act of 2000, P.L. No. 106-185, gives the federal government several incentives to pursue criminal forfeitures rather than civil forfeitures. The statute expands the authority to seek criminal forfeitures as part of the sentence for any crime where civil forfeiture is authorized. It also makes it easier for the government to seize assets connected to a crime after obtaining the criminal conviction.

**Page 1172 (Prosecution paperback page 368).    Add this material at the end of the first full paragraph on the page.**

One of the most important features of the Civil Asset Forfeiture Reform Act of 2000, P.L. No. 106-185, was its elimination of the bond requirement for parties challenging a forfeiture in federal court. The federal law also allows claimants to file tort claims for any damage to the property that the government causes while it holds the property during the time that forfeiture proceedings are pending.

## 1.　Parties and Innocent Owners

**Page 1177 (Prosecution paperback page 373).　Add this material after Problem 15-3 (Problem 5-3 in the Prosecution paperback) and eliminate note 1.**

## 18 U.S.C. §983(d)

(1) An innocent owner's interest in property shall not be forfeited under any civil forfeiture statute. The claimant shall have the burden of proving that the claimant is an innocent owner by a preponderance of the evidence.

(2)　(A) With respect to a property interest in existence at the time the illegal conduct giving rise to forfeiture took place, the term "innocent owner" means an owner who—

(i) did not know of the conduct giving rise to forfeiture; or

(ii) upon learning of the conduct giving rise to the forfeiture, did all that reasonably could be expected under the circumstances to terminate such use of the property.

(B)　(i) For the purposes of this paragraph, ways in which a person may show that such person did all that reasonably could be expected may include demonstrating that such person, to the extent permitted by law—(I) gave timely notice to an appropriate law enforcement agency of information that led the person to know the conduct giving rise to a forfeiture would occur or has occurred; and (II) in a timely fashion revoked or made a good faith attempt to revoke permission for those engaging in such conduct to use the property or took reasonable actions in consultation with a law enforcement agency to discourage or prevent the illegal use of the property.

(ii) A person is not required by this subparagraph to take steps that the person reasonably believes would be likely to subject any person (other than the person whose conduct gave rise to the forfeiture) to physical danger.

(3)　(A) With respect to a property interest acquired after the conduct giving rise to the forfeiture has taken place, the term "innocent owner" means a person who, at the time that person acquired the interest in the property—

(i) was a bona fide purchaser or seller for value (including a purchaser or seller of goods or services for value); and

(ii) did not know and was reasonably without cause to believe that the property was subject to forfeiture.

(B) An otherwise valid claim under subparagraph (A) shall not be denied on the ground that the claimant gave nothing of value in exchange for the property if—

(i) the property is the primary residence of the claimant;

(ii) depriving the claimant of the property would deprive the claimant of the means to maintain reasonable shelter in the community for the claimant and all dependents residing with the claimant;

(iii) the property is not, and is not traceable to, the proceeds of any criminal offense; and

(iv) the claimant acquired his or her interest in the property through marriage, divorce, or legal separation, or the claimant was the spouse or legal dependent of a person whose death resulted in the transfer of the property to the claimant through inheritance or probate, except that the court shall limit the value of any real property interest for which innocent ownership is recognized under this subparagraph to the value necessary to maintain reasonable shelter in the community for such claimant and all dependents residing with the claimant....

(5) If the court determines, in accordance with this section, that an innocent owner has a partial interest in property otherwise subject to forfeiture, or a joint tenancy or tenancy by the entirety in such property, the court may enter an appropriate order—

(A) severing the property;

(B) transferring the property to the Government with a provision that the Government compensate the innocent owner to the extent of his or her ownership interest once a final order of forfeiture has been entered and the property has been reduced to liquid assets; or

(C) permitting the innocent owner to retain the property subject to a lien in favor of the Government to the extent of the forfeitable interest in the property.

(6) In this subsection, the term owner—

(A) means a person with an ownership interest in the specific property sought to be forfeited, including a leasehold, lien, mortgage, recorded security interest, or valid assignment of an ownership interest; and

(B) does not include—

(i) a person with only a general unsecured interest in, or claim against, the property or estate of another;

(ii) a bailee unless the bailor is identified and the bailee shows a colorable legitimate interest in the property seized; or

(iii) a nominee who exercises no dominion or control over the property.

## NOTES

1. *Innocent owners under federal statutes.* The principal federal forfeiture statute includes the "innocent owner defense" reprinted above. As part of the Civil Asset Forfeiture Reform Act of 2000, P.L. No. 106-185, this statute changes the availability of the defense. Under the former version of the federal statute, the property owner had to show by a preponderance of the evidence that the relevant criminal acts occurred "without the knowledge, consent or willful blindness of the owner." 21 U.S.C. §881(a)(4)(C) (defense applicable to innocent owners of conveyances). See also 21 U.S.C. §§881(a)(6), (7) (owners of real and personal property used to facilitate illegal drug activity must show no "knowledge or consent"). How would you describe the precise differences between the innocent owner defense under the old and new statutes?

## 2.   Proof and Presumptions

**Page 1180 (Prosecution paperback page 376).    Replace the first two paragraphs in this section with the following material.**

Forfeiture statutes take various positions on the relevant burden of proof and standard of proof. At the start of the proceedings, the government must establish for the court that the property is subject to forfeiture. Sometimes, as under a few state statutes, the government carries this burden by showing probable cause to believe the property is forfeitable. More commonly, forfeiture statutes require the government to meet a preponderance of the evidence test; a few require clear and convincing evidence, or even proof beyond a reasonable doubt.

If the government fails to carry its initial burden, the action is dismissed. If the government succeeds, the burden of proof shifts to the property claimant, who must establish (usually by a preponderance of the evidence) that one of the relevant exemptions (such as the innocent owner defense) applies. In some states, the claimant might also have to prove by a preponderance that the property is not sufficiently connected to the crime and therefore is not subject to forfeiture. See Ill. Rev. Stat. ch. 725, para. 159/9.

## 18 U.S.C. §983(c)

In a suit or action brought under any civil forfeiture statute for the civil forfeiture of any property—

(1) the burden of proof is on the Government to establish, by a preponderance of the evidence, that the property is subject to forfeiture;

(2) the Government may use evidence gathered after the filing of a complaint for forfeiture to establish, by a preponderance of the evidence, that property is subject to forfeiture; and

(3) if the Government's theory of forfeiture is that the property was used to commit or facilitate the commission of a criminal offense, or was involved in the commission of a criminal offense, the Government shall establish that there was a substantial connection between the property and the offense.

**Page 1184 (Prosecution paperback page 380).    Replace notes 1 and 2 with the following material.**

1. *Burden of proof: majority position.*  It is most common for civil forfeiture statutes to place the burden of proof on the state to demonstrate that the property is forfeitable; the claimant then has the

burden of proof to demonstrate that any exemptions or exceptions apply. The federal government and more than 30 states allocate the burden in this way. However, roughly a dozen states follow a different approach to the burden of proof: After the prosecution establishes probable cause to believe that property is forfeitable, the claimant carries the burden of persuasion and must show that the property is not forfeitable. Court challenges to the constitutionality of this burden of proof have mostly failed. A few states, such as Tennessee and Washington, place the burden of proof on the government for real property seizures and on the claimant for personal property seizures.

In the federal system, the Civil Asset Forfeiture Reform Act of 2000, P.L. No. 106-185, changed the burden of proof in civil forfeiture. Before this amendment to the federal statutes, the burden of proof on the question of forfeitability shifted to a claimant after the government showed probable cause to believe that the property was forfeitable. Look again at the provisions of 18 U.S.C. §983(c), reprinted above. Would you expect this statutory amendment to lead to a different outcome in many cases? Will this amendment change more outcomes than the expanded "innocent owner" defense? More than the elimination of the bond requirement?

2. *Standard of proof: majority position.* In more than 30 states, civil forfeiture statutes require the party carrying the burden of proof to establish facts by a preponderance of the evidence. For criminal forfeiture actions, which are resolved after a criminal conviction for the underlying crime, the government of course must prove the elements of the crime beyond a reasonable doubt. But after conviction, in the sentencing phase, the government usually must establish the forfeitability of the property only by a preponderance of the evidence rather than beyond a reasonable doubt. See 21 U.S.C. §853(d). Clear and convincing evidence is the government's standard of proof in the civil forfeiture statutes of about a half-dozen states. See Minn. Stat. §609.531(6a)(a). A handful require proof beyond a reasonable doubt for some civil forfeitures. E.g., Neb. Rev. Stat. §28-431(4). Why would a prosecutor ever use a civil forfeiture statute that requires proof beyond a reasonable doubt?

The Florida decision in the *Real Property* case was unusual in requiring a particular burden of proof and standard of proof as a matter of constitutional law. The Florida constitution forbids one of the branches of government from invading the province of another. Did the court invade the province of the legislature with its decision in *Real Property*? Or did it instead create law within its area of special expertise—procedural fairness—at the implicit invitation of the legislature? Would the court have upheld a statute if it had explicitly required the government to carry the burden of proof by a preponderance of the evidence? The Florida legislature amended the statute dealing with civil forfeiture actions in 1992 and 1995, without changing the "due proof" language relating to the procedure at trial.

**Page 1187 (page 383 in Prosecution paperback).   Add this material after Problem 15-5 (Problem 5-5 in the Prosecution paperback).**

### Problem 15-6 (5-6). Weapons on Wheels

In 1999, New York City began a "Zero Tolerance Drinking and Driving Initiative." Under this policy, police officers who arrest someone for driving while intoxicated (registering .10 or higher on a breathalyzer test) may seize the automobile. The policy prevents the police from seizing a vehicle in cases where drivers are arrested for the lesser offense of "driving while impaired" (registering between .06 and .10 on a breathalyzer test). The seized car is searched and stored in a city facility. If the driver is either the owner or principal user of the car, the city will begin a civil forfeiture proceeding to take the car away. If the owner of the car knows it will be used to commit a crime (including driving while intoxicated) the car is also subject to forfeiture. Before the city adopted this new policy, the police held the cars of people arrested for drunken driving until some other person arrived at the station to pick up the car. The city could seek forfeiture of the car after a criminal conviction.

Within 25 days of the seizure, the driver can fill out a form requesting that the city return the car. Civil forfeiture proceedings in the Supreme Court take about six months. If the city prevails in the forfeiture proceedings, the car is sold at auction and the proceeds go into the city's general fund.

An acquittal of the driver on the criminal charges does not necessarily mean that the city will lose its civil forfeiture action. Nor does a criminal conviction necessarily mean that the city will go forward with a forfeiture action. Drivers whose cars have been seized for other offenses (such as soliciting prostitutes or purchasing small amounts of drugs) can sometimes get the cars returned by "settling" the forfeiture action for about 25 percent of the value of the car. It is not yet clear whether the city will allow such settlements in cases involving drunk driving. There were 6,368 arrests of drunken drivers in New York City in 1998, and 31 fatalities attributed to driving while intoxicated.

The new policy is based on an existing provision of the Administrative Code of the City of New York. Section 14-140 provides that the Police Property Clerk may take possession of "all property . . . suspected of having been used as a means of committing crime or employed in aid or furtherance of crime." A person who uses property in aid or furtherance of crime "or suffered the same to be used, . . . or who was a participant or accomplice in any such act . . . shall not be deemed to be the lawful claimant entitled to any such money or property."

Norman Siegel, the executive director of the New York Civil Liberties Union, responded to the plan this way: "The executive branch can't add punishment to the drunk driving laws. The police should not be in the business of being judge, jury and used-car salesman." Professor Alan Dershowitz offered this opinion of the law: "I am very much afraid that the presumption of innocence is being eroded, that police will be encouraged to arrest people for purposes of getting their cars, getting to seize material. I want to wait until the presumption of innocence is overcome by evidence of guilt. I am thrilled that the city of New York has finally taken drunken driving as seriously as it takes other kinds of crimes. Just wait until conviction."

Mayor Rudolph Giuliani responded to critics of the new policy as follows: "It isn't punishment. It's remedial. The car is seized in order to protect society against this car being driven around in the communities of New York City because it's been demonstrated that this car will be operated unsafely." According to Police Commissioner Howard Safir, the forfeiture action is "a way of preventing the use of what, in fact, is a weapon when driven while intoxicated against the public."

Francisco Almote, one of the first motorists whose vehicles was seized under the new policy, had been convicted five times previously on charges that he drove while intoxicated. Police seized his 1987 Toyota when they arrested him. A second driver whose car was seized was Pavel Grinberg, who was driving with his wife in Brooklyn one night when he was pulled over for not wearing a seat belt. Police officers said that a breathalyzer test showed a blood alcohol level of 0.11 percent. The officers arrested Grinberg and seized his 1988 Acura Integra (with a book value of about $1,650). "I was at my good friend's daughter's first birthday party and I had one beer — that was it," Grinberg said.

You are an attorney in the office of the Corporation Counsel for New York City. What difficulties (if any) do you foresee in enforcing this policy? Do you have any advice for how it should be enforced? How should the city respond in cases where the defendant charged with driving while intoxicated is willing to plead guilty to the lesser charge of driving while impaired (a charge that is not a basis for seizing the car under the city's policy)?

# Chapter 16 / 6

# Discovery and Speedy Trial

## A. Discovery

### 1. Prosecution Disclosures

**Page 1203 (Prosecution paperback page 399).   Add this material at the end of note 1.**

The Supreme Court applied the *Brady* rule in Strickler v. Greene, 527 U.S. 263 (1999). In a capital murder case, Virginia prosecutors failed to disclose materials casting doubt on the testimony of an eyewitness to the alleged crime. The exculpatory material appeared in interview notes and in letters the witness wrote to a detective. Because of the evidence of guilt independent of the eyewitness testimony, the Court held that the failure to disclose did not create a "reasonable probability" of a different outcome at trial.

**Page 1203 (Prosecution paperback page 399).   Add this material at the end of note 2.**

Who should carry the burden of proof on the question of whether the withheld evidence was material? On questions of ineffective assistance of counsel under *Strickland,* the defense carries the burden of showing prejudice; the prosecution carries the burden of proving that errors were "harmless" in most other settings. Because a failure to disclose under *Brady* is more within the control of the prosecution than ineffective assistance of counsel, does this mean that the burden should rest with the government? Surprisingly few courts have addressed this question directly. Most (but not all) courts simply assume without discussion that the burden lies on the defendant. See State v. Anderson, 410 N.W.2d 231 (Iowa 1987) (places burden on defendant); State v. Williamson, 562 A.2d 470 (Conn. 1987) (burden on government).

**Page 1204 (Prosecution paperback page 400).    Add this material at the end of note 4.**

The preservation of evidence has made a critical difference in more cases lately as DNA testing procedures become available. These tests make it possible to reevaluate the convictions of some defendants in cases (such as rape and murder cases) where blood or other biological material from the perpetrator is available at the crime scene or from the victim. The incentive to test this material and to match it to the convicted defendant is very strong in capital cases, and a few capital defendants have been released on the basis of DNA test information. See Roger Parloff, Gone But Not Forgotten, The American Lawyer, Jan./ Feb. 1999 (discussing ruling by Virginia courts allowing prosecutors to destroy evidence of executed defendant prior to DNA testing).

**Page 1213 (Prosecution paperback 409).    Add this material after note 8.**

9. *The extent of discovery violations.* How often do prosecutors and defense attorneys fail to disclose the information that they should to the opposing party? Periodic newspaper reports on "prosecutorial misconduct" focus on discovery violations; they suggest (inconclusively) that discovery violations by prosecutors occur regularly. The *Chicago Tribune* conducted an ambitious analysis of nationwide court records in 1999. It found records of 381 reversals of homicide cases since 1963, due to prosecutors concealing exculpatory evidence or using false evidence at trial. While this was an extremely small percentage of the homicide convictions during this time, the report notes that such violations are difficult to document and rarely lead to reversals of a conviction. See Ken Armstrong and Maurice Possley, The Verdict:

Dishonor, Chicago Tribune, Jan. 8, 1999; see also Cris Carmody, The *Brady* Rule: Is It Working? National L.J., May 17, 1993, at 30.

Prosecutors' offices sometimes evaluate the performance of their own attorneys and create systems to sanction wrongdoers and to train less experienced attorneys to avoid discovery violations. One such mechanism is the Office for Professional Responsibility (OPR) within the U.S. Department of Justice. A spate of news reports has argued that OPR has been ineffective in countering a "win at all costs" mentality among federal prosecutors. See Special Report: OPR in Transition, 4 No. 1 DOJ Alert 3 (Jan. 3–17, 1994); Jim McGee, Prosecutor Oversight Is Often Hidden from Sight, Washington Post, Jan. 15, 1993, at A1. How would you measure in a reliable way whether prosecutors are now committing more discovery violations than in the past? If such a trend were proven, how would you explain it? Could it be traced to the number of new prosecutors hired in a given time period?

# B.  Speedy Trial Preparation

## 2.  Speedy Trial After Accusation

**Page 1268 (Prosecution paperback page 464).    Add this material at the end of Problem 16-5 (Problem 6-5 in the Prosecution paperback).**

Cf. New York v. Hill, 528 U.S. 110 (2000) (defense counsel could effectively waive defendant's right to be brought to trial within 180-day period specified under Interstate Agreement on Detainers, by agreeing to a trial date outside that time period, even without express consent by defendant).

# Chapter 17 / 7

# Pleas and Bargains

## A. Why Bargain?

Page 1275 (Prosecution paperback page 471).   Add this material after the
*Seaberg* opinion.

MEMORANDUM FOR ALL
UNITED STATES ATTORNEYS

| | |
|---|---|
| FROM: | John Keeney, Acting Assistant Attorney General |
| SUBJECT: | Use of Sentencing Appeal Waivers to Reduce the Number of Sentencing Appeals |
| DATE: | October 4, 1995 |

This memorandum provides guidance regarding the possible use of
waivers of sentencing appeal rights and post-conviction rights in plea
agreements. The Department recognizes that many districts currently
incorporate such waivers into plea agreements. We believe that the use
of these waivers in appropriate cases can be helpful in reducing the
burden of appellate and collateral litigation involving sentencing issues.
    . . . At the outset, it is important to note that the Supreme Court has
repeatedly held that a criminal defendant can elect to waive many
important constitutional and statutory rights during the plea bargaining
process. Consistent with that principle, the courts of appeals have upheld
the general validity of a sentencing appeal waiver in a plea agreement.

A sentencing appeal waiver provision does not waive all claims on appeal. The courts of appeals have held that [a defendant's claim] that he was denied the effective assistance of counsel at sentencing, that he was sentenced on the basis of his race, or that his sentence exceeded the statutory maximum, will be reviewed on the merits by a court of appeals despite the existence of a sentencing appeal waiver in a plea agreement.

A plea bargain is a contract between the prosecutor and the defendant. Thus, the scope of a sentencing appeal waiver in a plea bargain will depend upon the precise language used in the sentencing appeal waiver provision.

A broad sentencing appeal waiver requires the defendant to waive any and all sentencing issues on appeal and through collateral attack. The following waiver provision is an example of a broad approach that may be used in plea agreements:

> The defendant is aware that Title 18, United States Code, Section 3742 affords a defendant the right to appeal the sentence imposed. Acknowledging all this, the defendant knowingly waives the right to appeal any sentence within the maximum provided in the statute(s) of conviction (or the manner in which that sentence was determined) on the grounds set forth in Title 18, United States Code, Section 3742 or on any ground whatever, in exchange for the concessions made by the United States in this plea agreement. The defendant also waives his right to challenge his sentence or the manner in which it was determined in any collateral attack . . . .

The advantage of a broad sentencing appeal waiver is that it will bar the appeal of virtually any sentencing guideline issue. . . . The disadvantage of the broad sentencing appeal waiver is that it could result in guideline-free sentencing of defendants in guilty plea cases, and it could encourage a lawless district court to impose sentences in violation of the guidelines. It is imperative to guard against the use of waivers of appeal to promote circumvention of the sentencing guidelines. . . .

Use of waiver of appeal rights in a manner resulting in sentences in violation of the sentencing guidelines could prompt a court of appeals to reconsider its decision to uphold the validity of a sentencing appeal waiver. Alternatively, the reviewing court could construe a sentencing appeal waiver narrowly in order to correct an obvious miscarriage of justice. To avoid these concerns, we recommend that, in a case involving an egregiously incorrect sentence, the prosecutor consider electing to disregard the waiver and to argue the merits of the appeal. That would avoid confronting the court of appeals with the difficult decision of enforcing a sentencing appeal waiver that might result in a miscarriage of justice.

A second kind of sentencing appeal waiver is limited in some respect, most likely with regard to a particular sentence, sentencing range, or guideline application. For example, a sentencing appeal waiver could preclude appeal of sentences consistent with a recommended sentence, sentencing range, or particular guideline application agreed to by the parties. Thus, if the plea agreement provides that the prosecutor will recommend the lower half of the available sentences for a particular offense level applicable to the case (subject to a determination of the criminal history category), the plea agreement could also provide for a waiver of the defendant's right to appeal any sentence imposed within the agreed-upon lower half of the applicable range. . . .

The advantage of a limited sentencing appeal waiver is that it is flexible and can be modified to meet the parties' needs. A limited sentencing appeal waiver may be useful when the government seeks a plea agreement, but the defendant is unwilling to plead guilty without some assurance that he will be entitled to appeal an erroneous sentence. The disadvantage of a limited appeal waiver is that it will not reduce the number of sentencing appeals as much as a sentencing appeal waiver that requires the defendant to relinquish appeal of all sentencing issues.

The use of a sentencing appeal waiver in a plea agreement to bar an appeal by the defendant does not require the government to waive its right to appeal an adverse sentencing ruling. The government's retention of its right to appeal the sentence while requiring the defendant to waive his right to appeal does not violate any right of the defendant. However, the Fourth Circuit has held that if the government wishes to retain its right to appeal the sentence while requiring the defendant to waive [the same right to appeal], the government must explicitly reserve its right to appeal the sentence in the plea agreement. The government's retention of its appeal rights will not be inferred by silence or omission in the plea agreement. United States v. Guevara, 941 F.2d 1299 (4th Cir. 1991). Of course, in the interest of striking a bargain, a United States Attorney's office may decide that it is necessary for the government to waive its appeal rights when the defendant takes such action. . . .

A waiver of an important constitutional or statutory right must be knowing and voluntary to be valid. Therefore, prosecutors should ensure that the record reflects that the defendant knowingly and voluntarily waived his right to appeal his sentence. It is recommended that both the plea agreement and the Rule 11 colloquy specifically spell out the sentencing appeal waiver. The plea agreement should expressly state that the defendant understands the meaning and effect of the agreement and that his waiver of rights is knowing and voluntary. The defendant and his counsel can be required to sign those provisions separately. . . .

Nonetheless, relying solely on the text of the plea agreement is risky. The better practice is for the district court to supplement the plea agreement by specifically referring the defendant to the sentencing appeal waiver provision and obtaining the defendant's express waiver of his right to appeal during the Rule 11 hearing. . . .

The general acceptance of the sentencing appeal waiver in the courts of appeals has caused criminal defendants to mount systematic challenges to the sentencing appeal waiver. One common and repeated challenge to the sentencing appeal waiver is the argument that a sentencing appeal waiver is involuntary as a matter of law because the defendant will not know his actual sentence at the time that he executes the waiver. [However,] the validity of a waiver does not depend on the defendant's knowledge of all of the consequences of the waiver to be valid. When a defendant agrees to plead guilty, he does not know whether the government can prove its case and how witnesses will testify. [T]hose uncertainties do not make the case invalid as a matter of law. For that same reason, the defendant's lack of knowledge of his actual sentence when he executes the waiver does not make a sentencing appeal waiver unknowing as a matter of law.

Criminal defendants are also attempting to find language in the plea agreement that allegedly authorizes them to appeal sentences despite the sentencing appeal waiver. For example, some sentencing appeal waiver provisions contain language that the defendant will be sentenced "in accordance" or "in conformity" with the sentencing guidelines. Although the obvious purpose of those provisions is to remind the defendant that he will be sentenced under the sentencing guidelines, some defendants have argued that the "in accordance" or "in conformity" language means that the defendant will be sentenced correctly under the sentencing guidelines. Thus, if the district court errs in applying the guidelines to sentence the defendant, the plea agreement has been violated which nullifies the sentencing appeal waiver. [This] position would effectively eviscerate the sentencing appeal waiver, which assumes that an error may be committed at sentencing. Of course, that problem might be avoided by redrafting the plea agreement to make clear that although the defendant will be sentenced under the sentencing guidelines, he will have no right to challenge an incorrect application of the guidelines. . . .

**Page 1279 (Prosecution paperback page 475).   Add this material to the end of note 6.**

For a discussion of the capacity of defendants to waive or extend statutes of limitations, see Donald Schapiro and Robert Schapiro, Face the Music, The New Republic, Nov. 16, 1998, at 11; Acevedo-Ramos v. United States, 961 F.2d 305 (1st Cir. 1992). Would a court be less willing to enforce the waiver if the defendant's statute of limitations defense is only available for the lesser crime of conviction, because the statute of limitations was longer for the crime as originally charged?

## B.   Categorical Restrictions on Bargaining

### 4.   Victim Consultation

**Page 1321 (Prosecution paperback page 517).   Add this material after note 2.**

3.   *The impact of victims' rights laws.* All 50 states have some statutory protections for the rights of victims during the criminal process, and about 30 states have amended their constitutions to provide for such rights. But some states have stronger requirements than others. Does the type of law at work in a state influence the way that government officials deal with the victim of an alleged crime? Does a stronger law change the likely reaction of the victim? A 1998 survey suggests that stronger victim protection laws do translate into some noteworthy differences in practice. For instance, victims in "strong-protection states" are more likely to learn about sentencing or parole hearings than victims in "weak-protection states." However, the strength of the victim protection laws did *not* affect the number of victims who learned about plea negotiations or a decision to dismiss charges. See

Dean Kilpatrick, David Beatty, and Susan Smith Howley, The Rights of Crime Victims — Does Legal Protection Make a Difference? (Research in Brief) (Dec. 1998, NCJ 173839). What barriers might stand in the way of notifying victims about the progress of plea negotiations?

## C. Validity of Individual Plea Bargains

### 1. Lack of Knowledge

**Page 1329 (Prosecution paperback page 525).    Add this material at the end of note 4.**

In United States v. Ruiz, 122 S. Ct. 2450 (2002), the U.S. Supreme Court upheld a "fast track" plea agreement even though the government, as a condition of the agreement, required the defendant to waive the right to receive impeachment information relating to any informants or other witnesses, as well as information supporting any affirmative defense she might raise. Although these disclosures were important parts of a fair trial, they were among the trial rights that a defendant is allowed to waive.

## E. The Future of Bargaining

### 1. Legitimacy of Bargaining

**Page 1367 (Prosecution paperback page 563).    Add this material after the notes.**

3. *Bargaining and bribery.* Sometimes the government will enter a plea bargain with a defendant in exchange for the defendant's cooperation in other criminal investigations, including testimony against other criminal defendants. Does this sort of plea bargain amount to bribing a witness? Courts have never taken such an argument seriously until recently, when a panel of the U.S. Court of Appeals for the Tenth Circuit reversed a money laundering conviction on the ground that the government had bribed the cooperating witness. A few months later, the

en banc court changed direction and upheld the conviction. The "anti-gratuity statute," 18 U.S.C. §201(c)(2), declares that

> Whoever . . . directly or indirectly, gives, offers, or promises anything of value to any person, for or because of the testimony under oath or affirmation given or to be given by such person as a witness upon a trial . . . shall be fined under this title or imprisoned. . . .

The defendant, Singleton, claimed that the government's cooperating witness, who testified after receiving a promise of lenient treatment in a pending drug case, had received something "of value" and therefore had a motive to testify untruthfully in favor of the government.

Although the statute was phrased generally, the en banc court read the word "whoever" to exclude prosecuting attorneys acting within the normal course of their authority. Any other result, the court said, would be a "a radical departure from the ingrained legal culture of our criminal justice system." United States v. Singleton, 165 F.3d 1297 (10th Cir. 1999) (en banc). In the Court's view, Congress did not intend to authorize such prosecutions of ordinary exercises of sovereignty. The dissenting opinion relied on the clear language of the statute and argued that it was intended to prevent exactly the sort of motive to lie that was involved in this case.

What would be the effects if prosecutors stopped promising to enter lenient plea agreements with cooperative witnesses? Would the effects of such a ban be any more or less profound that the advent of the exclusionary rule? Try to formulate alternatives that prosecutors might adopt to obtain cooperation from witnesses who were involved in alleged crimes.

## 2.   Efforts to Ban Bargaining

**Page 1367 (Prosecution paperback page 563).      Add this material at the end of the first paragraph in this section.**

Professor George Fisher, through careful study of the origins of plea bargaining in nineteenth-century Massachusetts, has revealed how plea bargaining first thrived for crimes that gave judges little choice over sentences (and therefore gave added importance to the prosecutor's choice of charges). Bargaining also became more attractive to prosecutors after the appearance of probation as a sentencing option. Judges became more amenable to plea bargaining after a flood of railroad tort suits created civil docket pressures. Fisher, Plea Bargaining's Triumph, 109 Yale L.J. 857 (2000).

**Page 1376 (Prosecution paperback page 572).     Add this material at the end of note 1.**

For an evaluation of the ban on post-indictment plea bargaining in the Bronx and Queens, see Kenneth Jost, Critics Blast New York Plea Ban, 9 CQ Researcher No. 6, at 124 (Feb. 12, 1999).

# Chapter 18 / 8

# Decisionmakers at Trial

## A. Judge or Jury?

### 2. Essential Nature of the Jury

**Page 1398 (Prosecution paperback page 594).** **Add this material to the end of note 3.**

See also Michael J. Saks and Mollie Weighner Marti, A Meta-Analysis of the Effects of Jury Size, 21 Law & Hum. Behav. 451 (1997). For a survey of jury practice in other countries (including New Zealand, Canada, Scotland, Ireland, Spain, Russia, and Japan), see the symposium in volume 62 of Law & Contemporary Problems.

## B. Selection of Jurors

### 2. Dismissals for Cause

**Page 1426 (Prosecution paperback page 622).** **Add this material to the end of note 2.**

The judge's decision about whether to excuse a juror for hardships interacts with rules about the length of service expected of jurors and the sanctions for citizens who do not appear for jury duty. How do you suppose a judge would react to a juror asking for a hardship excuse in a system requiring 10 days of service from jurors, and where only 5 percent of all citizens who are summoned actually appear for jury duty? Would the judge's response to the hardship request change in a "one day or one trial" system? Under the "one day or one trial" system, prospective jurors serve in a maximum of one trial and complete their service after one day if they are not chosen for a trial. About 40 percent of the U.S. population lives in counties with a "one day or one trial" system. See Caitlin Liu, Making Jury Duty Less Trying, L.A. Times, Jan. 28, 2000.

## 3.    Peremptory Challenges

**Page 1448 (Prosecution paperback page 644).    Add this material to the end of note 1.**

In United States v. Martinez-Salazar, 528 U.S. 304 (2000), the trial judge failed to excuse a juror for cause, so the defense lawyers used a peremptory to remove the biased juror. The Court held that the federal procedural rules on peremptory challenges do not require a defendant to use a peremptory challenge to exclude a juror who should have been removed for cause. If the defense attorney decides to leave the biased juror on the panel and the jury convicts, an appeal based on the right to an impartial jury is available. However, if the defense attorney decides to use a peremptory challenge to remove the biased juror, rather than taking her chances later on appeal, there is no reversible error. The constitution and the federal procedural rules do not guarantee that the defendant will be able to use all peremptory challenges on qualified jurors. In other words, full access to peremptory challenges is not necessary to protect the overarching goal of an impartial jury.

**Page 1457 (Prosecution paperback page 653).    Add this material to the end of note 4.**

See Nancy J. King, *Batson* for the Bench? Regulating the Peremptory Challenge of Judges, 73 Chi.-Kent L. Rev. 509 (1998).

# C.  *Jury Deliberations and Verdicts*

## 1.  Instructions to Deadlocked Juries

**Page 1467 (Prosecution paperback page 663).   Add this material to the end of note 2.**

See also Richardson v. United States, 526 U.S. 813 (1999) (interpreting the federal Continuing Criminal Enterprise statute to require jury to agree unanimously on the "violations" that make up the "series of continuing violations" that define the enterprise; violations are elements of the offense, not merely the means of committing an element).

**Page 1468 (Prosecution paperback page 664).   Add this material to the end of note 5.**

See People v. Hues, 704 N.E.2d 546 (N.Y. 1998) (survey of cases on issue of jurors taking notes).

## 2.  Jury Nullification

**Page 1475 (Prosecution paperback page 671).   Add this material to the end of note 1.**

For thorough examinations of the historical origins of jury nullification in the United States, see Clay S. Conrad, Jury Nullification: The Evolution of a Doctrine (1998); Stanton D. Krauss, An Inquiry Into the Right of Criminal Juries to Determine the Law in Colonial America, 89 J. Crim. L. & Criminology 111 (1998). It appears that many of the older cases affirming the power of the jury to "find the law" were intended to limit a judicial practice of directing the jury how to apply the law to particular facts.

**Page 1477 (Prosecution paperback page 673).    Add this material to the end of note 4.**

The jury may receive information about its power to "nullify" from sources other than the judge or the defense attorney, including pamphleteers outside the courthouse. Judges and prosecutors from time to time take action (such as the filing of contempt or jury tampering charges) against these advocates. Professor Nancy King has analyzed these tactics and concludes that they are constitutionally acceptable. King, Silencing Nullification Advocacy Inside the Jury Room and Outside the Courtroom 65 U. Chi. L. Rev. 433 (1998).

# Chapter 19 / 9

# Witnesses and Proof

## A. Burden of Proof

### 2. Reasonable Doubt About What?

**Page 1519 (Prosecution paperback, page 715). Add the following materials to the end of note 3.**

The Supreme Court has spoken again recently on the question of whether particular facts are "elements" of a crime (to be decided by a trial jury using the beyond a reasonable doubt standard) or are instead "sentencing enhancement" (to be decided after trial using a lower standard of proof). The decision in Apprendi v. New Jersey, 530 U.S. 466 (2000), is reprinted in Chapter 20 of this supplement.

### 3. Presumptions

**Page 1527 (Prosecution paperback, page 723). Add the following material after note 2.**

3. *Statutory definitions of sufficient evidence.* As we have seen, a legislature is free by and large to define the elements of crimes; it is more limited in its power to declare what inferences about crime elements that a jury must draw from the proven facts. However, the legislature may specify the type of evidence that is *not* sufficient to

prove the elements. For instance, some statutes specify the minimum number of witnesses the prosecution must present to support a conviction for a particular crime (e.g., the traditional "two witness rule" for perjury convictions). In Carmell v. Texas, 529 U.S. 513 (2000), the Texas legislature amended its criminal statutes to authorize conviction of certain sexual offenses based on the victim's testimony alone; before that time, the statute required the victim's testimony plus other corroborating evidence to convict the offender. The Court held that when a legislature changes such rules dealing with the sufficiency of evidence, the change may only apply prospectively. Any retroactive application of such a law would amount to an ex post facto law.

## B.  Confrontation of Witnesses

### 2.   Unavailable Witnesses

Page 1547 (Hardback edition).    Replace State v. Gray and notes 1 and 2 with the following material.

### Kevin Gray v. Maryland
523 U.S. 185 (1998)

BREYER, J.
The issue in this case concerns the application of Bruton v. United States, 391 U.S. 123 (1968). *Bruton* involved two defendants accused of participating in the same crime and tried jointly before the same jury. One of the defendants had confessed. His confession named and incriminated the other defendant. The trial judge issued a limiting instruction, telling the jury that it should consider the confession as evidence only against the codefendant who had confessed and not against the defendant named in the confession. *Bruton* held that, despite the limiting instruction, the Constitution forbids the use of such a confession in the joint trial.
The case before us differs from *Bruton* in that the prosecution here redacted the codefendant's confession by substituting for the defendant's name in the confession a blank space or the word "deleted." We must

decide whether these substitutions make a significant legal difference. We hold that they do not and that *Bruton*'s protective rule applies.

In 1993, Stacy Williams died after a severe beating. Anthony Bell gave a confession, to the Baltimore City police, in which he said that he (Bell), Kevin Gray, and Jacquin "Tank" Vanlandingham had participated in the beating that resulted in Williams' death. Vanlandingham later died. A Maryland grand jury indicted Bell and Gray for murder. The State of Maryland tried them jointly.

The trial judge, after denying Gray's motion for a separate trial, permitted the State to introduce Bell's confession into evidence at trial. But the judge ordered the confession redacted. Consequently, the police detective who read the confession into evidence said the word "deleted" or "deletion" whenever Gray's name or Vanlandingham's name appeared. Immediately after the police detective read the redacted confession to the jury, the prosecutor asked, "after he gave you that information, you subsequently were able to arrest Mr. Kevin Gray; is that correct?" The officer responded, "That's correct." The State also introduced into evidence a written copy of the confession with those two names omitted, leaving in their place blank white spaces separated by commas. The State produced other witnesses, who said that six persons (including Bell, Gray, and Vanlandingham) participated in the beating. Gray testified and denied his participation. Bell did not testify.

When instructing the jury, the trial judge specified that the confession was evidence only against Bell; the instructions said that the jury should not use the confession as evidence against Gray. The jury convicted both Bell and Gray. Gray appealed. . . .

*Bruton*, as we have said, involved two defendants—Evans and Bruton—tried jointly for robbery. Evans did not testify, but the Government introduced into evidence Evans' confession, which stated that both he (Evans) and Bruton together had committed the robbery. The trial judge told the jury it could consider the confession as evidence only against Evans, not against Bruton.

This Court held that, despite the limiting instruction, the introduction of Evans' out-of-court confession at Bruton's trial had violated Bruton's right, protected by the Sixth Amendment, to cross-examine witnesses. The Court recognized that in many circumstances a limiting instruction will adequately protect one defendant from the prejudicial effects of the introduction at a joint trial of evidence intended for use only against a different defendant. But it said that

> there are some contexts in which the risk that the jury will not, or cannot, follow instructions is so great, and the consequences of failure so vital to the defendant, that the practical and human limitations of the jury system cannot be ignored. Such a context is presented here, where the powerfully incriminating extrajudicial statements of a codefendant, who stands accused side-by-side with the defendant, are deliberately spread before the jury in a joint trial. Not only are the incriminations devastating to the defendant but their credibility is inevitably suspect. . . . The unreliability of such evidence is intolerably compounded when the alleged accomplice, as here, does not testify and cannot be tested by cross-examination. [391 U.S. at 135-136.]

In Richardson v. Marsh, 481 U.S. 200 (1987), the Court considered a redacted confession. The case involved a joint murder trial of Marsh and Williams. The State had redacted the confession of one defendant, Williams, so as to "omit all reference" to his codefendant, Marsh — indeed, to omit all indication that anyone other than Williams and a third person had participated in the crime. The trial court also instructed the jury not to consider the confession against Marsh. As redacted, the confession indicated that Williams and the third person had discussed the murder in the front seat of a car while they traveled to the victim's house. The redacted confession contained no indication that Marsh — or any other person — was in the car. Later in the trial, however, Marsh testified that she was in the back seat of the car. For that reason, in context, the confession still could have helped convince the jury that Marsh knew about the murder in advance and therefore had participated knowingly in the crime.

The Court held that this redacted confession fell outside *Bruton*'s scope and was admissible (with appropriate limiting instructions) at the joint trial. The Court distinguished Evans' confession in *Bruton* as a confession that was "incriminating on its face," and which had "expressly implicat[ed]" *Bruton*. By contrast, Williams' confession amounted to "evidence requiring linkage" in that it became incriminating in respect to Marsh "only when linked with evidence introduced later at trial." The Court held that "the Confrontation Clause is not violated by the admission of a nontestifying codefendant's confession with a proper limiting instruction when, as here, the confession is redacted to eliminate not only the defendant's name, but any reference to his or her existence."

The Court added: "We express no opinion on the admissibility of a confession in which the defendant's name has been replaced with a symbol or neutral pronoun."

Originally, the codefendant's confession in the case before us, like that in *Bruton*, referred to, and directly implicated another defendant. The State, however, redacted that confession by removing the nonconfessing defendant's name. Nonetheless, unlike *Richardson*'s redacted confession, this confession refers directly to the "existence" of the nonconfessing defendant. The State has simply replaced the nonconfessing defendant's name with a kind of symbol, namely the word "deleted" or a blank space set off by commas. The redacted confession, for example, responded to the question "Who was in the group that beat Stacey," with the phrase, "Me, _____, and a few other guys." And when the police witness read the confession in court, he said the word "deleted" or "deletion" where the blank spaces appear. . . .

*Bruton*, as interpreted by *Richardson*, holds that certain "powerfully incriminating extrajudicial statements of a codefendant" — those naming another defendant — considered as a class, are so prejudicial that limiting instructions cannot work. Unless the prosecutor wishes to hold separate trials or to use separate juries or to abandon use of the confession, he must redact the confession to reduce significantly or to eliminate the special prejudice that the *Bruton* Court found. Redactions that simply replace a name with an obvious blank space or a word such as "deleted" or a symbol or other similarly obvious indications of alteration, however, leave statements that, considered as a class, so closely resemble *Bruton's* unredacted statements that, in our view, the law must require the same result.

For one thing, a jury will often react similarly to an unredacted confession and a confession redacted in this way, for the jury will often realize that the confession refers specifically to the defendant. This is true even when the State does not blatantly link the defendant to the deleted name, as it did in this case by asking whether Gray was arrested on the basis of information in Bell's confession as soon as the officer had finished reading the redacted statement. Consider a simplified but typical example, a confession that reads "I, Bob Smith, along with Sam Jones, robbed the bank." To replace the words "Sam Jones" with an obvious blank will not likely fool anyone. A juror somewhat familiar with criminal law would know immediately that the blank, in the phrase

"I, Bob Smith, along with _____ , robbed the bank," refers to defendant Jones. A juror who does not know the law and who therefore wonders to whom the blank might refer need only lift his eyes to Jones, sitting at counsel table, to find what will seem the obvious answer, at least if the juror hears the judge's instruction not to consider the confession as evidence against Jones, for that instruction will provide an obvious reason for the blank. A more sophisticated juror, wondering if the blank refers to someone else, might also wonder how, if it did, the prosecutor could argue the confession is reliable, for the prosecutor, after all, has been arguing that Jones, not someone else, helped Smith commit the crime. For another thing, the obvious deletion may well call the jurors' attention specially to the removed name. By encouraging the jury to speculate about the reference, the redaction may overemphasize the importance of the confession's accusation — once the jurors work out the reference. . . .

Finally, *Bruton*'s protected statements and statements redacted to leave a blank or some other similarly obvious alteration, function the same way grammatically. They are directly accusatory. Evans' statement in *Bruton* used a proper name to point explicitly to an accused defendant. And *Bruton* held that the "powerfully incriminating" effect of . . . an out-of-court accusation creates a special, and vital, need for cross-examination — a need that would be immediately obvious had the codefendant pointed directly to the defendant in the courtroom itself. The blank space in an obviously redacted confession also points directly to the defendant, and it accuses the defendant in a manner similar to Evans' use of Bruton's name or to a testifying codefendant's accusatory finger. By way of contrast, the factual statement at issue in *Richardson* — a statement about what others said in the front seat of a car — differs from directly accusatory evidence in this respect, for it does not point directly to a defendant at all.

We concede certain differences between *Bruton* and this case. A confession that uses a blank or the word "delete" (or, for that matter, a first name or a nickname) less obviously refers to the defendant than a confession that uses the defendant's full and proper name. Moreover, in some instances the person to whom the blank refers may not be clear: Although the follow-up question asked by the State in this case eliminated all doubt, the reference might not be transparent in other cases in which a confession, like the present confession, uses two (or more) blanks, even though only one other defendant appears at trial, and in which the trial indicates that there are more participants than the confession has named. . . . We also concede that the jury must use inference to connect the statement in this redacted confession with the defendant. But inference pure and simple cannot make the critical difference, for if it did, then *Richardson* would also place outside *Bruton*'s scope confessions that use shortened first names, nicknames, descriptions as unique as the "red-haired, bearded, one-eyed man-with-a-limp," and perhaps even full names of defendants who are always known by a nickname. This Court has assumed, however, that nicknames and specific descriptions fall inside, not outside, *Bruton*'s protection. . . .

That being so, *Richardson* must depend in significant part upon the kind of, not the simple fact of, inference. *Richardson*'s inferences involved statements that did not refer directly to the defendant himself and which became incriminating "only when linked with evidence introduced later at trial." The inferences at issue here involve statements that, despite redaction, obviously refer directly to someone, often obviously the defendant, and which involve inferences that a jury ordinarily could make immediately, even were the confession the very first item introduced at trial. Moreover, the redacted confession with the blank prominent on its face, in *Richardson*'s words, "facially incriminat[es]" the codefendant. . . .

Nor are the policy reasons that *Richardson* provided in support of its conclusion applicable here. *Richardson* expressed concern lest application of *Bruton*'s rule apply where "redaction" of confessions, particularly "confessions incriminating by connection," would often "not [be] possible," thereby forcing prosecutors too often to abandon use either of the confession or of a joint trial. Additional redaction of a confession that uses a blank space, the word "delete," or a symbol, however, normally is possible. Consider as an example a portion of the confession before us: The witness who read the confession told the jury that the confession (among other things) said, "Question: Who was in the group that beat Stacey? Answer: Me, deleted, deleted, and a few other guys." Why could the witness not, instead, have said: "Question: Who was in the group that beat Stacey? Answer: Me and a few other guys." . . .

The *Richardson* Court also feared that the inclusion, within *Bruton's* protective rule, of confessions that incriminated "by connection" too often would provoke mistrials, or would unnecessarily lead prosecutors to abandon the confession or joint trial, because neither the prosecutors nor the judge could easily predict, until after the introduction of all the evidence, whether or not *Bruton* had barred use of the confession. To include the use of blanks, the word "delete," symbols, or other indications of redaction, within *Bruton's* protections, however, runs no such risk. Their use is easily identified prior to trial and does not depend, in any special way, upon the other evidence introduced in the case. . . .

For these reasons, we hold that the confession here at issue, which substituted blanks and the word "delete" for the respondent's proper name, falls within the class of statements to which *Bruton's* protections apply. . . .

SCALIA, J., dissenting.

In Richardson v. Marsh, we declined to extend the "narrow exception" of Bruton v. United States beyond confessions that facially incriminate a defendant. . . . The almost invariable assumption of the law is that jurors follow their instructions. This rule "is a pragmatic one, rooted less in the absolute certitude that the presumption is true than in the belief that it represents a reasonable practical accommodation of the interests of the state and the defendant in the criminal justice process." *Richardson.* . . . In *Bruton*, we recognized a "narrow exception" to this rule. . . .

We declined in *Richardson*, however, to extend *Bruton* to confessions that incriminate only by inference from other evidence. When incrimination is inferential, "it is a less valid generalization that the jury will not likely obey the instruction to disregard the evidence." Today the Court struggles to decide whether a confession redacted to omit the defendant's name is incriminating on its face or by inference. [T]he statement "Me, deleted, deleted, and a few other guys" does not facially incriminate anyone but the speaker. The Court's analogizing of "deleted" to a physical description that clearly identifies the defendant does not survive scrutiny. By "facially incriminating," we have meant incriminating independent of other evidence introduced at trial. Since the defendant's appearance at counsel table is not evidence, the description "red-haired, bearded, one-eyed man-with-a-limp" would be facially incriminating — unless, of course, the defendant had dyed his hair black and shaved his beard before trial, and the prosecution introduced evidence concerning his former appearance. . . . By contrast, the person to whom "deleted" refers in "Me, deleted, deleted, and a few other guys" is not apparent from anything the jury knows independent of the evidence at trial. Though the jury may speculate, the statement expressly implicates no one but the speaker.

Of course the Court is correct that confessions redacted to omit the defendant's name are more likely to incriminate than confessions redacted to omit any reference to his existence. But it is also true — and more relevant here — that confessions redacted to omit the defendant's name are less likely to incriminate than confessions that expressly state it. The latter are "powerfully incriminating" as a class; the former are not so. Here, for instance, there were two names deleted, five or more participants in the crime, and only one other defendant on trial. The jury no doubt may "speculate about the reference" as it speculates when evidence connects a defendant to a confession that does not refer to his existence. The issue, however, is not whether the confession incriminated petitioner, but whether the incrimination is so "powerful" that we must depart from the normal presumption that the jury follows its instructions. I think it is not — and I am certain that drawing the line for departing from the ordinary rule at the facial identification of the defendant makes more sense than drawing it anywhere else.

We explained in *Richardson* that forgoing use of codefendant confessions or joint trials was too high a price to insure that juries never disregard their instructions. The Court minimizes the damage that it does by suggesting that additional redaction of a confession that uses a blank space . . . normally is possible. In the present case, it asks, why could the police officer not have testified that Bell's answer was "Me and a few other guys"? The answer, it seems obvious to me, is because that is not what Bell said. Bell's answer was "Me, Tank, Kevin and a few other guys." Introducing the statement with full disclosure of deletions is one thing; introducing as the complete statement what was in fact only a part is something else. And of course even concealed deletions from the text will often not do the job that the Court demands. For inchoate offenses—conspiracy in particular—redaction to delete all reference to a confederate would often render the confession nonsensical. If the question was "Who agreed to beat Stacey?", and the answer was "Me and Kevin," we might redact the answer to "Me and [deleted]," or perhaps to "Me and somebody else," but surely not to just "Me"—for that would no longer be a confession to the conspiracy charge, but rather the foundation for an insanity defense. . . . The risk to the integrity of our system (not to mention the increase in its complexity) posed by the approval of such freelance editing seems to me infinitely greater than the risk posed by the entirely honest reproduction that the Court disapproves.

The United States Constitution guarantees, not a perfect system of criminal justice (as to which there can be considerable disagreement), but a minimum standard of fairness. Lest we lose sight of the forest for the trees, it should be borne in mind that federal and state rules of criminal procedure—which can afford to seek perfection because they can be more readily changed—exclude nontestifying-codefendant confessions even where the Sixth Amendment does not. Under the Federal Rules of Criminal Procedure (and Maryland's), a trial court may order separate trials if joinder will prejudice a defendant. . . . . Federal and most state trial courts (including Maryland's) also have the discretion to exclude unfairly prejudicial (albeit probative) evidence. Fed. Rule Evid. 403; Md. Rule Evid. 5-403. Here, petitioner moved for a severance on the ground that the admission of Bell's confession would be unfairly prejudicial. The trial court denied the motion, explaining that where a confession names two others, and the evidence is that five or six others participated, redaction of petitioner's name would not leave the jury with the "unavoidable inference" that Bell implicated Gray.

I do not understand the Court to disagree that the redaction itself left unclear to whom the blank referred. That being so, the rule set forth in *Richardson* applies, and the statement could constitutionally be admitted with limiting instruction. . . .

## NOTES

1. *Out-of-court statements by codefendants: majority position.* A codefendant who has confessed and implicated the defendant may be unavailable for testimony or cross-examination at trial because of the codefendant's privilege against self-incrimination. In Bruton v. United States, 391 U.S. 123 (1968), the Court prevented the use of the

codefendant's statement in a joint jury trial, even if the judge cautions the jury to consider the confession as evidence only against the codefendant. When the codefendant takes the stand at trial (and is therefore available for cross-examination), or when the defendant has also confessed and offered enough similar details to make the two confessions "interlocking," the codefendant's confession may come into evidence. Cruz v. New York, 481 U.S. 186 (1987) (similarities in interlocking confessions provide enough indicia of reliability to satisfy confrontation clause); Nelson v. O'Neil, 402 U.S. 622 (1971) (testimony of codefendant). Virtually all state courts allow the government to introduce codefendant confessions under circumstances such as these.

2. *Redacted statements.* The decision in Gray v. Maryland considered the types of redactions to a codefendant confession that would make the statement admissible against the codefendant in a joint trial. Before the Supreme Court announced its decision in *Gray*, state courts divided on the question of whether to admit codefendant confessions when the defendant's name is simply replaced with a neutral pronoun or a word such as "deleted." One group of courts (describing themselves as "facial incrimination" jurisdictions) concluded that replacement of the defendant's name in the confession is enough to prevent the jury from using the evidence improperly. The *Bruton* bar, they said, applies only to codefendant confessions that facially incriminate the defendant by naming him or making some equivalent identification. Another group of courts (the "contextual" jurisdictions) looked to the other evidence in the case to determine the probability that the jury would use the other evidence to identify the defendant as the unnamed person mentioned in the codefendant's confession. See People v. Fletcher, 917 P.2d 187 (Cal. 1996). Did the U.S. Supreme Court in *Gray* side with one of these groups of state courts, or did it create a new method of analysis?

Does a prosecutor redacting a confession for use in a joint trial now have to consider the other evidence to be admitted in the trial? The type of defense that each codefendant will raise? For instance, suppose that one of the four codefendants in a joint trial for robbery and murder has confessed. Part of the interrogation transcript reads as follows:

*Q.* You knew they were going over there to rob the place. You knew that was going to happen.
*A.* They were talking about it.

*Q*. When you went up there, who had a gun?
*A*. Everybody.
*Q*. But you did go with the others knowing that they were going to go up there and rob that place.
*A*. Uh huh.
*Q*. Where did you get your .38?
*A*. They got it.

Would you edit this transcript before offering it into evidence? If so, how? Would it matter to you that the codefendants will argue that they did not know about any plans to kill the robbery victims? That they were unarmed? See State v. Leutfaimany, 585 N.W.2d 200 (Iowa 1998).

Justice Scalia's dissent in *Gray* points out that joinder and severance rules give trial judges discretion to order separate trials for codefendants if a joint trial would be prejudicial. Would the need to edit a codefendant's confession convince you, as a trial judge, to adopt a strong presumption in favor of separate trials? Does the operation of the *Bruton* rule call for any changes in joinder and severance rules?

**Page 1556 (Prosecution paperback page 752).    Add the following material at the end of note 3.**

In Lilly v. Virginia, 527 U.S. 116 (1999), the Supreme Court decided that a defendant's Sixth Amendment right of confrontation prevented the use at trial of the statement made to police by an alleged accomplice, admitting some criminal activity but blaming the defendant for the most serious criminal acts. The accomplice refused to testify at trial and the prosecution sought to introduce the out-of-court statement under an exception to the bar on hearsay evidence, because the statement was against the speaker's penal interest. Four justices (Stevens, Souter, Ginsburg, and Breyer) declared that such statements are not reliable for confrontation clause purposes as falling into a "firmly rooted" exception to the hearsay rule. They reasoned that statements can only qualify as a firmly rooted exception to the hearsay bar when they are "so trustworthy that adversarial testing can be expected to add little to [the statements'] reliability." Nor did the statements bear any "particularized guarantees of trustworthiness." The accomplice was in custody for his involvement in serious crimes, and made his statements when responding to leading questions from interrogators. Justice Scalia joined in the result, concluding that the use of the tape-recorded statements to police at trial without making him available for cross-examination is a "paradigmatic" confrontation clause violation. Other justices concluded that the accomplice's confession does not satisfy a firmly rooted hearsay exception because the statements that were against his penal interest were separate from the statements exculpating him and inculpating Lilly. The case, in their view, did not raise the question whether the confrontation clause permits the admission of a genuinely self-inculpatory statement that also inculpates a codefendant.

## C.  The Self-Incrimination Privilege at Trial

### 1.   Comments on Silence

**Page 1584 (page 781 in the Prosecution paperback).    Add the following material after note 4.**

5. *Comments on presence at trial.*  In Portuondo v. Agard, 529 U.S. 61 (2000), the prosecutor pointed out to the jury that the defendant, who was present in the courtroom, had the opportunity to hear all other witnesses and to tailor his testimony accordingly. Agard claimed that the prosecutor's comments violated his Fifth Amendment right to be present at trial and his Sixth Amendment right to confront his accusers. He drew an analogy to Griffin v. California, suggesting that in his case, just as in *Griffin*, the prosecutor was making the exercise of these constitutional trial rights more costly. Are there meaningful differences between this prosecutor's comment and a comment about a defendant's refusal to testify?  The Supreme Court found no constitutional violation.

## D.  Ethics and Lies at Trial

**Page 1599 (page 796 in the Prosecution paperback).    Add the following material at the end of the notes.**

The recent investigations of the Los Angeles Police Department offer many examples of police officers who fabricated evidence and lied during trial testimony. By some accounts, there could be hundreds or perhaps thousands of tainted criminal convictions. See Matt Lait, Scott Glover, and Tina Daunt, Scandal Could Taint Hundreds of Convictions, L.A. Times, Feb. 17, 2000.

# Chapter 20 / 10

# Sentencing

## A. Who Sentences?

### 1. Indeterminate Sentencing

**Page 1620 (Prosecution paperback page 816).** **Add this material to the end of note 5.**

For a proposal to expand the use of jury sentencing, see Adriaan Lanni, Note, Jury Sentencing in Noncapital Cases: An Idea Whose Time Has Come (Again)? 108 Yale L.J. 1775 (1999).

### 2. Legislative Sentencing

**Page 1631 (Prosecution paperback page 827).** **Add this material to the end of note 1.**

More state courts have shown a willingness to insist, under various provisions of their state constitutions, that the legislature select a punishment that is proportionate to the crime. People v. Davis, 687 N.E.2d 24 (Ill. 1997) (statutory penalty for felons convicted of failing to register a firearm violates due process clauses of state and federal constitutions, because penalty is far less severe for more serious offense of unlawful use of weapon by a felon); State v. Moss-Dwyer, 686 N.E.2d 109 (Ind. 1997) (recognizing possible proportionality challenges under state constitution, but refusing to declare a sentence disproportionate where statute made misinformation on a handgun permit application a greater crime than carrying a handgun without a license). State courts have also applied the *Harmelin* test under the Eighth Amendment of the federal constitution to bar some disproportionate sentences. State v. Bonner, 577 N.W.2d 575 (S.D. 1998) (15-year sentence for second-degree burglary was disproportionate, cruel and unusual; offender with no prior record was developmentally disabled and accomplices received probation). Other courts have used nonconstitutional methods of reducing sentences in particular cases without declaring a punishment disproportionate for an entire class of cases. See State v. DePiano, 926 P.2d 494 (Ariz. 1996) (despondent mother's unsuccessful attempt to commit suicide and infanticide by asphyxiation was punished by 34-year prison term; court reduced sentence under statute allowing reduction if "the punishment imposed is greater than under the circumstances of the case ought to be inflicted").

## 3.   Sentencing Commissions

**Page 1643 (Prosecution paperback page 839).    Add this material to the end of note 4.**

For two thoughtful proposals to increase the role of federal judges in the creation of federal sentencing rules, see Douglas A. Berman, A Common Law for this Age of Federal Sentencing: The Opportunity and Need for Judicial Lawmaking, 11 Stan. L. & Pol'y Rev. 93 (1999); Joseph W. Luby, Reining in the "Junior Varsity Congress": A Call for Meaningful Judicial Review of the Federal Sentencing Guidelines, 77 Wash. U. L.Q. 1199 (1999)

**Page 1644 (Prosecution paperback page 840).    Add this material to the end of note 6.**

Prison officials also have some influence over the amount of a prison sentence served. In most states, prison officials have the power to reduce the sentence by up to one-third or one-half of the maximum sentence set by the judge or the parole authority. Prison authorities use this discretion to reward good behavior by inmates: The reductions are known as "good time." Jim Jacobs has pointed out the anomaly of placing legal controls on other sentencing decisions, while leaving good time decisions unregulated. Jacobs, Sentencing by Prison Personnel: Good Time, 30 UCLA L. Rev. 217 (1982). Which institutions would be best suited to create legal constraints on good time decisions?

# B.  Revisiting Investigations and Charges

## 2.  Revisiting Charging Decisions: Relevant Conduct

**Page 1661 (Prosecution paperback page 857).**     **Add this material at the end of note 1.**

In Monge v. California, 524 U.S. 721 (1998), the Supreme Court decided that the double jeopardy clause does not apply at all to noncapital sentencing proceedings. California's "three-strikes" law provides that a convicted felon with one prior conviction for a serious felony will have her prison term doubled. When Monge was convicted of narcotics crimes, the government asked the court to enhance his sentence based on a previous assault conviction. The trial court did so, but a state appeals court later concluded that there was insufficient proof of the details of the assault. Monge then argued that a remand for retrial on the sentence enhancement would violate double jeopardy principles. The U.S. Supreme Court disagreed, because double jeopardy protections are inapplicable to sentencing proceedings: The determinations at a sentencing hearing do not place a defendant in jeopardy for an "offense." In an earlier case, the Court had decided that double jeopardy would prevent a prosecutor in a capital case from seeking the death penalty on a retrial after an appeal, if the original trial had resulted in a sentence less than death. Bullington v. Missouri, 451 U.S. 430 (1981). However, noncapital sentencing involves less severe consequences, and the court refused to extend the *Bullington* decision to the noncapital setting.

# C.  Revisiting Pleas and Trials

## 1.  Revisiting Proof at Trial

**Page 1671 (Prosecution paperback page 867).   Add this material before the notes.**

### Charles Apprendi v. New Jersey
530 U.S. 466 (2000)

STEVENS, J.

A New Jersey statute classifies the possession of a firearm for an unlawful purpose as a "second-degree" offense. Such an offense is punishable by imprisonment for between five years and ten years. A separate statute, described by that State's Supreme Court as a "hate crime" law, provides for an "extended term" of imprisonment if the trial judge finds, by a preponderance of the evidence, that the "defendant in committing the crime acted with a purpose to intimidate an individual or group of individuals because of race, color, gender, handicap, religion, sexual orientation or ethnicity." N.J. Stat. Ann. §2C:44-3(e). The extended term authorized by the hate crime law for second-degree offenses is imprisonment for between 10 and 20 years.

The question presented is whether the Due Process Clause of the Fourteenth Amendment requires that a factual determination authorizing an increase in the maximum prison sentence for an offense from 10 to 20 years be made by a jury on the basis of proof beyond a reasonable doubt.

At 2:04 A.M. on December 22, 1994, petitioner Charles C. Apprendi, Jr., fired several .22-caliber bullets into the home of an African-American family that had recently moved into a previously all-white neighborhood in Vineland, New Jersey. Apprendi was promptly arrested and, at 3:05 A.M., admitted that he was the shooter. After further questioning, at 6:04 A.M., he made a statement—which he later retracted—that even though he did not know the occupants of the house personally, "because they are black in color he does not want them in the neighborhood."

A New Jersey grand jury returned a 23-count indictment charging

262

Apprendi with [crimes growing out of] shootings on four different dates, as well as the unlawful possession of various weapons. None of the counts referred to the hate crime statute, and none alleged that Apprendi acted with a racially biased purpose.

The parties entered into a plea agreement, pursuant to which Apprendi pleaded guilty to two counts of second-degree possession of a firearm for an unlawful purpose, and one count of the third-degree offense of unlawful possession of an antipersonnel bomb; the prosecutor dismissed the other 20 counts. Under state law, a second-degree offense carries a penalty range of 5 to 10 years; a third-degree offense carries a penalty range of between 3 and 5 years. As part of the plea agreement, however, the State reserved the right to request the court to impose a higher "enhanced" sentence on [the possession count based on the December 22 shooting] on the ground that that offense was committed with a biased purpose. . . .

At the plea hearing, the trial judge heard sufficient evidence to establish Apprendi's guilt. . . . Because the plea agreement provided that the sentence on the sole third-degree offense would run concurrently with the other sentences, the potential sentences on the two second-degree counts were critical. If the judge found no basis for the biased purpose enhancement, the maximum consecutive sentences on those counts would amount to 20 years in aggregate; if, however, the judge enhanced the sentence on [the December 22 count], the maximum on that count alone would be 20 years and the maximum for the two counts in aggregate would be 30 years, with a 15-year period of parole ineligibility.

After the trial judge accepted the three guilty pleas, the prosecutor filed a formal motion for an extended term. The trial judge thereafter held an evidentiary hearing on the issue of Apprendi's "purpose" for the shooting on December 22. Apprendi adduced evidence from a psychologist and from seven character witnesses who testified that he did not have a reputation for racial bias. He also took the stand himself, explaining that the incident was an unintended consequence of overindulgence in alcohol, denying that he was in any way biased against African-Americans, and denying that his statement to the police had been accurately described. The judge, however, found the police officer's testimony credible, and concluded that the evidence supported a finding that the crime was motivated by racial bias. Having found by a preponderance of the evidence that Apprendi's actions were taken "with a purpose to intimidate" as provided by the statute, the trial judge held that the hate crime enhancement applied [and] sentenced him to a 12-year term of imprisonment on [the December 22 count], and to shorter concurrent sentences on the other two counts. [The New Jersey appellate courts upheld the sentence.]

In his 1881 lecture on the criminal law, Oliver Wendell Holmes, Jr., observed: "The law threatens certain pains if you do certain things, intending thereby to give you a new motive for not doing them. If you persist in doing them, it has to inflict the pains in order that its threats may continue to be believed." New Jersey threatened Apprendi with certain pains if he unlawfully possessed a weapon and with additional pains if he selected his victims with a purpose to intimidate them because of their race. As a matter of simple justice, it seems obvious that the procedural safeguards designed to protect Apprendi from unwarranted pains should apply equally to the two acts that New Jersey has singled out for punishment. Merely using the label "sentence enhancement" to describe the latter surely does not provide a principled basis for treating them differently.

At stake in this case are constitutional protections of surpassing importance: the proscription of any deprivation of liberty without "due process of law," and the [Sixth Amendment] guarantee that "[i]n all criminal prosecutions, the accused shall enjoy the right to a speedy and public trial, by an impartial jury." Taken together, these rights indisputably entitle a criminal defendant to a jury determination that he is guilty of every element of the crime with which he is charged, beyond a reasonable doubt. [T]he historical foundation for our recognition of these principles extends down centuries into the common law. . . . Equally well founded is the companion right to have the jury verdict based on proof beyond a reasonable doubt. . . .

Any possible distinction between an "element" of a felony offense and a "sentencing factor" was unknown to the practice of criminal indictment, trial by jury, and judgment by court as it existed during the years surrounding our Nation's founding. As a general rule, criminal proceedings were submitted to a jury after being initiated by an indictment containing "all the facts and circumstances which constitute the offence, stated with such certainty and precision, that the defendant may be enabled to determine the species of offence they constitute, in order that he may prepare his defence accordingly and that there may be no doubt as to the judgment which should be given, if the defendant be convicted." J. Archbold, Pleading and Evidence in Criminal Cases 44 (15th ed. 1862). . . .

Thus, with respect to the criminal law of felonious conduct, "the English trial judge of the later eighteenth century had very little explicit discretion in sentencing. The substantive criminal law . . . prescribed a particular sentence for each offense. . . ." Langbein, The English Criminal Trial Jury on the Eve of the French Revolution, in The Trial Jury in England, France, Germany 1700-1900, pp. 36-37 (A. Schioppa ed. 1987). . . .

This practice at common law held true when indictments were issued pursuant to statute. Just as the circumstances of the crime and the intent of the defendant at the time of commission were often essential elements to be alleged in the indictment, so too were the circumstances mandating a particular punishment. "Where a statute annexes a higher degree of punishment to a common-law felony, if committed under particular circumstances, an indictment for the offence, in order to bring the defendant within that higher degree of punishment, must expressly charge it to have been committed under those circumstances, and must state the circumstances with certainty and precision. [2 M. Hale, Pleas of the Crown *170]." Archbold, Pleading and Evidence in Criminal Cases, at 51. . . .

We should be clear that nothing in this history suggests that it is impermissible for judges to exercise discretion—taking into consideration various factors relating both to offense and offender—in imposing a judgment within the range prescribed by statute. We have often noted that judges in this country have long exercised discretion of this nature in imposing sentence within statutory limits in the individual case. [O]ur periodic recognition of judges' broad discretion in sentencing—since the nineteenth-century shift in this country from statutes providing fixed-term sentences to those providing judges discretion within a permissible range—has been regularly accompanied by the qualification that that discretion was bound by the range of sentencing options prescribed by the legislature. . . .

We do not suggest that trial practices cannot change in the course of centuries and still remain true to the principles that emerged from the Framers' fears "that the jury right could be lost not only by gross denial, but by erosion." Jones v. United States, 526 U. S. 227 (1999). But practice must at least adhere to the basic principles undergirding the requirements of trying to a jury all facts necessary to constitute a statutory offense, and proving those facts beyond reasonable doubt. As we made clear in In re Winship, 397 U. S. 358 (1970), the "reasonable doubt" requirement has a vital role in our criminal procedure for cogent reasons. Prosecution subjects the criminal defendant both to the possibility that he may lose his liberty upon conviction and the certainty that he would be stigmatized by the conviction. We thus require this, among other, procedural protections in order to "provide concrete substance for the presumption of innocence," and to reduce the risk of imposing such deprivations erroneously. If a defendant faces punishment beyond that provided by statute when an offense is committed under certain circumstances but not others, it is obvious that both the loss of liberty and the stigma attaching to the offense are heightened; it necessarily follows that the defendant should not—at the moment the State is put to proof of those circumstances—be deprived of protections that have, until that point, unquestionably attached.

Since *Winship*, we have made clear beyond peradventure that *Winship*'s due process and associated jury protections extend, to some degree, to determinations that go not to a defendant's guilt or innocence, but simply to the length of his sentence. This was a primary lesson of Mullaney v. Wilbur, 421 U. S. 684 (1975), in which we invalidated a Maine statute that presumed that a defendant who acted with an intent to kill possessed the "malice aforethought" necessary to constitute the State's murder offense (and therefore, was subject to that crime's associated punishment of life imprisonment). The statute placed the burden on the defendant of proving, in rebutting the statutory presumption, that he acted with a lesser degree of culpability, such as in the heat of passion, to win a reduction in the offense from murder to manslaughter (and thus a reduction of the maximum punishment of 20 years).

The State had posited in *Mullaney* that requiring a defendant to prove heat-of-passion intent to overcome a presumption of murderous intent did not implicate *Winship* protections because, upon conviction of either offense, the defendant would lose his liberty and face societal stigma just the same. Rejecting this argument, we acknowledged that criminal law "is concerned not only with guilt or innocence in the abstract, but also with the degree of criminal culpability" assessed. Because the "consequences" of a guilty verdict for murder and for manslaughter differed substantially, we dismissed the possibility that a State could circumvent the protections of *Winship* merely by redefining the elements that constitute different crimes, characterizing them as factors that bear solely on the extent of punishment.

It was in McMillan v. Pennsylvania, 477 U. S. 79 (1986), that this Court, for the first time, coined the term "sentencing factor" to refer to a fact that was not found by a jury but that could affect the sentence imposed by the judge. That case involved a challenge to the State's Mandatory Minimum Sentencing Act. According to its provisions, anyone convicted of certain felonies would be subject to a mandatory minimum penalty of five years imprisonment if the judge found, by a preponderance of the evidence, that the person "visibly possessed a firearm" in the course of committing one of the specified felonies. Articulating for the first time, and then applying, a multifactor set of criteria for determining whether the *Winship* protections applied to bar such a system, we concluded that the Pennsylvania statute did not run afoul of our previous admonitions against relieving the State of its burden of proving guilt, or tailoring the mere form of a criminal statute solely to avoid *Winship*'s strictures.

We did not, however, there budge from the position that (1) constitutional limits exist to States' authority to define away facts necessary to constitute a criminal offense, and (2) that a state scheme that keeps from the jury facts that expose defendants to greater or additional punishment may raise serious constitutional concern. . . .

Finally, . . . Almendarez-Torres v. United States, 523 U. S. 224 (1998), represents at best an exceptional departure from the historic practice that we have described. In that case, we considered a federal grand jury indictment, which charged the petitioner with "having been found in the United States after being deported," in violation of 8 U.S.C. §1326(a)—an offense carrying a maximum sentence of two years. Almendarez-Torres pleaded guilty to the indictment, admitting at the plea hearing that he had been deported, that he had unlawfully reentered this country, and that the earlier deportation had taken place "pursuant to" three earlier convictions for aggravated felonies. The Government then filed a presentence report indicating that Almendarez-Torres' offense fell within the bounds of §1326(b) because, as specified in that provision, his original deportation had been subsequent to an aggravated felony conviction; accordingly, Almendarez-Torres could be subject to a sentence of up to 20 years. Almendarez-Torres objected, contending that because the indictment "had not mentioned his earlier aggravated felony convictions," he could be sentenced to no more than two years in prison.

Rejecting Almendarez-Torres' objection, we concluded that sentencing him to a term higher than that attached to the offense alleged in the indictment did not violate the strictures of *Winship* in that case. Because Almendarez-Torres had admitted the three earlier convictions for aggravated felonies—all of which had been entered pursuant to proceedings with substantial procedural safeguards of their own—no question concerning the right to a jury trial or the standard of proof that would apply to a contested issue of fact was before the Court. [A]s *Jones* made crystal clear, our conclusion in *Almendarez-Torres* turned heavily upon the fact that the additional sentence to which the defendant was subject was the prior commission of a serious crime. 523 U. S. at 243 (explaining that recidivism is "a traditional, if not the most traditional, basis for a sentencing court's increasing an offender's sentence"); id., at 244 (emphasizing the fact that recidivism "does not relate to the commission of the offense"). Both the certainty that procedural safeguards attached to any "fact" of prior conviction, and the reality that Almendarez-Torres did not challenge the accuracy of that fact in his case, mitigated the due process and Sixth Amendment concerns otherwise implicated in allowing a judge to determine a fact increasing punishment beyond the maximum of the statutory range. . . .

In sum, our reexamination of our cases in this area, and of the history upon which they rely, confirms [that] any fact that increases the penalty for a crime beyond the prescribed statutory maximum [except for the fact of a prior conviction] must be submitted to a jury, and proved beyond a reasonable doubt.

The New Jersey statutory scheme that Apprendi asks us to invalidate allows a jury to convict a defendant of a second-degree offense based on its finding beyond a reasonable doubt that he unlawfully possessed a prohibited weapon; after a subsequent and separate proceeding, it then allows a judge to impose punishment identical to that New Jersey provides for crimes of the first degree, based upon the judge's finding, by a preponderance of the evidence, that the defendant's "purpose" for unlawfully possessing the weapon was to intimidate his victim on the basis of a particular characteristic the victim possessed. In light of the constitutional rule explained above, and all of the cases supporting it, this practice cannot stand.[16]

[New Jersey argues that] the required finding of biased purpose is not an "element" of a distinct hate crime offense, but rather the traditional "sentencing factor" of motive . . . . The text of the statute requires the factfinder to determine whether the defendant possessed, at the time he committed the subject act, a "purpose to intimidate" on account of, inter alia, race. By its very terms, this statute mandates an examination of the defendant's state of mind—a concept known well to the criminal law as the defendant's mens rea.

[Furthermore,] it does not matter whether the required finding is characterized as one of intent or of motive, because labels do not afford an acceptable answer. That point applies as well to the constitutionally novel and elusive distinction between "elements" and "sentencing factors." Despite what appears to us the clear "elemental" nature of the factor here, the relevant inquiry is one not of form, but of effect—does

---

16. The principal dissent would reject the Court's rule as a "meaningless formalism," because it can conceive of hypothetical statutes that would comply with the rule and achieve the same result as the New Jersey statute. While a State could, hypothetically, undertake to revise its entire criminal code in the manner the dissent suggests, post, at 18—extending all statutory maximum sentences to, for example, 50 years and giving judges guided discretion as to a few specially selected factors within that range—this possibility seems remote. Among other reasons, structural democratic constraints exist to discourage legislatures from enacting penal statutes that expose every defendant convicted of, for example, weapons possession, to a maximum sentence exceeding that which is, in the legislature's judgment, generally proportional to the crime. This is as it should be. Our rule ensures that a State is obliged "to make its choices concerning the substantive content of its criminal laws with full awareness of the consequence, unable to mask substantive policy choices" of exposing all who are convicted to the maximum sentence it provides. Patterson v. New York, 432 U. S., at 228- 229, n. 13 (Powell, J., dissenting). So exposed, "the political check on potentially harsh legislative action is then more likely to operate." . . . Finally, the principal dissent ignores the distinction the Court has often recognized between facts in aggravation of punishment and facts in mitigation. If facts found by a jury support a guilty verdict of murder, the judge is authorized by that jury verdict to sentence the defendant to the maximum sentence provided by the murder statute. If the defendant can escape the statutory maximum by showing, for example, that he is a war veteran, then a judge that finds the fact of veteran status is neither exposing the defendant to a deprivation of liberty greater than that authorized by the verdict according to statute, nor is the Judge imposing upon the defendant a greater stigma than that accompanying the jury verdict alone. Core concerns animating the jury and burden-of-proof requirements are thus absent from such a scheme.

the required finding expose the defendant to a greater punishment than that authorized by the jury's guilty verdict? [T]he effect of New Jersey's sentencing "enhancement" here is unquestionably to turn a second-degree offense into a first-degree offense, under the State's own criminal code. . . .

The New Jersey procedure challenged in this case is an unacceptable departure from the jury tradition that is an indispensable part of our criminal justice system. Accordingly, the judgment of the Supreme Court of New Jersey is reversed, and the case is remanded for further proceedings not inconsistent with this opinion.

SCALIA, J., concurring.

. . . I think it not unfair to tell a prospective felon that if he commits his contemplated crime he is exposing himself to a jail sentence of 30 years—and that if, upon conviction, he gets anything less than that he may thank the mercy of a tenderhearted judge (just as he may thank the mercy of a tenderhearted parole commission if he is let out inordinately early, or the mercy of a tenderhearted governor if his sentence is commuted). Will there be disparities? Of course. But the criminal will never get more punishment than he bargained for when he did the crime, and his guilt of the crime (and hence the length of the sentence to which he is exposed) will be determined beyond a reasonable doubt by the unanimous vote of 12 of his fellow citizens. In Justice Breyer's bureaucratic realm of perfect equity, by contrast, the facts that determine the length of sentence to which the defendant is exposed will be determined to exist (on a more-likely-than-not basis) by a single employee of the State. . . .

What ultimately demolishes the case for the dissenters is that they are unable to say what the right to trial by jury does guarantee if, as they assert, it does not guarantee—what it has been assumed to guarantee throughout our history—the right to have a jury determine those facts that determine the maximum sentence the law allows. They provide no coherent alternative. . . .

THOMAS, J., concurring.

I join the opinion of the Court in full. I write separately to explain my view that the Constitution requires a broader rule than the Court adopts. . . .

Sentencing enhancements may be new creatures, but the question that they create for courts is not. Courts have long had to consider which facts are elements in order to determine the sufficiency of an accusation (usually an indictment). The answer that courts have provided regarding the accusation tells us what an element is, and it is then a simple matter to apply that answer to whatever constitutional right may be at issue in a case—here, *Winship* and the right to trial by jury. A long line of essentially uniform authority addressing accusations, and stretching from the earliest reported cases after the founding until well into the 20th century, establishes that the original understanding of which facts are elements was even broader than the rule that the Court adopts today.

This authority establishes that a "crime" includes every fact that is by law a basis for imposing or increasing punishment (in contrast with a fact that mitigates punishment). Thus, if the legislature defines some core crime and then provides for increasing the punishment of that crime upon a finding of some aggravating fact—of whatever sort, including the fact of a prior conviction—the core crime and the aggravating fact together constitute an aggravated crime, just as much as grand larceny is an aggravated form of petit larceny. The aggravating fact is an element of the aggravated crime. Similarly, if the legislature, rather than creating grades of crimes, has provided for setting the punishment of a crime based on some fact—such as a fine that is proportional to the value of stolen goods—that fact is also an element. No multi-factor parsing of statutes, of the sort that we have attempted since *McMillan*, is necessary. One need only look to the kind, degree, or range of punishment to which the prosecution is by law entitled for a given set of facts. Each fact necessary for that entitlement is an element.

[I]t is fair to say that *McMillan* began a revolution in the law regarding the definition of "crime." Today's decision, far from being a sharp break with the past, marks nothing more than a return to the status quo ante—the status quo that reflected the original meaning of the Fifth and Sixth Amendments. . . .

O'CONNOR, J., dissenting.

. . . Our Court has long recognized that not every fact that bears on a defendant's punishment need be charged in an indictment, submitted to a jury, and proved by the government beyond a reasonable doubt. Rather, we have held that the legislature's definition of the elements of the offense is usually dispositive. Although we have recognized that there are obviously constitutional limits beyond which the States may not go in this regard, . . . we have proceeded with caution before deciding that a certain fact must be treated as an offense element despite the legislature's choice not to characterize it as such. We have therefore declined to establish any bright-line rule for making such judgments and have instead approached each case individually, sifting through the considerations most relevant to determining whether the legislature has acted properly within its broad power to define crimes and their punishments or instead has sought to evade the constitutional requirements associated with the characterization of a fact as an offense element. In one bold stroke the Court today casts aside our traditional cautious approach and instead embraces a universal and seemingly bright-line rule limiting the power of Congress and state legislatures to define criminal offenses and the sentences that follow from convictions thereunder. . . .

None of the history contained in the Court's opinion requires the rule it ultimately adopts. [The excerpts from the nineteenth-century Archbold treatise] pertain to circumstances in which a common-law felony had also been made a separate statutory offense carrying a greater penalty. Taken together, the statements from the Archbold treatise demonstrate nothing more than the unremarkable proposition that a defendant could receive the greater statutory punishment only if the indictment expressly charged and the prosecutor proved the facts that made up the statutory offense, as opposed to simply those facts that made up the common-law offense. . . .

In his concurring opinion, Justice Thomas cites additional historical evidence. [H]e claims that the Fifth and Sixth Amendments "codified" preexisting common law [and] he contends that the relevant common law treated any fact that served to increase a defendant's punishment as an element of an offense. Even if Justice Thomas' first assertion were correct—a proposition this Court has not before embraced—he fails to gather the evidence necessary to support his second assertion. Indeed, for an opinion that purports to be founded upon the original understanding of the Fifth and Sixth Amendments, Justice Thomas' concurrence is notable for its failure to discuss any historical practice, or to cite any decisions, predating (or contemporary with) the ratification of the Bill of Rights. Rather, Justice Thomas divines the common-law

- 295 of 334

understanding of the Fifth and Sixth Amendment rights by consulting decisions rendered by American courts well after the ratification of the Bill of Rights, ranging primarily from the 1840s to the 1890s. Whatever those decisions might reveal about the way American state courts resolved questions regarding the distinction between a crime and its punishment under general rules of criminal pleading or their own state constitutions, the decisions fail to demonstrate any settled understanding with respect to the definition of a crime under the relevant, preexisting common law. . . .

The Court . . . cites our decision in Mullaney v. Wilbur, 421 U. S. 684 (1975), to demonstrate the "lesson" that due process and jury protections extend beyond those factual determinations that affect a defendant's guilt or innocence. The Court explains *Mullaney* as having held that the due process proof beyond a reasonable doubt requirement applies to those factual determinations that, under a State's criminal law, make a difference in the degree of punishment the defendant receives. The Court chooses to ignore, however, the decision we issued two years later, Patterson v. New York, 432 U. S. 197 (1977), which clearly rejected the Court's broad reading of *Mullaney*.

In *Patterson*, the jury found the defendant guilty of second-degree murder. Under New York law, the fact that a person intentionally killed another while under the influence of extreme emotional disturbance distinguished the reduced offense of first-degree manslaughter from the more serious offense of second-degree murder. Thus, the presence or absence of this one fact was the defining factor separating a greater from a lesser punishment. Under New York law, however, the State did not need to prove the absence of extreme emotional disturbance beyond a reasonable doubt. Rather, state law imposed the burden of proving the presence of extreme emotional disturbance on the defendant, and required that the fact be proved by a preponderance of the evidence. We rejected Patterson's due process challenge to his conviction.

[T]he fact that *Patterson* did not act under the influence of extreme emotional disturbance, in substance, increased the penalty for his crime beyond the prescribed statutory maximum for first-degree manslaughter. Nonetheless, we held that New York's requirement that the defendant, rather than the State, bear the burden of proof on this factual determination comported with the Fourteenth Amendment's Due Process Clause.

273

[I]t is possible that the Court's "increase in the maximum penalty" rule rests on a meaningless formalism that accords, at best, marginal protection for the constitutional rights that it seeks to effectuate. [One reading of the Court's holding] requires that a fact be submitted to a jury and proved beyond a reasonable doubt only if that fact, as a formal matter, extends the range of punishment beyond the prescribed statutory maximum. A State could, however, remove from the jury (and subject to a standard of proof below "beyond a reasonable doubt") the assessment of those facts that define narrower ranges of punishment, within the overall statutory range, to which the defendant may be sentenced. Thus, apparently New Jersey could cure its sentencing scheme, and achieve virtually the same results, by drafting its weapons possession statute in the following manner: First, New Jersey could prescribe, in the weapons possession statute itself, a range of 5 to 20 years' imprisonment for one who commits that criminal offense. Second, New Jersey could provide that only those defendants convicted under the statute who are found by a judge, by a preponderance of the evidence, to have acted with a purpose to intimidate an individual on the basis of race may receive a sentence greater than 10 years' imprisonment.

Under another reading of the Court's decision, it may mean only that the Constitution requires that a fact be submitted to a jury and proved beyond a reasonable doubt if it, as a formal matter, increases the range of punishment beyond that which could legally be imposed absent that fact. A State could, however, remove from the jury (and subject to a standard of proof below 'beyond a reasonable doubt') the assessment of those facts that, as a formal matter, decrease the range of punishment below that which could legally be imposed absent that fact. Thus, . . . New Jersey could cure its sentencing scheme, and achieve virtually the same results, by drafting its weapons possession statute in the following manner: First, New Jersey could prescribe, in the weapons possession statute itself, a range of 5 to 20 years' imprisonment for one who commits that criminal offense. Second, New Jersey could provide that a defendant convicted under the statute whom a judge finds, by a preponderance of the evidence, not to have acted with a purpose to intimidate an individual on the basis of race may receive a sentence no greater than 10 years' imprisonment. . . .

If New Jersey can, consistent with the Constitution, make precisely the same differences in punishment turn on precisely the same facts, and can remove the assessment of those facts from the jury and subject them to a standard of proof below beyond a reasonable doubt, it is impossible to say that the Fifth, Sixth, and Fourteenth Amendments require the Court's rule. For the same reason, the "structural democratic constraints" that might discourage a legislature from enacting either of the above hypothetical statutes would be no more significant than those that would discourage the enactment of New Jersey's present sentence-enhancement statute. . . .

Given the pure formalism of the above readings of the Court's opinion, one suspects that the constitutional principle underlying its decision is more far reaching. The actual principle underlying the Court's decision may be that any fact (other than prior conviction) that has the effect, in real terms, of increasing the maximum punishment beyond an otherwise applicable range must be submitted to a jury and proved beyond a reasonable doubt. . . . The principle thus would apply not only to schemes like New Jersey's, under which a factual determination exposes the defendant to a sentence beyond the prescribed statutory maximum, but also to all determinate sentencing schemes in which the length of a defendant's sentence within the statutory range turns on specific factual determinations (e.g., the federal Sentencing Guidelines).

[T]he apparent effect of the Court's opinion today is to halt the current debate on sentencing reform in its tracks and to invalidate with the stroke of a pen three decades' worth of nationwide reform, all in the name of a principle with a questionable constitutional pedigree. [Perhaps] the most significant impact of the Court's decision will be a practical one—its unsettling effect on sentencing conducted under current federal and state determinate-sentencing schemes. [W]ith respect to past sentences handed down by judges under determinate sentencing schemes, the Court's decision threatens to unleash a flood of petitions by convicted defendants seeking to invalidate their sentences in whole or in part on the authority of the Court's decision today. . . . Because many States, like New Jersey, have determinate-sentencing schemes, the number of individual sentences drawn into question by the Court's decision could be colossal. . . .

BREYER, J., dissenting.
[The majority's] rule would seem to promote a procedural ideal—

that of juries, not judges, determining the existence of those facts upon which increased punishment turns. But the real world of criminal justice cannot hope to meet any such ideal. It can function only with the help of procedural compromises, particularly in respect to sentencing. . . .

In modern times the law has left it to the sentencing judge to find those facts which (within broad sentencing limits set by the legislature) determine the sentence of a convicted offender. The judge's factfinding role is not inevitable. One could imagine, for example, a pure "charge offense" sentencing system in which the degree of punishment depended only upon the crime charged (e.g., eight mandatory years for robbery, six for arson, three for assault). But such a system would ignore many harms and risks of harm that the offender caused or created, and it would ignore many relevant offender characteristics. Hence, that imaginary charge offense system would not be a fair system, for it would lack proportionality, i.e., it would treat different offenders similarly despite major differences in the manner in which each committed the same crime.

[It] is important for present purposes to understand why judges, rather than juries, traditionally have determined the presence or absence of such sentence-affecting facts in any given case. And it is important to realize that the reason is not a theoretical one, but a practical one. . . . There are, to put it simply, far too many potentially relevant sentencing factors to permit submission of all (or even many) of them to a jury. . . .

At the same time, to require jury consideration of all such factors— say, during trial where the issue is guilt or innocence—could easily place the defendant in the awkward (and conceivably unfair) position of having to deny he committed the crime yet offer proof about how he committed it, e.g., "I did not sell drugs, but I sold no more than 500 grams." And while special postverdict sentencing juries could cure this problem, they have seemed (but for capital cases) not worth their administrative costs. Hence, before the Guidelines, federal sentencing judges typically would obtain relevant factual sentencing information from probation officers' presentence reports, while permitting a convicted offender to challenge the information's accuracy at a hearing before the judge without benefit of trial-type evidentiary rules. . . .

The majority raises no objection to traditional pre-Guidelines sentencing procedures under which judges, not juries, made the factual findings that would lead to an increase in an individual offender's sentence. How does a legislative determination differ in any significant way? For example, if a judge may on his or her own decide that victim injury or bad motive should increase a bank robber's sentence from 5 years to 10, why does it matter that a legislature instead enacts a statute that increases a bank robber's sentence from 5 years to 10 based on this same judicial finding?

[T]he majority also makes no constitutional objection to a legislative delegation to a commission of the authority to create guidelines that determine how a judge is to exercise sentencing discretion. But if the Constitution permits Guidelines, why does it not permit Congress similarly to guide the exercise of a judge's sentencing discretion?

[The majority] argues for a limiting principle that would prevent a legislature with broad authority from transforming (jury-determined) facts that constitute elements of a crime into (judge-determined) sentencing factors, thereby removing procedural protections that the Constitution would otherwise require. The majority's cure, however, is not aimed at the disease.

The same "transformational" problem exists under traditional sentencing law, where legislation, silent as to sentencing factors, grants the judge virtually unchecked discretion to sentence within a broad range. Under such a system, judges or prosecutors can similarly transform crimes, punishing an offender convicted of one crime as if he had committed another. A prosecutor, for example, might charge an offender with five counts of embezzlement (each subject to a 10-year maximum penalty), while asking the judge to impose maximum and consecutive sentences because the embezzler murdered his employer. And, as part of the traditional sentencing discretion that the majority concedes judges retain, the judge, not a jury, would determine the last-mentioned relevant fact, i.e., that the murder actually occurred.

This egregious example shows the problem's complexity. The source of the problem lies not in a legislature's power to enact sentencing factors, but in the traditional legislative power to select elements defining a crime, the traditional legislative power to set broad sentencing ranges, and the traditional judicial power to choose a sentence within that range on the basis of relevant offender conduct. Conversely, the solution to the problem lies, not in prohibiting legislatures from enacting sentencing factors, but in sentencing rules that determine punishments on the basis of properly defined relevant conduct, with sensitivity to the need for procedural protections where sentencing factors are determined by a judge (for example, use of a reasonable doubt standard), and invocation of the Due Process Clause where the history of the crime at issue, together with the nature of the facts to be proved, reveals unusual and serious procedural unfairness.

[T]he majority's rule would provide a degree of increased procedural protection in respect to those particular sentencing factors currently embodied in statutes. I nonetheless believe that any such increased protection provides little practical help and comes at too high a price. For one thing, by leaving mandatory minimum sentences untouched, the majority's rule simply encourages any legislature interested in asserting control over the sentencing process to do so by creating those minimums. That result would mean significantly less procedural fairness, not more. . . .

**Page 1672 (Prosecution paperback page 868).    Add this material at the end of note 1.**

The *Apprendi* decision has created a great deal of upheaval in the state and federal courts. Many defendants have pointed out particular factual findings, especially in drug cases, that increase their sentence in some way or another. Thus, they argue, a jury must make the relevant factual findings. For facts that merely increase a sentence within the designated statutory range, these claims have not succeeded. But what about facts that increase the minimum sentence that could apply to the crime? In Harris v. United States, 122 S. Ct. 2406 (2002), the Supreme Court reaffirmed *McMillan* and held that a judge rather than a jury could find the facts necessary to increase the minimum sentence. How might you distinguish the increased minimum sentence involved in *Harris* from the increased maximum sentence involved in *Apprendi*?

The *Apprendi* ruling also has implications for capital sentencing, where findings about "aggravating factors" are a precondition to the court imposing the death penalty. See Ring v. Arizona, 122 S. Ct. 2428 (2002) (jury rather than judge must find an aggravating circumstance necessary for imposition of the death penalty).

## 3.   Revisiting Guilty Pleas and Refusals to Plead

**Page 1684 (Prosecution paperback page 880).**   **Add this material at the end of note 2.**

If perjury at trial can enhance a sentence, this adds to the long list of incentives for defendants not to testify at trial. As we saw in the previous chapter, the Fifth Amendment declares that a factfinder may not draw adverse inferences from this silence at trial. Does the same protection apply to silence at sentencing? In Mitchell v. United States, 526 U.S. 314 (1999), the Supreme Court decided that a guilty plea in federal court does not extinguish the defendant's Fifth Amendment right to remain silent at sentencing. The government in this narcotics case presented testimony from codefendants at Mitchell's sentencing hearing; the codefendants claimed that she had sold 1.5 to 2 ounces of cocaine twice a week for 18 months. The sentencing judge found that this testimony established the 5-kilogram threshold for a mandatory 10-year minimum, and noted that Mitchell's failure to testify was a factor in persuading the court to rely on the codefendants' testimony. The Supreme Court declared that a sentencing judge may not draw adverse inferences from the defendant's silence at the sentencing hearing in selecting a sentence for the defendant.

## D.  *New Information About the Offender and the Victim*

### 1.   Offender Information

#### b.   *Cooperation in Other Investigations*

**Page 1699 (Prosecution paperback page 895).**   **Add this material at the end of the note.**

For an exploration of possible nonconstitutional limits on the prosecutor's power over sentencing discounts for cooperation in investigations, see Cynthia Y. K. Lee, From Gatekeeper to Concierge:

Reigning in the Federal Prosecutor's Expanding Power over Substantial Assistance Departures, 50 Rutgers L. Rev. 199 (1997). Professor Frank Bowman has documented and analyzed major recent changes in federal sentencing in cases of defendants cooperating in other investigations. Bowman, Departing is Such Sweet Sorrow: A Year of Judicial Revolt on "Substantial Assistance" Departures Follows a Decade of Prosecutorial Indiscipline, 29 Stetson L. Rev. 7 (1999).

# Chapter 21 / 11

# Race and Punishment

## A. *An American Dilemma*

**Page 1730 (Prosecution paperback page 926).** **Add this material after note 2.**

3. *Cumulative effects.* A May 2000 report from the Leadership Conference on Civil Rights, "Justice on Trial: Racial Disparities in the American Criminal Justice System," attempted to summarize the evidence of racial disparities throughout the criminal justice system. Some of the observations of the report were as follows:

> Police departments disproportionately target minorities as criminal suspects, skewing at the outset the racial composition of the population ultimately charged, convicted and incarcerated. And too often the police employed tactics against minorities that simply shock the conscience. . . . For example, a growing body of statistical evidence demonstrates that black motorists are disproportionately stopped for minor traffic offenses because the police assumed they are more likely to be engaged in more serious criminal activity. . . . The practice is widespread. Under a federal court consent decree, traffic stops by the Maryland State Police on Interstate 95 were monitored. In the two-year period from January 1995 to December 1997, 70 percent of the drivers stopped and searched by the police were black, while only 17.5 percent of overall drivers—as well as overall speeders—were black. . . .
>
> Racial profiling is also carried out in forms other than pretextual traffic stops. Enforcement of the controlled substances laws, in general, seems premised on the bizarre perception that drug trafficking is exclusively a minority-owned business. Drug courier profiles have regularly included race as an explicit element of suspicion. In sworn testimony, DEA agents have at various times in recent years stated their belief that most drug couriers are

black females, and that being Hispanic or black was part of the profile they used to identify drug traffickers. . . .

[In the late 1990s, the New York City Police Department began to aggressively "stop and frisk" city residents.] Predictably, black and Hispanic New Yorkers were disproportionately targeted for "stop and frisk" pat-downs. A December 1999 report by the New York State Attorney General found that of the 175,000 "stops" engaged in by NYPD officers from January 1998 through March 1999, almost 84 percent were of blacks and Hispanics, despite the fact that those groups comprised less than half of the City's population; by contrast, only 13 percent of stops were of white New Yorkers, a group that comprises 43 percent of the City's population. . . .

At every subsequent stage of the criminal process—from the first plea negotiations with a prosecutor, to the imposition of the prison sentence by a judge—the subtle biases and stereotypes that cause police officers to rely on racial profiling are compounded by the racially skewed decisions of other key actors. . . . Prosecutors have the authority to decline prosecution altogether, or to authorize diversion, under which completion of drug treatment or community service results in the dismissal of the charges. But such displays of prosecutorial mercy appear to be exercised in a manner that disproportionately benefits whites.

In 1991 the *San Jose Mercury News* reviewed almost 700,000 criminal cases from California between 1981 and 1990 and uncovered statistically significant disparities at several different stages of the criminal justice process. Among the study's findings was that six percent of whites, as compared to only four percent of minorities, won "interest of justice" dismissals, in which prosecutors dropped the criminal case entirely. Moreover, the study found, 20 percent of white defendants charged with crimes providing for the option of diversion received that benefit, while only 14 percent of similarly situated blacks and 11 percent of similarly situated Hispanics were placed in such programs.

Related to the decision to decline prosecution is the decision to charge the defendant in state or federal court. [The] prosecutorial decision to bring charges in federal court, or leave the case to the state system, is often exercised to the detriment of America's minorities. . . . From 1992 to 1994, approximately 96.5 percent of all federal crack prosecutions were of nonwhites. A 1992 U.S. Sentencing Commission report determined that *only* minorities were prosecuted for crack offenses in over half of the federal judicial districts that handled crack cases. . . . These discrepancies are remarkable because the crack epidemic knew no racial bounds. Despite stereotypes perpetuated by the media and pop culture, government statistics show that more whites overall used crack than blacks. . . .

Once a prosecutor decides to bring charges against an individual, plea negotiations present the next opportunity for a prosecutor to grant some degree of leniency to a defendant, or to insist on maximum punishment. [O]nce again the exercise of discretion is characterized by racially disparate results. The *San Jose Mercury News* report discussed above revealed consistent discrepancies in the treatment of white and nonwhite criminal defendants at the pretrial negotiation stage of the criminal process. During 1989-1990, a white felony defendant with no criminal record stood a 33 percent chance of having a charge reduced to a misdemeanor or infraction, compared to 25 percent for a similarly situated black or Hispanic. Statistics from other jurisdictions confirm that prosecutorial discretion may result in disparate treatment of minorities and whites. . . .

Another turning point in the criminal justice process, one that can mean the difference between freedom and incarceration for criminal defendants, is the bail determination. While the decision to set bail is ultimately a judicial function, prosecutors play an important role in determining whether a criminal defendant will be released on bail or detained in jail prior to trial by recommending detention or release to the court. A New York State study examined the extent to which black and Hispanic state criminal defendants were treated differently from similarly situated white criminal defendants with respect to pretrial detention, and concluded that statewide, minorities charged with felonies were detained more often than white defendants charged with felonies. Indeed, the study found that 10 percent of all minorities held in jail at felony indictment in New York City, and 33 percent of all minorities held in jail at felony indictment in the rest of New York State, would be released before arraignment if minorities were detained as often as comparably situated whites.

Another study reviewed bail determinations for criminal defendants in New Haven, Connecticut, and concluded that the bail rates set for black criminal defendants exceeded those set for similarly situated white criminal defendants. In short, the study concluded, lower bail rates could have been set for black defendants without incurring the risk of flight that bail rates are designed to avoid. . . .

Sentencing is arguably the most important stage of the criminal justice system. [O]ne of the chief failings of undue reliance on imprisonment to solve social problems is that this approach results in serious racial disparities. The "tough on crime" movement of the past several decades has led to incarceration rates for minorities far out of proportion to their percentage of the U.S. population.

One of the most thorough studies of sentencing disparities was undertaken by the New York State Division of Criminal Justice Services, which studied felony sentencing outcomes in New York courts between 1990 and 1992. The state concluded that one-third of minorities sentenced to prison would have received a shorter or nonincarcerative sentence if they had been treated like similarly situated white defendants. . . .

Racial disparities can be found not only in the fact of incarceration, but in the length of prison or jail time served. According to a Justice Department review of state sentencing, whites who serve time for felony drug offenses serve shorter prison terms than their black counterparts: an average of 27 months for whites, and 46 months for blacks. These discrepancies are mirrored with regard to nondrug crimes. . . .

There is a self-perpetuating, cyclical quality to the treatment of black and Hispanic Americans in the criminal justice system. Much of the unfairness visited upon these groups stems from the perceptions of criminal justice decision-makers that (1) most crimes are committed by minorities, and (2) most minorities commit crimes. Although empirically false, these perceptions cause a disproportionate share of law-enforcement attention to be directed at minorities, which in turn leads to more arrests of blacks and Hispanics. Disproportionate arrests fuel prosecutorial and judicial decisions that disproportionately affect minorities and result in disproportionate incarceration rates and prison sentence lengths for those minorities. The cumulative effect is to create a prison population in which blacks and Hispanics increasingly predominate, which in turn lends credence to the misperceptions that justify racial profiling and "tough on crime" policies. There are innumerable consequences to this vicious cycle of inequality—for incarcerated minorities, for their families and communities, and for the continued legitimacy of the criminal justice system.

This report revealed no new findings; it simply collected together the findings of earlier studies. Nevertheless, its sponsors hoped that the findings would be more powerful when pulled together into one report. Study: Race Affects Justice, N.Y. Times, May 4, 2000. When it comes to evidence of racial bias in criminal justice, does the whole body of evidence amount to more than the sum of its parts?

## B.   Race and the Victims of Crime

**Page 1742 (Prosecution paperback page 938).**   **Add this material after note 4.**

5.   *Victims and images of criminals.* Katheryn Russell explores incidents of "racial hoaxes," in which the apparent victim of a crime attempts to pin blame on an imaginary black "predator" or white "super-racist," and contrasts the motives, methods, and costs of "white-on-black" and "black-on-white" hoaxes. Russell, The Color of Crime (1998). Does the legal system's reaction to statistics such as those presented in *McCleskey* ignore or reinforce common images of criminals and victims of crime? See also David Cole, No Equal Justice: Race and Class in American Criminal Justice (1999); Jody David Armour, Negrophobia and Reasonable Racism: The Hidden Costs of Being Black in America (1997).

## D. *Race and Discretionary Decisions Affecting Punishment*

**Page 1776 (Prosecution paperback page 969).**   **Add this material at the end of note 1.**

Joseph Gastwirth and Tapan Nayak analyzed the data in *Stephens* using statistical techniques and concluded that the difference in treatment of black and white drug offenders in the case cannot be explained on grounds other than race. See Gastwirth and Nayak, Statistical Aspects of Cases Concerning Racial Discrimination in Drug Sentencing: Stephens v. State and U.S. v. Armstrong, 87 J. Crim. L. & Criminology 583 (1997).

**Page 1777 (Prosecution paperback page 970).**   **Add this material after note 4.**

5.   *Remedy at sentencing.* If a sentencing judge believes that racial discrimination is at least partly responsible for a pattern of cases that she notices, what is the proper remedy? In some circumstances, the judge cannot adjust the sentence because the crime of conviction carries a mandatory minimum sentence. But if the judge does have some sentencing discretion, should she reduce the sentence for one defendant in light of racially discriminatory practices taking place earlier in the system? See United States v. Leviner, 31 F. Supp. 2d 23 (D. Mass. 1998) (judge departs down from guideline sentence in narcotics case because defendant's lengthy arrest record consisted mostly of motor vehicle and small narcotics cases, crimes that generally reflect a tendency by police to stop black motorists more often than whites). See also Pamela Karlan, Race, Rights, and Remedies in Criminal Adjudication, 96 Mich. L. Rev. 2001 (1998).

6.   *Remedies outside the courts.*   When the evidence becomes clear that a particular institutional player is contributing to racial inequity in the criminal justice arena, a remedy will sometimes arrive through the political process, without any need for litigation or court rulings. Consider the case of Col. Carl Williams, the former Super-intendent of the New Jersey State Police. Governor Christie Whitman

dismissed Williams after a published report quoted him as saying that it was "naïve" to think race was not associated with the commission of some crimes, and that cocaine and marijuana traffickers were most likely members of minority groups.   See Robert D. McFadden, Whitman Dismisses State Police Chief for Race Remarks, N.Y. Times, Mar. 1, 1999 at A1.

# Chapter 22 / 12

# Appeals

## A. Who Appeals?

### 1. Right to Appeal

Page 1784 (Prosecution paperback page 976).   Add this material after the notes.

### George Smith v. Lee Robbins
528 U.S. 259 (2000)

THOMAS, J.

Not infrequently, an attorney appointed to represent an indigent defendant on appeal concludes that an appeal would be frivolous and requests that the appellate court allow him to withdraw or that the court dispose of the case without the filing of merits briefs. In Anders v. California, 386 U.S. 738 (1967), we held that, in order to protect indigent defendants' constitutional right to appellate counsel, courts must safeguard against the risk of granting such requests in cases where the appeal is not actually frivolous. We found inadequate California's procedure—which permitted appellate counsel to withdraw upon filing a conclusory letter stating that the appeal had "no merit" and permitted the appellate court to affirm the conviction upon reaching the same conclusion following a review of the record. We went on to set forth an acceptable procedure. California has since adopted a new procedure, which departs in some respects from the one that we delineated in *Anders*. The question is whether that departure is fatal. We hold that it is not. The procedure we sketched in *Anders* is a prophylactic one; the States are free to adopt different procedures, so long as those procedures adequately safeguard a defendant's right to appellate counsel.

Under California's new procedure, established in People v. Wende, 600 P.2d 1071 (Calif. 1979) . . . counsel, upon concluding that an appeal would be frivolous, files a brief with the appellate court that summarizes the procedural and factual history of the case, with citations of the record. He also attests that he has reviewed the record, explained his evaluation of the case to his client, provided the client with a copy of the brief, and informed the client of his right to file a pro se supplemental brief. He further requests that the court independently examine the record for arguable issues. Unlike under the *Anders* procedure, counsel following *Wende* neither explicitly states that his review has led him to conclude that an appeal would be frivolous ... nor requests leave to withdraw. Instead, he is silent on the merits of the case and expresses his availability to brief any issues on which the court might desire briefing.

The appellate court, upon receiving a "*Wende* brief," must conduct a review of the entire record, regardless of whether the defendant has filed a pro se brief. . . . If the appellate court, after its review of the record pursuant to *Wende*, also finds the appeal to be frivolous, it may affirm. If, however, it finds an arguable (i.e., nonfrivolous) issue, it orders briefing on that issue.

In 1990, a California state-court jury convicted respondent Lee Robbins of second-degree murder (for fatally shooting his former roommate) and of grand theft of an automobile (for stealing a truck that he used to flee the State after committing the murder). Robbins was sentenced to 17 years to life. He elected to represent himself at trial, but on appeal he received appointed counsel. His appointed counsel, concluding that an appeal would be frivolous, filed with the California Court of Appeal a brief that complied with the *Wende* procedure. Robbins also availed himself of his right under *Wende* to file a pro se supplemental brief, filing a brief in which he contended that there was insufficient evidence to support his conviction and that the prosecutor violated Brady v. Maryland, 373 U.S. 83 (1963), by failing to disclose exculpatory evidence. The California Court of Appeal, agreeing with counsel's assessment of the case, affirmed. The court explained that it had "examined the entire record" and [found no support for the two issues that Robbins raised]. After exhausting state postconviction remedies, Robbins filed in [federal district court] for a writ of habeas corpus. . . .

The District Court [concluded] that there were at least two issues that, pursuant to *Anders*, counsel should have raised in his brief (in a *Wende* brief, as noted above, counsel is not required to raise issues): first, whether the prison law library was adequate for Robbins's needs in preparing his defense after he elected to dismiss his appointed counsel and proceed pro se at trial, and, second, whether the trial court erred in refusing to allow him to withdraw his waiver of counsel. The District Court did not attempt to determine the likelihood that either of these two issues would have prevailed in an appeal. Rather, it simply concluded that, in the language of the *Anders* procedure, these issues "might arguably" have supported the appeal. . . . The court concluded that such a deviation amounted to deficient performance by counsel. . . .

In *Anders*, we reviewed an earlier California procedure for handling appeals by convicted indigents. Pursuant to that procedure, Anders's appointed appellate counsel had filed a letter stating that he had concluded that there was "no merit to the appeal." Anders, in response, sought new counsel; the State Court of Appeal denied the request, and Anders filed a pro se appellate brief. That court then issued an opinion that reviewed the four claims in his pro se brief and affirmed, finding no error (or no prejudicial error). . . .

We held that "California's action does not comport with fair procedure and lacks that equality that is required by the Fourteenth Amendment." We placed the case within a line of precedent beginning with Griffin v. Illinois, 351 U.S. 12 (1956), and continuing with Douglas v. California, 372 U.S. 353 (1963), that imposed constitutional constraints on States when they choose to create appellate review. In finding the California procedure to have breached these constraints, we compared it to other procedures we had found invalid and to statutory requirements in the federal courts governing appeals by indigents with appointed counsel. We relied in particular on Ellis v. United States, 356 U.S. 674 (1958) (per curiam), a case involving federal statutory requirements, and quoted the following passage from it:

> If counsel is convinced, after conscientious investigation, that the appeal is frivolous, of course, he may ask to withdraw on that account. If the court is

satisfied that counsel has diligently investigated the possible grounds of appeal, and agrees with counsel's evaluation of the case, then leave to withdraw may be allowed and leave to appeal may be denied. 356 U.S. at 675.

In *Anders*, neither counsel, the state appellate court on direct appeal, nor the state habeas courts had made any finding of frivolity. We concluded that a finding that the appeal had "no merit" was not adequate, because it did not mean that the appeal was so lacking in prospects as to be "frivolous." [We] proceeded, in a final, separate section, to set out what would be an acceptable procedure for treating frivolous appeals:

> [I]f counsel finds his case to be wholly frivolous, after a conscientious examination of it, he should so advise the court and request permission to withdraw. That request must, however, be accompanied by a brief referring to anything in the record that might arguably support the appeal. A copy of counsel's brief should be furnished the indigent and time allowed him to raise any points that he chooses; the court—not counsel—then proceeds, after a full examination of all the proceedings, to decide whether the case is wholly frivolous. If it so finds it may grant counsel's request to withdraw and dismiss the appeal insofar as federal requirements are concerned, or proceed to a decision on the merits, if state law so requires. On the other hand, if it finds any of the legal points arguable on their merits (and therefore not frivolous) it must, prior to decision, afford the indigent the assistance of counsel to argue the appeal.

We then concluded by explaining how this procedure would be better than the California one that we had found deficient. Among other things, we thought that it would "induce the court to pursue all the more vigorously its own review because of the ready references not only to the record but also to the legal authorities as furnished it by counsel."

The Ninth Circuit ruled that this final section of *Anders*, even though unnecessary to our holding in that case, was obligatory upon the States. We disagree. We have never so held . . . and the Ninth Circuit's view runs contrary to our established practice of permitting the States, within the broad bounds of the Constitution, to experiment with solutions to difficult questions of policy.

In McCoy v. Court of Appeals of Wisconsin, Dist. 1, 486 U.S. 429 (1988), we rejected a challenge to Wisconsin's variation on the *Anders* procedure. Wisconsin had departed from *Anders* by requiring *Anders* briefs to discuss why each issue raised lacked merit. The defendant argued that this rule was contrary to *Anders* and forced counsel to violate his ethical obligations to his client. We, however, emphasized that the right to appellate representation does not include a right to present frivolous arguments to the court. [The Wisconsin procedure], by providing for one-sided briefing by counsel against his own client's best claims, probably made a court more likely to rule against the indigent than if the court had simply received an *Anders* brief.

[A]ny view of the procedure we described in the last section of *Anders* that converted it from a suggestion into a straitjacket would contravene our established practice, rooted in federalism, of allowing the States wide discretion, subject to the minimum requirements of the Fourteenth Amendment, to experiment with solutions to difficult problems of policy. In Griffin v. Illinois, 351 U.S. 12 (1956), which we invoked as the foundational case for our holding in *Anders*, we expressly disclaimed any pretensions to rulemaking authority for the States in the area of indigent criminal appeals.

[It] is more in keeping with our status as a court, and particularly with our status as a court in a federal system, to avoid imposing a single solution on the States from the top down. . . . Accordingly, we hold that the *Anders* procedure is merely one method of satisfying the requirements of the Constitution for indigent criminal appeals. States may—and, we are confident, will—craft procedures that, in terms of policy, are superior to, or at least as good as, that in *Anders*. The Constitution erects no barrier to their doing so.

Having determined that California's *Wende* procedure is not unconstitutional merely because it diverges from the *Anders* procedure, we turn to consider the *Wende* procedure on its own merits. We think it clear that California's system does not violate the Fourteenth Amendment, for it provides a criminal appellant pursuing a first appeal as of right the minimum safeguards necessary to make that appeal adequate and effective. . . . A State's procedure provides [adequate and effective] review so long as it reasonably ensures that an indigent's appeal will be resolved in a way that is related to the merit of that appeal. . . .

In determining whether a particular state procedure satisfies this standard, it is important to focus on the underlying goals that the procedure should serve—to ensure that those indigents whose appeals are not frivolous receive the counsel and merits brief required by *Douglas*, and also to enable the State to protect itself so that frivolous appeals are not subsidized and public moneys not needlessly spent. For although, under *Douglas*, indigents generally have a right to counsel on a first appeal as of right, it is equally true that this right does not include the right to bring a frivolous appeal and, concomitantly, does not include the right to counsel for bringing a frivolous appeal. . . . The obvious goal of *Anders* was to prevent this limitation on the right to appellate counsel from swallowing the right itself, and we do not retreat from that goal today.

We think the *Wende* procedure reasonably ensures that an indigent's appeal will be resolved in a way that is related to the merit of that appeal. Whatever its strengths or weaknesses as a matter of policy, we cannot say that it fails to afford indigents the adequate and effective appellate review that the Fourteenth Amendment requires. . . .

The *Wende* procedure is undoubtedly far better than those procedures we have found inadequate. . . . Although we did not, in *Anders*, explain in detail why the California procedure was inadequate under each of these precedents, . . . a significant factor was that the old California procedure did not require either counsel or the court to determine that the appeal was frivolous; instead, the procedure required only that they determine that the defendant was unlikely to prevail on appeal. . . . *Wende*, by contrast, requires both counsel and the court to find the appeal to be lacking in arguable issues, which is to say, frivolous.

An additional problem with the old California procedure was that it apparently permitted an appellate court to allow counsel to withdraw and thereafter to decide the appeal without appointing new counsel. . . . Under *Wende*, by contrast, *Douglas* violations do not occur, both because counsel does not move to withdraw and because the court orders briefing if it finds arguable issues.

In *Anders*, we also disapproved the old California procedure because we thought that a one paragraph letter from counsel stating only his "bare conclusion" that the appeal had no merit was insufficient. [T]he *Wende* brief provides more than a one-paragraph "bare conclusion." Counsel's summary of the case's procedural and factual history, with citations of the record, both ensures that a trained legal eye has searched the record for arguable issues and assists the reviewing court in its own evaluation of the case.

[The *Anders* procedure] has, from the beginning, faced consistent and severe criticism. One of the most consistent criticisms … is that *Anders* is in some tension both with counsel's ethical duty as an officer of the court (which requires him not to present frivolous arguments) and also with his duty to further his client's interests (which might not permit counsel to characterize his client's claims as frivolous). California, through the *Wende* procedure, has made a good-faith effort to mitigate this problem by not requiring the *Wende* brief to raise legal issues and by not requiring counsel to explicitly describe the case as frivolous.

Another criticism of the *Anders* procedure has been that it is incoherent and thus impossible to follow. Those making this criticism point to our language in *Anders* suggesting that an appeal could be both "wholly frivolous" and at the same time contain arguable issues, even though we also said that an issue that was arguable was "therefore not frivolous." In other words, the *Anders* procedure appears to adopt gradations of frivolity and to use two different meanings for the phrase "arguable issue." The *Wende* procedure attempts to resolve this problem as well, by drawing the line at frivolity and by defining arguable issues as those that are not frivolous.[13] . . .

Our purpose is not to resolve any of these arguments. The Constitution does not resolve them, nor does it require us to do so. . . . It is enough to say that the *Wende* procedure . . . affords adequate and effective appellate review for criminal indigents. . . .

Since Robbins's counsel complied with a valid procedure for determining when an indigent's direct appeal is frivolous, we reverse the Ninth Circuit's judgment that the *Wende* procedure fails adequately to serve the constitutional principles we identified in *Anders*. But our reversal does not necessarily mean that Robbins's claim that his appellate counsel rendered constitutionally ineffective assistance fails.

---

13. A further criticism of *Anders* has been that it is unjust. More particularly, critics have claimed that, in setting out the *Anders* procedure, we were oblivious to the problem of scarce resources (with regard to both counsel and courts) and, as a result, crafted a rule that diverts attention from meritorious appeals of indigents and ensures poor representation for all indigents. See, e.g., Pritchard, Auctioning Justice: Legal and Market Mechanisms for Allocating Criminal Appellate Counsel, 34 Am. Crim. L. Rev. 1161, 1167-1168 (1997) (*Anders* has created a "tragedy of the commons" that, "far from guaranteeing adequate appellate representation for all criminal defendants, instead ensures that indigent criminal defendants will receive mediocre appellate representation, whether their claims are good or bad"). . . .

For it may be, as Robbins argues, that his appeal was not frivolous and that he was thus entitled to a merits brief rather than to a *Wende* brief. Indeed, both the District Court and the Ninth Circuit found that there were two arguable issues on direct appeal. The meaning of "arguable issue" as used in the opinions below, however, is far from clear. The courts below most likely used the phrase in the unusual way that we used it in *Anders*—an issue arguably supporting the appeal even though the appeal was wholly frivolous. Such an issue does not warrant a merits brief. But the courts below may have used the term to signify issues that were "arguable" in the more normal sense of being nonfrivolous and thus warranting a merits brief. Further, the courts below, in determining whether there were arguable issues, did not address petitioner's argument that, at least with regard to the adequacy of the prison law library, Robbins waived the issue for appeal by failing to object at trial. Thus, it will be necessary on remand to clarify just how strong these two issues are.

On remand, the proper standard for evaluating Robbins's claim that appellate counsel was ineffective in neglecting to file a merits brief is that enunciated in Strickland v. Washington, 466 U.S. 668 (1984). Respondent must first show that his counsel was objectively unreasonable in failing to find arguable issues to appeal—that is, that counsel unreasonably failed to discover nonfrivolous issues and to file a merits brief raising them. If Robbins succeeds in such a showing, he then has the burden of demonstrating prejudice. That is, he must show a reasonable probability that, but for his counsel's unreasonable failure to file a merits brief, he would have prevailed on his appeal. . . .

SOUTER, J., dissenting.

In a line of cases beginning with Griffin v. Illinois, this Court examined appellate procedural schemes under the principle that justice may not be conditioned on ability to pay. Even though absolute equality is not required, we held in Douglas v. California that when state criminal defendants are free to retain counsel for a first appeal as of right, the Fourteenth Amendment requires that indigent appellants be placed on a substantially equal footing through the appointment of counsel at the State's expense.

Two services of appellate counsel are on point here. Appellate counsel examines the trial record with an advocate's eye, identifying and weighing potential issues for appeal. This is review not by a dispassionate legal mind but by a committed representative, pledged to his client's interests, primed to attack the conviction on any ground the record may reveal. If counsel's review reveals arguable trial error, he prepares and submits a brief on the merits and argues the appeal.

The right to the first of these services, a partisan scrutiny of the record and assessment of potential issues, goes to the irreducible core of the lawyer's obligation to a litigant in an adversary system, and we have consistently held it essential to substantial equality of representation by assigned counsel. . . . The right is unqualified when a defendant has retained counsel, and I can imagine no reason that it should not be so when counsel has been appointed.

Because the right to the second service, merits briefing, is not similarly unqualified, however, the issue we address today arises. The limitation on the right to a merits brief is that no one has a right to a wholly frivolous appeal, against which the judicial system's first line of defense is its lawyers. Being officers of the court, members of the bar are bound not to clog the courts with frivolous motions or appeals, and this is of course true regardless of a lawyer's retained or appointed status in a given case. The problem to which *Anders* responds arises when counsel views his client's appeal as frivolous, leaving him duty barred from pressing it upon a court.

The rub is that although counsel may properly refuse to brief a frivolous issue and a court may just as properly deny leave to take a frivolous appeal, there needs to be some reasonable assurance that the lawyer has not relaxed his partisan instinct prior to refusing, in which case the court's review could never compensate for the lawyer's failure of advocacy. A simple statement by counsel that an appeal has no merit, coupled with an appellate court's endorsement of counsel's conclusion, gives no affirmative indication that anyone has sought out the appellant's best arguments or championed his cause to the degree contemplated by the adversary system. . . . To guard against the possibility, then, that counsel has not done the advocate's work of looking hard for potential issues, there must be some prod to find any reclusive merit in an ostensibly unpromising case and some process to assess the lawyer's efforts after the fact. A judicial process that renders constitutional error invisible is, after all, itself an affront to the Constitution.

In *Anders*, we devised such a mechanism to ensure respect for an appellant's rights. [C]ounsel must do his partisan best, short of calling black white, to flag the points that come closest to being appealable; the lawyer's job is to state the issues that give the defendant his best chances to prevail, even if the best comes up short under the rule against trifling with the court. "[T]he court—not counsel—," we continued, "then proceeds, after a full examination of all the proceedings, to decide whether the case is wholly frivolous."

*Anders* thus contemplates two reviews of the record, each of a markedly different character. First comes review by the advocate, the defendant's interested representative. His job is to identify the best issues the partisan eye can spot. Then comes judicial review from a disinterested judge, who asks two questions: whether the lawyer really did function as a committed advocate, and whether he misjudged the legitimate appealability of any issue. In reviewing the advocate's work, the court is responsible for assuring that counsel has gone as far as advocacy will take him with the best issues undiscounted. . . .

Without the assurance that assigned counsel has done his best as a partisan, his substantial equality to a lawyer retained at a defendant's expense cannot be assumed. And without the benefit of the lawyer's statement of strongest claims, the appellate panel cannot act as a reviewing court, but is relegated to an inquisitorial role.

It is owing to the importance of assuring that an adversarial, not an inquisitorial, system is at work that I disagree with the Court's statement today that our cases approve of any state procedure that "reasonably ensures that an indigent's appeal will be resolved in a way that is related to the merit of that appeal." A purely inquisitorial system could satisfy that criterion, and so could one that appoints counsel only if the appellate court deems it useful. But we have rejected the former and have explicitly held the latter unconstitutional, the reason in each case being that the Constitution looks to the means as well as to the ends.

. . . With *Anders* thus as a benchmark, California's *Wende* procedure fails to measure up. Its primary failing is in permitting counsel to refrain as a matter of course from mentioning possibly arguable issues in a no-merit brief; its second deficiency is a correlative of the first, in obliging an appellate court to search the record for arguable issues without benefit of an issue-spotting, no-merit brief to review. . . .

The *Wende* procedure does not assure even the most minimal

assistance of counsel in an adversarial role. The Constitution demands such assurances, and I would hold Robbins entitled to an appeal that provides them.

## NOTES

1. *Counsel for indigent appellants.* Although defendants have no federal constitutional right to an appeal, the federal equal protection clause does require states to make its chosen appeals process available to all defendants, even those without the financial resources to pay for an appeal. According to Griffin v. Illinois, 351 U.S. 12 (1956), the state must provide a defendant with a free transcript of a trial record, if such a transcript is necessary to file an appeal. In Douglas v. California, 372 U.S. 353 (1963), the Court extended *Griffin* to require the government to provide indigent appellants with an attorney for an initial "appeal as of right." Compare Ross v. Moffitt, 417 U.S. 600 (1974) (no constitutional requirement to provide counsel for preparation of petitions for discretionary appellate review). As with the right to appointed counsel at trial, many states expand the availability of counsel on appeal beyond what the federal constitution requires. As the Supreme Court explained in Smith v. Robbins, when appellate counsel for an indigent defendant believes the defendant could raise only frivolous issues on appeal, states still must have some mechanism for bringing potential issues to the court's attention. Do the mechanisms described in *Anders* and in the *Wende* case from California give indigent defendants the functional equivalent of retained appellate counsel?

2. *Self-representation on appeal.* In Martinez v. Court of Appeal of California, 528 U.S. 152 (2000), the Supreme Court refused to extend the right of self-representation at trial—established in Faretta v. California, 422 U.S. 806 (1975)—to a direct appeal. The appellate courts may properly appoint counsel for the appellant, even if the appellant objects. One of the Court's reasons to embrace the right of self-representation at trial was "respect for individual autonomy." Are there any differences between the interests of a defendant at trial and the interests of an appellant when it comes to self-representation?

# B.  Scope of Appeal

## 1.  Review of Factual Findings

**Page 1806 (Prosecution paperback page 998).    Add this material before the notes.**

### Problem 22-2 (12-2). Wrong Place, Wrong Time?

An undercover police officer approached an apartment on Sixth Avenue in Saginaw, Michigan, at about 8:30 P.M. on a December evening. He asked a man inside the apartment for a "$10 rock" of crack cocaine and passed two marked $5 bills through an open window. He heard some conversation inside the apartment, then received a small plastic bag containing crack cocaine. Within two hours, the undercover officer returned with a search warrant and several other officers. They found four men inside the apartment: Lemiel Wolfe, Darren Rogers, Alan Wise, and Leonard James.

When the officers entered the apartment, all four of the men in the apartment ran to the back bedroom. The officers found a loaded twelve-gauge shotgun on the floor in the front room. When the police officers entered the back bedroom of the apartment they saw Wise standing over an open vent in the floor, with the grate removed. The officers recovered 27 plastic baggies of crack cocaine from the vent, amounting to less than 50 grams of cocaine. They found no glass pipes or other paraphernalia typically used to smoke cocaine. It appeared to the officers that no one was living in the apartment. The front room contained only a couch, a refrigerator, and a broken television set. The apartment had no running water and the toilet was not in working condition. The bath tub was being used as a toilet.

The officers arrested and searched all four of the men in the apartment. Wolfe was holding $265 in cash, including the two marked $5 bills. In addition, he had a beeper and a key to the back door of the apartment. The search of Rogers revealed a piece of paper with the number of Wolfe's beeper written on it and a shotgun shell of the same type as the shotgun they found in the front room.

The government charged Wolfe and Rogers with possession with intent to deliver less than 50 grams of cocaine, and possession of a firearm during the commission of a felony. Police officers testified at trial to establish the events as described above.

Wolfe testified at trial that he went to Saginaw to visit a friend. He arrived around 6:00 P.M. that evening and went to the Sixth Avenue apartments to visit Sharon Johnson, whose relatives lived in the apartment next to the apartment where the arrest took place. Wolfe visited with her for about five minutes.

Wolfe said that he had invited several friends from Detroit (Rogers, James, and Wise) to visit Johnson. Around 8:00 P.M., he saw his Detroit friends approaching on the street outside the apartments, and he called out to them from the front porch because they were not familiar with the location. Wolfe testified that he left after a few minutes to visit another friend's house. When he returned to Sixth Avenue around 10:00 P.M., Wolfe spoke briefly with the next-door residents, then joined his friends for a party. He went to the local store for food and beer, after collecting money from the others. When Wolfe returned from the store, Leonard James repaid a prior $20 debt with four $5 bills, two of which were the marked bills that James had received earlier that night from the undercover police officer. As the group sat and watched television, Wolfe saw James smoking cocaine, but testified that he saw no other drugs in the apartment. Shortly after his return from the convenience store, the police raided the apartment and arrested Wolfe, along with several others.

Rogers testified as follows:

> *Q.* Wolfe testified that it was about eight o'clock when he saw you. Is he correct?
> *A.* I don't really know what time it was, but when we got there, it was about six when we saw him standing outside. . . .
> *Q.* And how long after Wolfe came back up did he stay upstairs with you?
> *A.* A good little while.
> *Q.* How long is a "good little while"?
> *A.* I'd say an hour, two hours.

Rogers also testified that Leonard James gave Wolfe the marked $5 bills before Wolfe left the Sixth Avenue apartment to visit his other friend.

Wolfe and Rogers were both convicted on both counts; Wolfe appealed. He argues that the government's evidence did not support either of the two charges, because the evidence did not prove that he possessed the cocaine with intent to distribute it, nor did it prove that he possessed a firearm. Under the case law of Michigan, the government can establish possession of cocaine by showing that the defendant physically possessed the cocaine, or that the defendant "had the right to exercise control of the cocaine and knew that it was present." A person's presence, by itself, at a location where drugs are found is insufficient to prove possession. Just as proof of actual possession of narcotics is not necessary to prove possession, actual delivery of narcotics is not required to prove intent to deliver. Intent to deliver has been inferred from the quantity of narcotics in a defendant's possession, from the way in which those narcotics are packaged, and from other circumstances surrounding the arrest.

How would you rule on appeal? Was the evidence sufficient to sustain one or both of the convictions? Were either of the convictions contrary to the weight of the evidence? Compare People v. Wolfe, 489 N.W.2d 748 (Mich. 1992).

## 2.   Retroactivity

**Page 1815 (Prosecution paperback page 1007).    Add this material at the end of note 2.**

See Taylor v. State, 10 S.W.3d 673 (Tex. Crim. App. 2000) (rejects federal retroactivity doctrine and adopts a multifactor approach to determine whether new rules of nonconstitutional state law should be retroactively applied in state post-conviction proceedings).

**Page 1816 (Prosecution paperback page 1008). Add this material at the end of note 3.**

In Rogers v. Tennessee, 532 U.S. 451 (2001), the state supreme court abolished a common law defense in a criminal case (the "year and a day" rule preventing homicide prosecutions for deaths occurring over a year after the infliction of the mortal injury) and applied the new rule retroactively to the defendant. The Supreme Court upheld the conviction, noting that the due process clause rather than the ex post facto clause controls this situation because it involves judicial rather than legislative action. The court also concluded that this change of the law was not so "unexpected and indefensible" as to violate the fair notice concept protected by due process. The Tennessee court's change in the common law defense tracked a similar development in many other jurisdictions.


## 3.   Harmless Error

**Page 1838 (Prosecution paperback page 1030).     Add this material at the end of note 2.**

See State v. Toney, 979 S.W.2d 642 (Tex. Crim. App. 1998) (sorting out the complex Texas cases on harmlessness of errors in reasonable doubt instructions).

Other deviations from the usual procedure for empanelling and instructing a jury are very often deemed to be structural errors in the trial. See State v. LaMere, 2000 Mt. 45 (2000) (summoning jurors by telephone rather than by mail in violation of statute governing juror summonses requires automatic reversal); State v. Garcia-Contreras, 953 P.2d 936 (Ariz. 1998) (forcing defendant to choose between attending voir dire in jail garb or missing the voir dire was a structural error, no harmless error analysis necessary); State v. Cleveland, 959 S.W.2d 948 (Tenn. 1997) (absence of juror during part of closing argument cannot ever be harmless error).

For recent discussions of "plain error" that allows an appellate court to rule on a question even though the appellant did not raise or preserve the issue at trial, see United States v. Cotton, 122 S. Ct. 1781 (2002) (omission from federal indictment of a fact that enhances the statutory maximum sentence does not amount to plain error); United States v. Vonn, 122 S. Ct. 1043 (2002) (federal defendant who allows Rule 11 error to pass without objections in trial court must satisfy Rule 52(b) plain error rule).

# Chapter 13

# Habeas Corpus

## B. The Availability of Postconviction Review

### 2. Procedural Bars

**Page 1070 of the Prosecution paperback.   Add the following material at the end of note 3.**

Remarkable foresight is necessary to assert some claims of "cause" in the federal system. According to Edwards v. Carpenter, 529 U.S. 446 (2000), when a habeas petitioner points to ineffective assistance of counsel as the reason for her failure to raise some challenge within the state system, the ineffective assistance claim itself is also subject to procedural default rules. That is, the petitioner must either follow all state procedural rules when raising the ineffective assistance argument, or show some "cause and prejudice" for failing to raise this "cause" argument in the proper way.

**Page 1074 of the Prosecution paperback.   Add the following material at the end of note 1.**

In the federal system, the Antiterrorism and Effective Death Penalty Act of 1996 makes it difficult for a federal court to hear claims for a second time. Under the statute, the merits of concluded criminal proceedings should not be revisited in federal court unless the petitioner makes a strong showing of "actual" or "factual" innocence. The Supreme Court has interpreted the federal statute to allow for at least one hearing on the merits in federal court, even if the issue is raised but not resolved in an initial federal petition. See Slack v. McDaniel, 529 U.S. 473 (2000) (federal habeas petition filed after an initial federal petition was dismissed without adjudication on the merits for failure to exhaust state remedies is not a "second or successive" petition; petitioner is not limited in refiled petition to the claims made in the original dismissed petition); Stewart v. Martinez-Villareal, 523 U.S. 637 (1998) (prisoner whose habeas petition was dismissed for failure to exhaust state remedies, and who then did exhaust those remedies and returned to federal court, is not filing a "successive" petition barred by statute; similarly, claim raised in federal court and dismissed as premature can be heard when raised in timely manner in later federal petition).

## 3.   Collateral Review of Ineffective Assistance Claims

**Page 1087 of the Prosecution paperback.    Add the following material at the end of note 5.**

In Calderon v. Thompson, 523 U.S. 538 (1998), the petitioner hoped to establish the ineffectiveness of his trial counsel because the attorney did not contest the conclusions of the state's forensic expert or impeach the credibility of two jailhouse informants. The federal appeals court originally refused to grant relief, but then "recalled the mandate" (that is, changed its mind) two days before the execution. The Supreme Court held that the appeals court had no power to recall the mandate, because there was no "miscarriage of justice" in this case. A miscarriage of justice occurs when the defendant presents new evidence of actual innocence not available at trial. Neither the additional evidence he presented to impeach the credibility of two jailhouse informants nor a pathologist's opinion about the forensic evidence was strong enough to show by "clear and convincing evidence" that no reasonable juror would have found him eligible for the death penalty.

# C.  Federal Habeas Corpus Review of State Convictions

## 1.  Expansion

**Page 1101 of the Prosecution paperback.**    **Add this material at the end of note 2.**

In Williams v. Taylor, 529 U.S. 420 (2000), the Supreme Court read the statute's "fails to develop" standard to require some showing of "fault" by the petitioner.  A failure to develop a claim's factual basis "is not established unless there is lack of diligence, or some greater fault, attributable to the prisoner or his counsel." The necessary "diligence" under the statute requires a petitioner to make "a reasonable attempt, in light of the information available at the time, to investigate and pursue claims in state court." The fact that a particular investigation would have been *successful* is not enough to show that it was a *necessary* part of any reasonable investigation.

**Page 1101 of the Prosecution paperback.**    **Add this material at the end of note 3.**

See O'Sullivan v. Boerckel, 526 U.S. 838 (1999) (to satisfy the exhaustion requirement, state prisoner must present claims to state supreme court in petition for discretionary review after a ruling by the intermediate appeals court, if that review is part of the state's "ordinary appellate review procedure"; because the time for requesting leave to appeal to the Illinois Supreme Court was long past, Boerckel's failure to present three of his claims to that court resulted in a procedural default).

## 2.   Contraction

**Page 1112 of the Prosecution paperback.    Add this material at the end of note 2.**

The defendant must show that he was prejudiced by a violation of some subconstitutional legal rule. In Peguero v. United States, 526 U.S. 23 (1999), the district court had failed to inform the defendant of his right to appeal, in violation of Federal Rule of Criminal Procedure 32(a)(2). However, because Peguero knew about his right to appeal, the violation of the rule was not enough to entitle him to collateral relief.

**Page 1113 of the Prosecution paperback.    Add this material at the end of note 3.**

The Supreme Court has begun to answer some of the questions about the meaning of the key statutory language: "a decision that was contrary to, or involved an unreasonable application of, clearly established Federal law."  In Williams v. Taylor, 529 U.S. 362 (2000), the Court declared that the 1996 statute placed a "new constraint" on the power of federal courts to hear challenges to state convictions.

Under the first clause (the "contrary to" clause), a federal habeas court may grant relief if the state court "arrives at a conclusion opposite to that reached by this Court on a question of law" or "confronts facts that are materially indistinguishable from a relevant Supreme Court precedent and arrives at a result opposite to ours." A routine application of the federal rule to different facts would not qualify for relief under the "contrary to" clause, even if a federal court might have applied the federal rule differently to those facts.

As for the second, "unreasonable application" clause, a federal habeas court should ask whether the state court's application of federal law was "objectively unreasonable." The federal habeas court should not simply ask whether any "reasonable jurist" would apply the federal rule in the same way as the state court did in the case at hand. On the other hand, "unreasonable" is not the same as "incorrect." A federal court might believe that the state court applied federal law incorrectly, and yet decide that the application was reasonable (and therefore unreviewable in habeas corpus).

Page 1114 of the Prosecution paperback.      Add this material after note 5.

6. *Appellate courts as gatekeepers.* The Antiterrorism and Effective Death Penalty Act of 1996 gives federal appeals courts the power to block some habeas petitions from reaching the appeals court. The statute says that a party cannot appeal the final order in a postconviction proceeding to a court of appeals, unless a circuit judge issues a "certificate of appealability," or "COA." The petitioner may obtain such a certificate only by making a substantial showing of the denial of a constitutional right. 28 U.S.C. §2253(c). The federal courts reading this provision broadly to allow appeals in a wide range of claims. See Hohn v. United States, 524 U.S. 236 (1998) (petitioner was complaining about sufficiency of evidence, a constitutional claim covered by COA statute). Petitioners may show a denial of a "constitutional right" even if the district court refused to hear the merits of the claim. According to Slack v. McDaniel, 529 U.S. 473 (2000), when the district court dismisses a petition on procedural grounds, the "substantial showing necessary to obtain a COA has two components. One component deals with the underlying constitutional claim, while another deals with the district court's procedural holding. A COA should issue if the petitioner shows that "jurists of reason" would find it "debatable" whether 1) the person was denied a constitutional right, and 2) the district court was correct in its procedural ruling.

7. *Judicial attitudes toward habeas corpus.* Do federal and state judges have different attitudes about the importance of federal habeas corpus review of state convictions? In a 1996 survey, federal and state judges were asked if elected state judges have "sufficient independence to make difficult decisions that may favor the rights of convicted offenders." Among federal judges, 74 percent replied "yes," while 81 percent of the state judges replied "yes." When asked if there is a "need for continued existence and availability" of federal habeas review of state convictions, 29 percent of the state judges answered "no," while only 7 percent of the federal judges gave the same answer. Most of the state and federal judges approved of the restrictions on federal habeas review created by Rehnquist Court decisions. See Christopher E. Smith & Darwin L. Burke, Judges' Views on Habeas Corpus: A Comparison of State and Federal Judges, 22 Okla. City U. L. Rev. 1125 (1997).

Should legislators consider the views of judges about habeas corpus when debating changes in the statutes governing post-conviction review? If so, for what specific purpose?